Touching Hearts

Touching Hearts

Michael F. Meister, FSC, Editor

The Christian Brothers Spirituality Seminar
Sponsored by the
Christian Brothers Conference
Landover, Maryland

Cover illustration by Carolyn St. George

Published by Christian Brothers Publications, Landover, MD 20785

Copyright © 1992 by Christian Brothers Conference, Landover, MD 20785

Printed by Saint Mary's Press, 702 Terrace Heights, Winona, MN 55987-1320

ISBN 0-9623-279-9-9

Contents

Introduction

Michael F. Meister, FSC, Editor

In his Meditation for Pentecost, John Baptist de La Salle exhorts us to consider the surprising change that came over the Apostles when they "began to speak in strange languages, as the Spirit gave utterance to each." This outpouring of God's Spirit upon them enlightened them so that they could "explain the Scriptures with the utmost depth and precision." As a result, they converted "a very great number" to the Gospel. Of the 77 Meditations the Founder wrote for all the Sundays, only five are without formal titles—among them this one, where he concludes: "You are engaged in a ministry wherein you have to touch hearts." This theme was the focus of the nineteenth annual Christian Brothers Spirituality Seminar, and the title of this volume, *Touching Hearts,* springs from that theme.

The ten articles presented here are a kind of Pentecost insofar as they offer a variety of challenging reflections that point to the ongoing presence of the Spirit in the Institute today. While the reader may encounter surprising changes and strange languages, be aware that these are not the marks of Pentecost the Founder would have us consider. Rather, the event reminds us that the principal motivation of our ministry—the touching of hearts—is a sure manifestation of the outpouring of God's Spirit. With this outpouring in mind, the articles in this volume appear in three divisions: Probing Personal Experience, Searching Sacred Texts, and Confronting Cultural Patterns.

Division One explores retrospective, risk, trust, and interdependence as ways of providing a view of concrete issues in Lasallian life. It begins with Armand Alcazar's insightful exploration of how we need to be in touch with ourselves before we can touch others in our ministry. Kevin Griffin's article is built on a set of sensitively portrayed reminiscences which relate to the themes of calling, caring, and loving as essential features of a mature Lasallian vocation. Edward Sheehy is a historian, and his article investigates the issue of obedience as the "vow of the nineties."

Division Two examines sacred texts, Scriptural and Lasallian, that are both normative and formative for Lasallian educators. Robert Berger's fine discussion centers on the prophet Jeremiah as Robert explores how we bring our students to see the action of God in their lives. My explication is presented as a way to access De La Salle's remarkable charisma by understanding the principles embodied in one of his central works. Robert Smith's theological discussion is a fine presentation of Saint Paul's ethics.

Division Three analyzes contemporary social concerns, exploring their structure and their effect on us as persons, as Christians, as Lasallians. James Ebner's article is a candid and provocative investigation of one of the great social evils in our society. Peter Gilmour brings his expertise as a narrative theologian to bear in his article, which is motivated by his view of the participatory nature of the relationship involved in touching hearts. William Hall's study is scintillating as he moves to his point that our students today are different from those of the Founder. On the way, he explores the difficulty of deepening versus the broadening of the heart. Finally, Thomas Lisack's thoughtful article raises our consciousness by contextualizing the plight of the homeless within the Lasallian ministry.

Inasmuch as the Pentecost experience offered all the opportunity to hear the Word in their own language, we hope that these ten articles will find a receptive place among the rich diversity of our confreres and colleagues in the Lasallian Family for whom they were written. If we are engaged together in a ministry where we touch hearts, may each of us first allow our own to be touched: by God's Spirit, by our colleagues, and by our students.

Touching Hearts

Probing Personal Experience

Only Hearts Touch Hearts

Armand Alcazar, FSC

One evening recently, Jimmy, a college student, was over for dinner. Afterward, he asked if he could stay for a while just to talk. A lot of questions and ideas were running through his mind about God, religion, and his own future after college. At one point in the conversation, he asked a question familiar to most of us, "Tell me, Brother, why did you become a Brother?"

I gave Jimmy some of my usual answers: I wanted to emulate a few of my teachers who were Brothers; I wanted to teach, to help others, to develop a closer relationship with God. Although these reasons for entering religious life were all true, further reflection revealed deeper and more subtle voices which called me into religious life. A few days later, when I asked myself Jimmy's question again in earnest, I came closer to articulating the fuller reasons for pursuing the life of a Christian Brother.

I believe that my reasons for entering religious life went beyond modelling myself after former Brothers, wanting to teach, or even desiring to help others, in general. These innermost motivations were also a little more immediate than establishing a better relationship with God. Although the aforementioned reasons were

---

BROTHER ARMAND ALCAZAR, FSC, PhD, is currently Assistant Professor of Religious Studies at Christian Brothers University in Memphis. Prior to this assignment he was a teacher, counselor, and campus minister in Nebraska, Missouri, and Tennessee. He has graduate degrees from Memphis State University (MA in Counseling), Seattle University (MA in Ministry), Holy Names College in Oakland, California (MA in Spirituality), and The Union Institute in Cincinnati, Ohio (PhD in Religious Studies).

noble enough for joining the Brothers, I have been aware of more pivotal motivations ever since I was 18. Yet, until now I have been unable to articulate these hidden aspirations. I have been afraid that my quests were not sublime, orthodox, or manly enough for choosing a religious life with the Christian Brothers.

Touching Hearts

Today, if Jimmy were here I could honestly tell him that I became a religious because I wanted to touch people deeply, to go below the surface of the everyday box-score conversations, actually to become a part of other people's inner lives, to model the compassion of Jesus and—do I dare admit it?—to deal with issues pertaining to love. Indeed, as an idealistic young Brother I was interested in touching the hearts of others.

Why has it been so difficult to realize and admit what I really wanted to do? What has taken me so long to articulate this original goal for entering religious life? I think it is because there have been other, more familiar and honorable roles, designed to be means to an end, which I confused with being an end unto themselves. Specifically, my aim was to be a well-informed, professional "teacher," and a holy, celibate, religious "saint." These were the two pathways which I turned into destinations along my religious journey. At times these pathways did, in fact, lead to *touching hearts*. Too often, however, when situations called for the give-and-take of true compassion and the relationship necessary for real personhood, I ran away.

This article will describe how two admirable roles of the Christian Brothers can actually fall short of our Lasallian tradition. Specifically, being a teacher and aiming toward sainthood are the tools which some of us use in order "to Brother." When these roles of teacher and saint are mistaken for our end or goal we can spend our lives working toward personal achievements without ever actually touching the hearts of others. This article suggests that if we desire to touch hearts, the only way to do this is by coming to terms with our own humanity.

Brothers as Teachers

The very title of our Institute, "The Brothers of the Christian Schools," speaks volumes about our work and life. Christian Brothers are associated with schools and education. "The end of this Institute is to give a **Christian** education to the young."[1] Naturally, then, teaching is emphasized.

I remember all too well the night before I first stepped into the classroom. I lay awake on my back most of the night terrified about that all-important first day in the classroom, while searching the cracks in the ceiling for secret instructions on how to survive the next morning's responsibilities. But I was prepared, I told myself. I had all those hours in theology and was certified through the education department. Just because I was teaching Spanish, which was neither my major nor my minor, was no reason to panic.[2] (Many of us have had a lot of experience with teaching outside our fields of expertise.)

The reason I mention this episode is to illustrate that the welfare of the students was not my original concern. I was worried about my own survival. In the high school classroom, therefore, discipline and order became a preoccupation for awhile. "You must sit alphabetically; you must be quiet; you must put down your pens as soon as I say 'pens down';" that is, "you must recognize my authority."

Of course there were moments when I recognized the individual worth of the students. I recall observing a classroom of my students while they were watching a film. My eyes and heart searched each of their faces as they, unaware of my scrutiny, innocently looked on. I remember having to fight back tears on that particular day, because I suddenly became aware of how much I loved them. I surprised myself! Without planning to do so, I was living out a Lasallian tradition.

> The Brother is totally immersed in the life of the students: he shares their interests, their worries, their hopes. He is not so much a school-master instilling a set of teachings as he is an older brother who helps them to be aware of what the Spirit is speaking within themselves,

what their own abilities are, and little by little how they may discover their true place in the world.[3]

The fact of the matter is, teaching is a tough job. Amidst preparing lessons, correcting tests, and conducting a disciplined class, it is easy to lose sight of why we do all that we do. The point here is not so much whether we are in the classroom, an administrative office, at the Catholic Worker, on the campus ministry team, or in a diocesan position. Rather the importance lies in our purpose: "As Christian educators, the Brothers are 'God's laborers' who are working out his great plan of love. . . ."[4]

There have been setbacks for me in working toward this "great plan of love" as a teacher. I remember making the conscious decision that it would be more worth my while to be known as shrewd and clever rather than as approachable and understanding. No student was ever going to make a fool of me! I would examine every alibi, quiz every excuse, follow up each suspicious story—and at that time in my life, every situation was a suspicious one. It did not take the students long to give me an appropriate nickname: "Brother Columbo." The sad part was that I enjoyed the reputation as well as the nickname. I was stuck in a role, sidetracked in a heartless tangent which I mislabeled effective teacher-student rapport.

As quoted earlier from *A Declaration,* "The end of this Institute is to give a **Christian** education to the young."[5] The word I would like to emphasize here is "Christian." What is the way of Christ? Could there be any bottom lines that were hallmarks of Jesus? There are many Christian hallmarks, to be sure. But in Matthew's Gospel, I found two instances where Jesus sums up the whole Law and the message of the prophets, which I consider to be his own hallmark.

1. So always treat others as you would like them to treat you; that is the meaning of the Law and the Prophets.[6]
2. You must love the Lord your God with all your heart, with all your soul, and with all your mind. This is the greatest and the first commandment. The second resembles it: You must love your neighbor as yourself. On these two commandments hang the whole Law, and the Prophets also.[7]

We are commanded to love God, ourselves, and our neighbor. To drive the message further home, in Matthew 25 there is the story of the sheep and the goats—the only place in the Gospels where one finds this story of The Last Judgment. The gravity of the title causes the reader to take note: act according to the sheep on the right and you will go to heaven; act according to the goats on the left and you will go to hell! The message of this story is so apparent that the only way Christians have been able to make it obscure is through limited exposure. What is less obvious, but particularly interesting, is that neither the sheep nor the goats recognized Jesus. Both groups ask the same question:

> Lord, when did we see you hungry and feed you; or thirsty and give you drink? When did we see you a stranger and make you welcome; naked and clothe you; sick or in prison and go to see you?[8]

In other words, the act of recognizing Jesus is not what determines eternal punishment or eternal life! Rather, whatever we do to the least one of these brothers or sisters is the criteria used for our final judgment[9]

Touching hearts is practicing the compassion of Jesus. Being a Christian teacher, a Christian Brother, requires compassionate, loving treatment for those we teach. Teaching, educating, working is the vehicle we use in order to love. When alumni get together to remember the Brothers, the stories which emerge most frequently concern a Brother who has *touched a heart:*

> "Brother Mike knew that my dad was laid off for a number of months. He called me into the office, gave me some money, and told me to buy gifts for all the family. I'll never forget that Christmas day and the looks on my family's faces," a student recalls.
>
> "Brother Richard knew that my wife and I were hurting. He sent a bouquet to my wife in my name. That meant so much to both of us," reports a faculty member.
>
> "When my son had his accident, Brother Tony was there. He didn't say much; he didn't need to. He somehow knew that I didn't expect answers to my hysterical demands of 'God, how could you let this happen?' When the decision was made to turn off the respirator, I said good-bye to my son and left before the machine was turned off. I just couldn't stay. I was so grateful that Brother did stay. Somehow,

I felt that with him there, everything would be okay," recounts a parent.

How many times have we heard about the community that gave a student a place to stay overnight after he had fought with his parents, or the Brother who gave extra attention and tutoring to a struggling student on Saturday mornings? We have all been told and have experienced that we are remembered by our students for the "extras" that we provided along with the education. Maybe it is the extras that have to do with Christianity. It is quite possible that we have been remembered more for being human and Christian than for being shrewd and clever taskmasters. I believe these recollections describe what it means for us to be Lasallian. We use teaching as our opportunity to *touch hearts* rather than as our breastplate of authority and professionalism.

Brothers as Saints

I remember one of my first discussions with a visiting superior while I was in the novitiate. We talked about mental prayer, academics, and the *Documents of Vatican II*. Finally, the superior asked: "Well, overall, Brother, how are you doing?"

I told him that although I did not think that I was homesick, I did miss my friends. In fact, I missed a number of things: going out to have a good time, knowing that there was someone I could call, knowing that someone else would call me. In essence, I told him I was lonely.

In a rather brusque manner the superior instructed me that the life of a Brother was the life of a scholar, and the life of a celibate scholar was a life that included loneliness. Somehow, I did not find these words very consoling. Nevertheless, it seemed that this superior was telling the truth.

Soon after my meeting with the superior, we novices started learning about "particular friendships." We did not learn how to have them, of course, we learned how to avoid them. Living a viable community life meant that we were supposed to be close to the community at large without getting too close to any person in particular.[10] I found this idea paradoxical.

In an attempt to uncover the obscurity of the talk with my superior and my attempts at living community life, I started reading the *Lives of the Saints*. I wanted to be holy. I wanted to be a religious brother. I wanted to be a saint. But I needed some models to see how it was done. Sure enough, with the exception of one standout, (whom I will mention later) almost all of these individuals lived more or less solitary lives. I remember no references to the saints' love for their best friends or spouses or anyone with whom they had a meaningful relationship. I was also amazed at how few married people were saints! Therefore, I decided that I had chosen a saintly lifestyle in the Christian Brothers.

As young Brothers we were taught that by choosing celibacy we were consecrated to God. Therefore, the more detached we were from persons and the more independent we were from relationships, the more time we would have to spend with God, with whom we were to have our primary relationship. At times, I felt that my primary relationship was with God. It was a good feeling not to need anyone else but God; somehow it promoted a great sense of poise and control. However, these satisfying, independent periods were few and far between. Periods of loneliness kept creeping into my life. As a celibate, I sometimes equated feeling lonely with being pleasing to God because if I was not close to anyone else then I was still aiming to have God as my primary love-object.

However, this loneliness started affecting my attitude and my work. I found myself resentful of persons I perceived as having a meaningful relationship. Why did they deserve to be so happy? I concluded that people in relationship with other people obviously did not allow for God to be the mainstay of their lives as I did. My relationship was aimed toward God. Then why did I not seem as satisfied as those whose relationship was with other persons?

The resentment continuing, I decided to see a spiritual counselor. The counselor said, "What can I do for you, Brother? Why are you here?" "I think that my faith in God is lacking," I said. "What makes you say that?" she queried. I answered, "Because I find myself lonely a lot."

So there were also times when I felt that my loneliness was indicative of an inadequate relationship with God. After all, shouldn't a relationship with God sustain me at least as much as a relationship with another human being? If I was feeling lonely, then I could not be having an adequate relationship with God. Naturally, this could not be God's fault, so I must be the one who is not giving enough in this spiritual relationship. What sense could I make out of loneliness being the fruit of my attempts to relate to God alone?

I had taken the familiar route of thinking that a lonely, stagnant heart was as honorable as a loving, risking heart. I perceived celibacy as living a life like an independent, John Wayne, "fifties kinda guy," who always rode out of town alone, remaining just out of reach of those who would love him. Secretly, I also hoped that others would admire how independent, self-possessed, and saintly I was as a self-contained celibate. If the truth be known, I thought that the loneliness I experienced through my celibacy would be my ticket to sainthood. If I loved only God in this life, surely I would be rewarded in the next.

I had forgotten how contradictory it is to think that I could love God **instead** of individuals. Anyone who says,

> "I love God," and hates his neighbor, is a liar, since a person who does not love the neighbor that is seen cannot love God, who is not seen. So this is the commandment that God has given us, that anyone who loves God must also love his neighbor.[11]

Side by Side

Recently, I moved into a quaint little house on the edge of the campus of Christian Brothers University. I had to learn the idiosyncrasies of my new home. A former occupant cautioned me about the wood-burning stove in the living room: "Whatever you do, don't ever stoke this stove; it can throw off an awful lot of heat and that's risky!" Obediently, once winter came, I layered the bottom of the stove with sand and carefully tic-tac-toed the top of the sandy base with kindling. Atop the kindling I gingerly placed one dried log. For three consecutive nights I repeated my attempts to start a "cautious" little fire in that stove and failed miserably each time. Then it hit me. There need to be at least two logs to start a fire. One log needs to reflect its heat onto the other, and vice versa, in order for the heat of the fire to continue to burn. By itself, it will not ignite.

Thinking of those logs reminded me of people. Is it not true that we also need others with whom to reflect? The danger for us is the same as it is for those logs in that stove; namely, the fire could get too hot, and the risk too great. Yet, what is the alternative?

For me, the whole matter of relationships involves the contest of risk versus control. It was relatively natural for me to be the cool and collected counselor, that confident expert who took in other people's problems and concerns. How other-centered I was; how above it all. (How lonely.)

Early in my teaching career a rather precocious alumnus wanted to talk. He had graduated from one of our high schools and then from a local university. While on a walk, John spoke of his impressions, successes, failures, and relationships. He opened himself up and risked the story of his life with me.

He then asked, "So how are you doing, Brother?" I told him about my classes, my students, and my coaching. John started laughing. He explained, "You know, Brother, you're the kind of guy that people meet at school or at a party and say 'He's pretty cool.' You like to laugh, you listen well, and you're interesting. But then, we see you the next time, go out with you another time, talk with you yet again, and we don't know any more about you than we did the first time we met you. I've known you for five years and I don't know any more about you now than I did when I was a senior in high school."

I was only four years older than John, and I actually did like him and thought we were friends. But I just could not risk sharing any of my life with him. I could take on the role of teacher, counselor, and religious. But I neither wanted to be nor knew how to be vulnerable with another person by sharing my life. I had trouble simply being human. I was too frightened and embarrassed. John and I have never visited since that time.

Our *Declaration* states:

> The brother ought to have no fear of losing God when he goes among the young to serve them (Mk 10:44), nor of being estranged from Christ when he spends himself for [others] (2 Cor 12:15).[12]

Indeed, I was afraid. Yet, on an intellectual level I scoffed at those who needed relationships other than with God. The line from the *Desiderata* haunted me: "Neither be cynical about love; for in the face of aridity it is as perennial as the grass." Oftentimes I was cynical about love. Love was for the common people who could not love God as I could. I was aiming toward sainthood; therefore, my love was for God alone.

The *Declaration* continues:

> It is advantageous that this witness be given by [Brothers] who are not estranged by their consecration from participating in the life of the world.[13]

Chasing after sainthood, my eyes were on the next world. It seems odd how God pursued me in this world while I looked for God in the next.

On the eve of his fiftieth birthday Thomas Merton wrote in his journal:

> I suppose I regret most my lack of love, my selfishness and glibness (covering a deep shyness and need of love) with girls who, after all, did love me, I think, for a time. My great fault was my inability, really, to believe it, and my efforts to get complete assurance and perfect fulfillment.
>
> So one thing on my mind is sex, as something I did not use maturely and well, something I gave up without having come to terms with it. . . .[14]

How many of us echo Merton's regret? So what do we do as celibates in the world we live in today? On the one hand, in a society now more sensitive to sexual indiscretions, molestations, and child abuse, how do we relate to other human beings? On the other hand, during a period in our history when large numbers of Brothers have left to marry or to search for intimacy, to what are we called?

I believe that the answer to these questions is found in the one standout I found when searching the *Lives of the Saints* for a model I could follow during my earlier years as a religious. I found one holy man who retreated to the wilderness but always returned to the market place teeming with people. He cried when a friend died because he loved him so much. He accepted love and tenderness from a known prostitute without judging her, realizing that he would then be judged. He had a disciple who was referred to as "the one whom he loved." He was not ashamed to be a human who both gave and received love.

Relationships are not easy. In fact, they are risky, dangerous, and highly volatile. It makes sense to keep our affective life dormant and safe; to stay cold and alone like that solitary log in the wood-burning stove. Still, if Jesus is to be our model, we are then called to do more—to risk, to love.

Brothers as Human Beings

For most people it is so obvious that it hardly seems worth mentioning that we are humans. But as religious brothers, I do not believe that we can proceed without being reminded that we are, in fact, human beings, body and soul. If we are tempted to deride our own humanness we would do well to remember that we are made in the "image and likeness" of God the Father and that "the word was made flesh" through the embodiment of Jesus Christ. Somehow, our human dignity is recognized more by God but less by many of us. We can get bogged down in the dualism that says God loves our souls but hates our bodies. At times it seems that we are playing the child's game of tag; God pursues us in our humanity on earth and we pursue God's divinity in heaven. This chase is reminiscent of the song title, "Looking for Love in All the Wrong Places." We are inhabitants of the earth. "Here is the place and now is the time." Rabbi Heschel reminds us that "the Hebrew word *erets* meaning earth, occurs at least five times as often in the Bible as the word *shamay-*

im, meaning heaven."[15] Scripture is earthy. Those times when heaven is referenced it is most often accompanied by the word earth. "Heaven and earth" are commonly linked in the Scriptures. Further scriptural partners are humankind and God, body and soul, living and loving.

Not uncommonly, Scripture reminds us that as God has loved us, so we are called to love one another.[16] From the times of the Hebrew Scriptures where we are told to have a special care for the widow, the orphan, and the foreigner, to Jesus' command to "love one another as I have loved you," we are reminded of the need to love. For those of us who do attempt to model God's love, it has been my experience that we love with the hope or expectation of giving without being affected by that giving, that is, without remaining open to a response. Sebastian Moore writes:

> The desire that moves human beings toward one another and toward God has a correlative in God's desire for human beings. . . . For until we have experienced that we are both capable of offering love and capable of inciting love, we wallow in a morass of doubt that greatly limits our ability to enjoy life and contribute to the common good.[17]

Is the God of the Hebrew Scriptures or Jesus of the Christian Scriptures immune to the responses of the human community? It hardly seems so. In Hesse's novel *Siddhartha,* the eponymous protagonist says that he "learned the art of love in which, more than anything else, giving and taking become one."[18]

We are human beings living on earth called to love. Even though within the word "love" lies a paradox in its call for us to give and receive simultaneously, my experience is that it is easier for religious to talk about how to give love without discussing how to receive love. Attempting first to describe giving love immediately contributes to a duality not appropriately attached to real love. Can we ever only give love? Is it fitting and noble to expect to give love without even an openness or acceptance to receiving it back? Despite the onerous nature of this discussion of give and take, let me move to the topic of loving within our communities.

Touching Hearts in Community[19]

Who in our communities does not have the need to be recognized and valued? Yet, how slow we can be to give one another that recognition. Why are we so reluctant to show our appreciation for one another while we are alive? I believe it is because we are afraid of the response we might receive. I have noticed that we are far more free with the truth in how positively we feel about one another once a Brother dies; we eulogize one another quite tenderly. Of course we risk neither response nor rejection from our deceased confreres. Do our Brothers in the next life need the recognition and valuing more than those in this life?

Our reluctance to give and receive surely has many roots. One origin of this reluctance could certainly be our earlier training, which encouraged us to look to the next world rather than this one. For example, a Brother recently told me he had found his scholasticate notebook. He was decluttering and almost discarded the book. He opened to the first page, where he had quoted the Director of Scholastics as saying: "The only time a Brother is to touch another Brother is with his fist, and hard." Statements like this must have been more or less part of a standard repertoire for some directors of initial formation. *"Noli me tangere"* is still the cry of some of the Brothers in our communities; at least that is the way they are perceived externally.

There are many ways we can touch each other, Brothers, but each and every way requires risk and trust. We can pass on compliments from others, tell of positive traits we recognize ourselves, thank a Brother for a noticeable contribution, let others in our community know of awards and honors bestowed on one another, or simply tell of our appreciation for who a Brother is regardless of what he does.

> It is safe to say that religion has a great deal to do with the disposition of trust. At the heart of religion there lies an attitude of confidence and assurance. . . . People do not become religious simply by performing automatic operations of logic. Religion instead is closer to interpersonal kinds of experience and knowledge. The latter require that we risk ourselves by going out to people in acts of trust.[20]

None of us needs manuals dictating how we could best touch one another's hearts. The blueprinting is there in our own hearts if we only take the time first to consider and then to risk an action.

As a result of our reluctance or inability to reach out to one another, we have some very lonely Brothers who are left talking to and about themselves. Some turn inward, dry up, and wither; others turn elsewhere for love and recognition; still others talk of their expertise and talents in an attempt to hide the hurt they feel at realizing their aloneness. Hearts are meant to be touched. But often we need to look at our own hearts first before we can attempt to touch other hearts.

Tending to Our Own Hearts

At this point it is necessary to back up. For even before we move to loving one another in community, we must give ourselves permission to have a huge compassion for ourselves. Perhaps the reluctance we have to trust others is based on our conviction that we have nothing to offer, that we are worth nothing. When we believe that we are insignificant, why would anyone else, even our own Brothers, want to take what we have to give? There is a brief poem by Derrick Wolcott that encourages us toward a healthy self-love. It is entitled, "Love After Love."

> The day will come, when with elation, you will greet yourself arriving at your own door. And each will smile at the others' welcome saying: Sit here, eat, you will soon love again the stranger who was yourself.
>
> Give wine, give bread, give back your heart to itself; to the stranger who has loved you all your life whom you ignored for another who knows you by heart. Take down the love letters from the bookshelf, the photographs, the desperate notes. Feel your own image from the mirror. Sit, feast on your life![21]

Many of us get a little tentative when we hear about self-love. Self-love has not been a part of our training. Yet, when Jesus commands us to "love your neighbor as your self" he is referring to a healthy self-love.[22] Some may argue that today what we need is a heavier dose of humility; that self-love and even conceit run rampant in the lives of many and therefore need to be tempered rather than encouraged. As a teacher, student, interviewer, spiritual guide, and counselor, I can say in all honesty that I have never met a person who had a *bona fide* superiority complex. In my opinion, every instance of persons who "thought too much of themselves" was inspired by a deeper dissatisfaction or contempt for themselves. Showing how intelligent, cultured, or talented one is can easily be a smokescreen engineered to hide the more important insecurities of the self.

Our hearts are hidden deeply within us. They are heavily protected and yet they long to be touched. If we expect genuinely to touch another's heart, we will succeed only when our own heart is open as well. *Only hearts touch hearts.* When we hide and keep our own hearts unreachable, the chances of our touching anyone else's heart are quite slim.

> To love another human being fully, deeply, responsibly is to be carried into the ocean of the divine love. To feel the divine love poured forth in one's heart by the Holy Spirit is to have one's heart made tender, turned from stone to flesh, regarding other human beings.[23]

If we have any hope of touching others' hearts, we have to risk having our own hearts touched in the process. We can touch hearts as a teacher or as a religious. But we are always both of those only after first and foremost being a human, loving individual. Our bodies and our personhood house our heart, and only a loving heart can touch another heart.

Notes

1. The *Rule* of 1705 as quoted in *The Brother of the Christian Schools in the World Today: A Declaration.* Thirty-Ninth General Chapter: Second Session, 1967, 42. The emphasis is mine.

2. Two weeks before school started, the Brother Principal said he needed to see me. "I notice from your transcript that you took a number of hours in Spanish while you were at Northern Illinois University. How is it that you received eight hours in one semester?" he queried. I explained that

I took an accelerated course where we met each weekday from 9:00–10:00 A.M. and from 1:00–2:00 P.M. "Fine," he said. "With your name and that background, you'll do wonders teaching first and second year Spanish."

There was no further discussion.

3. *A Declaration*, p. 49.

4. Ibid., 44.

5. Ibid., 42. The emphasis is mine.

6. Mt 7:12.

7. Mt 32: 37–40.

8. Mt 25: 37–40.

9. This realization was identified through a conversation with Robert Zorad, religion teacher at De La Salle High School, Concord, California.

10. The title of this year's Spirituality Seminar, "Touching Hearts," probably would not have been appropriate before and during the sixties. (Some might argue that it is not an appropriate title today.)

11. 1 Jn 4: 20–21.

12. *A Declaration*, 28.

13. Ibid., 30.

14. Quoted in Joseph Carmody, "Monks Pond," *The Critic* (Winter 1992) 11.

15. Quoted in Robert McAfee Brown, *Spirituality and Liberation: Overcoming the Great Fallacy* (Louisville, KY: Westminster Press, 1988) 61.

16. These references are abundant, particularly in 1 Jn 4:7–21.

17. Quoted in John Carmody, "The Challenge of Intimacy," in *Studies in Formative Spirituality,* Vol. 12:3, (November 1991) 285.

18. Herman Hesse, *Siddhartha* (New York: Bantam Books, 1951) 71.

19. Without realizing, I left this heading until the end of this article. Perhaps its placement is indicative of where many of us put our concern for how we relate to each other as Brothers—as an afterthought.

20. John Haught, *What Is Religion?* (New York: Paulist Press, 1990) 91.

21. Derrick Wolcott, "Love After Love," from the audiotape *Songs for Coming Home* by David Whyte.

22. Raymond E. Brown et al., *The New Jerome Biblical Commentary* (Englewood Cliffs NJ: Prentice Hall, 1990) 666. For further references on this same theme, see Mt 5:43; 19:19; Rom 13:8–10; Gal 5:14; Jas 2:8.

23. John Carmody, "The Challenge of Intimacy," 278

Questions for Reflection and Discussion

1. If asked the question, "Why did you become a Christian Brother?" could you give reasons you have never before given that are just as relevant as your usual reasons? If yes, what would they be? If no, why?
2. Do you see the goal of "touching hearts" through our teaching as detracting from the role of teacher or enhancing it? Why?
3. As religious celibates, we must dare to risk that our own hearts will be touched if that is what it takes genuinely to touch others' hearts. Do you agree? If so, why? If not, why not?
4. Is celibacy a call to loneliness? If so, why? If not, why not?
5. It is not possible to love God without being vulnerable to relationships with other human beings. Do you agree? If so, why? If not, why not?
6. In what ways might Thomas Merton's regret be a relevant one for you?

A Jubilee for J.J.: A Quartet of Musings on Life's Relationships

Kevin J. Griffin, FSC

It was a lovely mid-October day with the morning sun highlighting the changing colors of autumn as Brother James Joseph Lanigan drove home from his swimming workout at the local "Y." His mind was racing in a thousand different directions. The "big day" had finally arrived. He was experiencing the emotional rush of joy, thanksgiving, and anxious anticipation while reviewing the upcoming events which would occur later that day at his Silver Jubilee celebration as a Christian Brother. J.J., as he was known by all, found it hard to believe that a quarter of a century of his life had been spent as a Lasallian educator in high schools throughout the Midwest. He marvelled at how quickly the time had gone by. It seemed like only a short while ago that he was saying good-bye to his best buddy from his youth, Red Reily, and explaining his decision to join the Christian Brothers that summer.

BROTHER KEVIN J. GRIFFIN, FSC, is currently teaching at Bethlehem University in the Holy Land. He is also an associate professor of education and communication arts at Christian Brothers University in Memphis. His doctorate is from St. Louis University in the areas of administration and teacher education.

1. The Golden Days of Youth

"Well, Red, I've got something I want to tell you. It may come as a surprise or a shock to learn that I have decided to join the Christian Brothers. I'll be leaving in a couple of days for some place called Glencoe, which is kind of like a boot camp for the 'Bros.'" J.J. felt relieved as the words flowed.

"J.J., you have to be pulling my leg! What happened to our plan of joining the Marines together this summer? Is this decision sudden or have you been thinking about it for a while?" queried Red.

J.J. thought for a moment. Here was his closest friend since the fourth grade. They had grown up together. Now they were coming to a crossroads in their lives. They had shared the ups and downs of becoming young men. There wasn't anything either one wouldn't do for the other. But Red's surprised facial expression and comments caused J.J. some frustration and pain. "Why does it have to be so difficult to share this vocation decision with Red," J.J. thought. There was an awkward silence. J.J. moved close to Red and put his hand on his shoulder. Both young men were finding it hard to know what to say at this point. Finally J.J. blurted out, "All I can say, Red, is that I have to follow this feeling I have to become a Brother. I don't know how everything will end up. I might leave Glencoe after two weeks or I might stay. All I know is that I have to go through with this decision now." J.J. stepped aside from Red and looked into space.

Red remained quiet for a minute, then he spoke. "Hey, J.J., if this is what you want to do with your life, I'm all for it a hundred percent! You know that it isn't going to be easy giving up the ladies, partying with your friends, and having your own spending money, and then having someone like Brother Bede the Bastard telling you what to do." (Brother Bede had been their high school principal.) "But it's your life and your decision and I want you to know I'm proud of you!"

The young men looked at each other. Then J.J. broke the silence. "Red, we'll keep in touch. It's not as if we'll never see each other again. I'm not going to outer space." Red nodded in agreement. They smiled broadly as they shook hands and patted each other on the back.

"Hey, Red," J.J. exclaimed, "this is enough serious talk for now. Let's go over to Joey's house to meet the rest of the guys. We can play cards and have some brews!" Red's face brightened at the suggestion and the two buddies headed toward Joey's place.

J.J. snapped back from his recollections as he pulled into the parking area next to the Brothers' home. A deep sense of gratitude and appreciation came over him. He could still count Red Reily as one of his dear friends. They had kept in touch over the years and their relationship had indeed prospered and matured. Both of them had worked at deepening their friendship throughout all of life's changes and challenges. This was not easy but both men were willing to give, to compromise, and to forgive so that their friendship could grow. He looked forward to seeing Red later that day at the celebration.

2. "Never Neglect the Third Kid in the Fifth Row!"

J.J. had just hung up the telephone in his room after speaking to his dear friend and mentor, Brother Charlie Kane. Brother Charlie wanted to check on some details relating to the jubilee banquet and the after-dinner talks, since he was going to be the principal "roaster" and "toaster" of J.J. later that day.

J.J. smiled to himself. Whenever he thought about Charlie, such wonderful memories and experiences came to mind. Of course, some of these recollections were bittersweet. J.J. first encountered Charlie at St. Benilde Prep, J.J.'s first community after four years of formation and his first teaching assignment. "The Prep" was a large, urban all-boys high school. It had long and glorious academic and athletic traditions. Its graduates were loyal and a credit to the Prep. All things considered, it was an exciting and challenging assignment for a first-year teacher.

It wasn't long before Charlie took the young, naive J.J. under his wing. J.J. had the potential to develop into an effective teacher but he was impulsive, headstrong, and had a strong temper. Studies always came easily to him and he sometimes lost patience with students who were struggling to learn or simply couldn't master the material in freshman English.

Charlie was the chairperson of the English Department and was assigned to be the "master" teacher for J.J. This was a fortunate occurrence because J.J. hadn't started off the year under the best of circumstances with some of his classes. A few discipline problems developed which came to the attention of the Dean of Students, Brother Jasper John, also known as "Jugular John" to the faculty and students. Brother "Jugular" developed a dislike for J.J., and this was not good. Charlie, however, worked patiently and firmly with J.J., and as the long, first year of teaching unfolded, J.J.'s classroom management and teaching began slowly and steadily to improve. Even "Jugular" modified his opinion of J.J.

Of all the lessons and sound pedagogical advice that Charlie imparted to J.J., one practice stood out so clearly in his mind. In each of J.J.'s classes were some students whom he was neglecting and not challenging because they simply sat there and didn't cause any problems. The difficulty was that they were not involved in the class, and they were getting farther and farther behind in their studies. Charlie brought the reality of this situation to J.J.'s attention.

"J.J., you've got to reach and to teach *all* your students in every class. Don't go after the best and the brightest all the time. Never neglect that third kid in the fifth row!" As J.J. developed into a more effective and confident teacher, he took Charlie's advice to heart and made it part of his teaching style. In fact, some of the students who responded most to J.J.'s teaching were initially shy, quiet lads who developed a love of English and a high regard for him as a teacher and as a Brother. As life would have it, J.J. became a mentor to young teachers later in his career and he was able to pass on effective teaching methods and discipline techniques that he had learned from Charlie and others. In fact, being a mentor to his religious and lay colleagues had been one of the most satisfying experiences in J.J.'s career.

Of course, Charlie also taught J.J. so much more about being a Lasallian educator and living as a religious Brother after Vatican II. Most of all, he taught J.J. the value of friendship in the Brothers. Charlie should be in good form today as a speaker, J.J. speculated. He had a great sense of humor, and he spoke from the heart. He was also a great teaser, so J.J. knew that he'd better not be too sensitive to Charlie's recollections and stories. J.J. resolved to sit back and laugh at himself and life at the celebration because, as Charlie frequently said, "Always keep a smile on your Irish face, J.J.; then they won't know what's on your mind." This was timely advice for any pilgrim on life's highway.

3. To Educate Them All My Days

J.J. was seated at a circular table in the school gym, which had been transformed into a banquet hall for the jubilee celebration. He was surrounded by his family, close friends, relatives, Brothers, lay colleagues, and former students. The Mass at the local parish church had gone off quite well. The serious and inspirational remarks by his Provincial and by the priest celebrant were well received and appreciated by J.J. and the congregation. Now that the social hour and dinner were completed, it was time to begin roasting and toasting the jubilarian.

Brother Charlie got right into his routine with a series of jokes, one-liners, and stories about J.J. over the past 25 years. There were lots of laughs from the appreciative audience plus knowing head motions in response to Charlie's remarks. J.J. laughed, had tears often, and felt humbled and affirmed throughout the talk.

Suddenly, Brother Charlie paused and swept the banquet hall with his eyes. Then he said, "We have a mystery guest with us today who wishes to congratulate and praise our beloved Brother J.J. I'm proud to present to you Dr. Vincent Salerno, Special Envoy from the United States to the Mideast Peace Talks."

J.J. couldn't believe what he was hearing and experiencing as the mystery guest came into the hall through a side door. Here was little Vinnie, all grown up with an important international position and a doctorate in international law under his belt, making his way to the speaker's podium. J.J. had kept in touch with Vinnie over the years by letters; they had enjoyed some wonderful times together in the Midwest and in Washington, DC. As a student in J.J.'s senior English class 22 years ago, Vinnie was quiet, shy, and not too sure of himself. J.J. had taken Charlie's advice to heart and sought to reach out to Vinnie as a person and as a student. The young man possessed a keen mind and a talent for writing. J.J. was instrumental in helping Vinnie develop his academic and personal abilities. In fact, J.J. was the key person in aiding Vinnie to obtain an academic scholarship to Saint Mary's College in Minnesota.

J.J. reflected that all of this had not been easy for Vinnie or himself. Vincent lost his father when he was a junior in high school. He had been close to his dad, and he took his death quite badly. He withdrew into himself and went through a long period of mild depression and self-pity. His widowed mother was beside herself, not knowing what to do to help her son. This dark time for Vinnie lasted nearly the entire second semester. In the late spring, Mrs. Salerno visited Brother John, the principal at Vincent's school, to seek help and advice. He listened to her story about Vinnie's behavior since his father's death. Of course, the principal knew that Vinnie's studies weren't going well and that he had been involved in some minor discipline problems.

Vinnie's class schedule for his senior year was finalized at the time of his mother's visit. Brother John told Mrs. Salerno that Vinnie would have Brother James Joseph as his homeroom advisor and his senior English teacher. J.J. was developing into an effective and caring educator, the principal assured Mrs. Salerno. She left Brother John's office with a hopeful feeling that Vinnie's senior year would be better, that he would come out of his grief and self-pity and get on with his life. A roar of laughter brought J.J. back to the hall.

J.J. smiled to himself as he listened to Vincent's comments about him as a teacher and as a Brother. Here was a former student extolling J.J. for reaching out and affirming him at a time in his life when he needed to be challenged and pushed into developing himself as a maturing young man and as a student. Vinnie remarked that J.J. was always there when he needed him. J.J.'s concern and care for Vinnie were firm, fair, and always compassionate. Vincent said, "After my dad, Brother James—J.J.—was the greatest influence on my life. I do not believe that I would be here speaking to you today if this special Brother hadn't come into my life when he did!"

Vinnie concluded his remarks, left the podium, and came over to J.J. Both men embraced warmly. The audience rose to its feet with thunderous applause.

Later that evening alone in his room, J.J. reflected on a quote from *The Education of Henry Adams:* "A teacher affects eternity; he can never tell where his influence stops." A rush of good feelings came over J.J. as he whispered a prayer of gratitude for his vocation as a Christian Brother educator.

4. "You Don't Really Mature as a Brother until You've Been in Love"

The morning after his jubilee celebration J.J. got up early to go through his mail from the day before. He really couldn't sleep because of all the wonderful experiences and the emotional high from the previous day's events. As he sat in the peaceful quiet of his room, he came across a greeting card from a certain Amy Driscoll. "My goodness," J.J. thought. "I haven't heard from her in ages." Amy was the daughter of a deceased woman named Kelly Marie Driscoll, who had been tragically killed in an auto accident at the age of 38. J.J. read the jubilee congratulations card with interest. Amy was eight years old when J.J. first met her mother, Kelly. J.J. was 28 years old at the time and was teaching Senior Religion and English at De La Salle Academy, where he had been assigned since making his final vows three years previously. Besides his teaching responsibilities, J.J. conducted the major fund-raising events at the Academy and was moderator of the Parents Club. Kelly had been widowed for three years after her husband died of cancer; her son was a freshman at the Academy. She was three years older than J.J., but she looked as if she were in her early 20s.

Kelly was a spirited volunteer worker for all the Academy events. Shortly after they met, J.J. realized that this woman was the kind of volunteer who comes along once in a great while. They planned and worked on many fund-raising projects and school events together. They were certainly a dynamic duo. J.J. got to know her son Patrick and her daughter Amy quite well. He regularly visited the Driscoll home for meals and planning sessions on current projects with Kelly. As time progressed, the bonds of friendship grew deeper between J.J. and the Driscolls, especially Kelly.

Then it happened. J.J. took Kelly out to dinner in appreciation for all her hard work on the Fall Festival. They had a delightful meal and thoroughly enjoyed being with each other. As they got ready to leave, Kelly reached over, touched J.J.'s hand, and said, "I just want you to know that working with you and being with you tonight are very special moments for me. You're one of the finest men I have ever met!"

They looked into each other's eyes; it was then they both knew that their friendship had deepened into love. J.J. broke the loving looks by saying, "Kelly, you know that I think the world of you. Your devotion and generosity to the Academy can't be described in words. You're very special to me and I would be lost without you at my side. I feel so complete when I'm around you."

Kelly blushed and grew silent. They both knew that it was time to leave. J.J. paid the bill while Kelly excused herself to go to the rest room. J.J. told her he'd wait for her outside the restaurant. He needed some fresh air, and as he got out into the crisp, fall evening, his mind was whirling. What should he do now? He really didn't believe in platonic relationships. Persons of the opposite sex either got more involved with each other or their relationship lost its intensity. J.J. knew that he was in a dilemma. He didn't want to stop working and being with Kelly. Look at all the wonderful projects they ran together. But deep down in his heart of hearts, he knew that he was falling in love with her. From what he could ascertain from her comments and feelings, she felt the same. At that moment Kelly emerged from the restaurant. It was evident that she had been crying in the rest room. If there was one weakness J.J. had, it was not knowing what to do when a woman cried. He just didn't handle tears too well. J.J. looked at Kelly and said, "Well, kid, how about a smile? You know that it isn't the end of the world. We're two mature human beings, trying our best to cope with life's ups and downs."

Kelly reached for J.J.'s hand as they walked to the parked car. Her grasp was tender and loving. She stopped by the car and said, "J.J., we're both in a difficult situation. I value you and respect you so much. I know how much being a Christian Brother means to you, and I do not want to be the person who comes between you and your vocation."

J.J. moved closer to Kelly and kissed her tenderly on the cheek and then on the forehead. He didn't dare kiss her on the lips because he knew he wouldn't be able to contain himself. They embraced quickly, and J.J. opened the car door for her.

The telephone rang and brought J.J. out of his day dream about that autumn evening with Kelly years ago. J.J. answered the call, which turned out to be a wrong number. He went back to reading Amy's card. He wondered if Amy knew about the deep love and respect he and Kelly had had for each other. Did Patrick suspect anything? These were all unanswered questions. Amy wrote in her card that J.J. always had a special place in her heart and in Patrick's too. In fact, she mentioned that she had a framed photo of J.J. with all the Driscolls at a University of Notre Dame football game. It was one of her prized possessions.

J.J.'s mind again raced back to the days and weeks after that fall dinner. Both Kelly and J.J. realized how far they could go before reaching a point of no return. J.J. went through some difficult times as did Kelly. This relationship was the biggest challenge to J.J.'s vocation so far in his life as a Brother. He couldn't sleep well; he was distracted in his daily activities in school; and he found it more challenging to pray. Getting more and more upset and frustrated by the situation, J.J. pondered on what to do. He had to talk to someone who could listen, not make judgments, and offer some wisdom. J.J. felt out of control and he knew that sharing a discussion of his relationship with Kelly was a great risk. Yet in his heart of hearts J.J. knew, despite his fear and embarrassment, that he had to seek counsel. After considering the Brothers he could speak to in confidence, J.J. selected Brother Julius Heller, a mature member of J.J.'s community. Julius was a friend and supporter of J.J., and he had a practical and realistic approach toward life. The two men agreed to meet in J.J.'s room one evening.

Julius sat back in the LazyBoy chair and looked reassuringly at J.J. He had a twinkle in his eyes and a grin on his Germanic face. J.J. had just told him about the intensity of his relationship with Kelly and was waiting for Julius' response.

"You know what, J.J.? What's happened to you happens to most Brothers over the course of their lives. In fact, our novice-master used to tell us that the best Brothers could make the best fathers. In my own experience of 34 years as a Brother, I have to tell you that a Brother doesn't really mature and grow up until he's been in love. Can you keep a secret? It's happened to me and it will probably happen again!"

After his conversation with Julius, J.J. felt somewhat relieved. The ideas and insights he received from Julius helped him put the situation into a less emotional context. But he continued to struggle with his love for Kelly and his desire to remain a Brother. He realized that his love for Kelly and her love for him was one of life's true joys. However, this love was such a challenge to him because he felt so divided and out of control. He knew that Kelly wasn't having an easy time of it, either. They mutually agreed not to be alone together and to maintain control over their physical expressions of love and affection. This joint agreement didn't come easily; however, with time Kelly and J.J. realized that it was in their mutual best interests to be friends but not lovers. Kelly never wanted to be the woman who caused J.J. to leave the Brothers. J.J., for his part, knew in his more rational moments that he wanted to remain a Brother. Out of all the pain, suffering, and frustration of falling in love with each other, both Kelly and J.J.'s friendship deepened and matured. They were both richer and better persons for having gone through this experience together.

Two years after they met, Kelly came into a healthy inheritance from a long lost uncle in Texas. Her newfound money made it possible to pursue a longstanding dream of getting academic degrees in business and interior design at a university in another state. Kelly's move was painful to both of them, but with time they realized that it was all for the best. They maintained their friendship by mail and by telephone. J.J. often reflected on the sound counsel he had received from Julius. He had no regrets about falling in love with Kelly. It had been one of the peak experiences in his life—one that was joyful, painful, exhilarating, and frustrating, but also affirming and maturing. He knew he was a better person because of risking to love and be loved, yet finally deciding to be true to himself and continue as a Brother. Through their many conversations together, J.J. knew that Kelly felt the same way. She was certainly one person he was looking forward to meeting in the next life.

What's It All About, Lord?

J.J. stood up and stretched in the solitude of his room. It had been a wonderful and exhilarating couple of days, he reflected. The song "People" came into his consciousness, and he began to hum the melody gently. One line from that song kept running through his mind: "People who need people are the luckiest people in the world." He suddenly fell down on his knees next to the bed and began praying—praising and thanking God for all the blessings, joys, relationships, difficulties, and challenges over the past quarter of a century. "What will the next 25 years bring," J.J. mused, as he stood up again. He suddenly felt the urge to have some strong black coffee and a little breakfast, so he headed toward the kitchen with a bounce in his steps.

Some Final Observations

In creating these four scenarios, I hoped to present real and even recognizable events and situations where a Brother has the opportunity to enter more fully into relationships with friends, Brothers, students, and women. J.J. was willing to take certain risks and be open with the persons he encountered throughout his life and in his ministry as a Christian Brother. As he reviewed his life and most especially, his vocation as a Brother, he had a mixture of memories. Some of his recollections were happy, positive, and joyful. Other memories were painful and distressing. However, J.J. isn't weighed down by his past. He is an optimistic individual who realistically knows that life has its share of happiness and joy together with pain and loss. He is mature enough to know that he has to let go of the brokenness and negativity in his life and make room in his heart and soul for the Lord's Spirit of joy, peace, and compassion. He is striving to be compassionate toward others as God has been, and is, compassionate with him. Grounded in his Lasallian roots, he is growing daily toward the challenging realization that his ministry and his life as a Christian Brother are most authentic and fruitful when he is touching hearts and when he is allowing his heart to be touched by others.

Suggested Reading

1. Robert Bly, *Iron John: A Book About Men* (New York: Addison-Wesley, 1990).
2. John Friel, *The Grown-Up Man* (Deerfield Beach, FL: Health Communications, 1991).
3. Sam Keen, *Fire In the Belly: On Being A Man* (New York: Bantam Books, 1991).

Questions for Reflection and Discussion

1. What is most challenging and most rewarding about being a man in our society today? About being a male religious? How do these challenges affect your relationships?

2. What are the factors in your personal and work life that cause the most stress? Do these stresses help or hinder your relationships?

3. In considering your relationships, how many go back to your elementary and high school days? How have you kept these relationships alive?

4. A wise individual has observed that as men get older (over age 30), they find it more challenging to develop relationships. What has been your experience in this area? How do you relate to your Brothers in community? As a Brother, do you have to be in control of your relationships with others? How willing are you to risk and to be open in your friendships and relationships?

5. Think of a student—current or former—whom you have influenced in some positive manner currently or over the years. How did you make a difference in this student's life? How do you know that you influenced this person? How do you feel about having such an experience, and how did this relationship affect you personally?

6. Have you had a mentor as a Brother? Has this made an impact on your career and personal life? Have you had the opportunity to be a mentor? Has this been a good experience for you? Do you look for opportunities to act as mentor to others?

7. How would you describe your relationship with women in your ministry and in your personal life? Do you have female friends and mentors? What challenges have you experienced as a Brother in "touching the hearts" of the women you encounter in your ministry? Do you look upon women as positive or negative influences on your growth as a Brother?

8. Who are the persons who have shared or share wisdom and hope with you as a person?

9. In the four scenarios, much of what J.J. learned and experienced came from outside the structure of a formal formation program. J.J. learned, grew, and matured as a person by experiencing life with its ups and downs. Has this been your experience also? Do you take advantage of the Region's continuing formation opportunities?

10. Do a life review for yourself regarding your relationships. How do you rate yourself? A success? A failure? How do you measure success and failure in relationships?

"But, Brother Visitor . . ."

Edward J. Sheehy, FSC

Introduction: The Meaning of Obedience

> The air force stood aside altogether, refusing orders to participate. As
> for the army, the 10 tank crews that defected to Boris Yeltsin sym-
> bolized the greater number of soldiers who refused to countenance
> the violent overthrow of the government. Even troopers nominally
> supporting the junta were reluctant to fight.[1]

Thus, the unwillingness of a Soviet army commander to *obey* triggered the collapse of the late summer coup attempt. Even more remarkable, perhaps, is the fact that his decision to disregard orders
does not seem to have been prompted by fear of the opposition:
Yeltsin's armor consisted primarily of rhetoric. Twice before in
Russian history, military commanders faced similar choices. On
Bloody Sunday (January 22, 1905), the Czar's troops fired on the
crowd—one of a series of events that triggered the revolution. But
as both history and *Doctor Zhivago* remind us, the revolutions of
1917 saw a much different outcome. In another vein, at the last Bal-
timore District Chapter, a general discussion ensued regarding the

---

BROTHER EDWARD J. SHEEHY, FSC, PHD, is currently Assistant Professor
of History at La Salle University in Philadelphia. Prior to this, he was an
instructor and an administrator in secondary schools in Maryland, Washington, DC, New Jersey, and Pennsylvania. He has graduate degrees from
Johns Hopkins University (MLA) and George Washington University (PhD
in American History). His book on the U.S. Navy and the early Cold War
was published in 1992.

missions. One viewpoint suggested a willingness to emphasize the Province's involvement in placement within the Province but maintain a spirit of volunteerism for overseas work.

These historical and personal reflections lead to a further examination of the issue and question (is there a question?) of obedience. What do obedience and the vow of obedience mean? How does a good religious approach obedience? How do we deal with each other in community? What are our perceptions of the decision-making process as well as the roles of the Director, Visitor, and Institute leadership at large? Are we beset by a "leave me alone" attitude? Do we need a "change of heart"?

Views of Obedience

Recently, we have exhibited justifiable pride in studies revolving around the anniversary celebration of the heroic vow of association made by the Founder and Brothers Gabriel Drolin and Nicolas Vuyart. My own suspicion (for want of a better word) is that obedience may be the heroic vow for the 1990s and beyond. Let me begin by focusing on an often-used simplistic analogy. Religious life (and by extension, obedience) mirrors the military. The tradition of strict, unwavering obedience to a superior's orders ranges from the anecdotal command to "water the stick" to terminology describing members of religious orders as soldiers. Certainly some military rhetoric supports the thesis. "There is nothing in war," Clausewitz wrote, "which is of greater importance than obedience." Alfred Tennyson immortalized the Light Brigade in the Crimean War with "theirs not to make reply, theirs not to reason why, theirs but to do and die." "The duty of obedience," Admiral Alfred Thayer Mahan graphically argued, "is not merely military but moral." Without obedience, "military organization would go to pieces, and military success [would] be impossible."[2]

Yet even in this field, obedience has its nuances. The defense of following orders has been riddled from Nuremburg to Vietnam. During World War II, Adolf Eichmann supervised the hunting down

and extermination of Jews. In 1960, the Israelis executed him d\
spite his impassioned resort to the chain of command. More recently, the world has ostracized Kurt Waldheim of Austria for similar
sentiments. The issue becomes more confused when we consider
that the winners set the rules. Somewhat parenthetically, we could
pursue the rationale for the Eighth Air Force's fire-bombing of Ger-
man cities and the atomic bombing of Hiroshima or Nagasaki, if
America had lost the war. The controversy engendered by the trial
and conviction of Lieutenant William Calley for killing innocent
civilians during the Vietnam conflict further illustrates this point. In
any case, even military obedience may require some judgment.[3]

From a religious standpoint, the Gospels and Paul's missives to
the young churches both emphasize obedience as required, not suggested. But as Geffrey Kelly notes, "It is doubtful if any obedience
other than that tendered the Father could be considered absolute."
Clearly, "laws were made for man and not vice versa, a point Jesus
deliberately made by his own disobedience." Kelly concludes that
our traditional view of strict obedience "would appear to be a mere
shadow, if not a distortion, of the Gospel challenge."[4]

As Kelly observes, the long-standing tradition of obedience
did appear to follow the military model, yet it also offered a simplistic view of the Scriptures. As expected, many spiritual writers
reinforced this theme. In the mid-fifteenth century, for example,
Thomas à Kempis equated obedience with the essence of Christianity. Thus, "He that strives to draw himself from this virtue with-
draws himself from grace." But even in lay spiritual writings,
nuances existed.

John Milton demanded "obedience to the spirit of God, rather
than to the fair seeming pretense of men" as "the best and most dutiful order that a Christian can observe." Even Savonarola argued
that when "the commands of superiors are contrary to God's commandments, and especially when contrary to the precepts of chari-
ty," then "no one is in such case bound to obedience." Further, we
must remember that we first hear of the three vows (obedience,
chastity, poverty) in terms of profession during the twelfth century.[5]

Obedience and the Brothers

Savonarola not withstanding, our view of De La Salle and obedience may be clear-cut. But here again is a richness and depth for reflection. Obedience is a cornerstone of the vows De La Salle,
Nicolas Vuyart, Gabriel Drolin, and ten additional Brothers took on
June 6, 1694. The emphasis on association is important, but these
first Brothers also stressed obedience as a key to their lives together. The formula of vows reads that our loyalty and obedience are to
both "the superiors who shall have the government thereof," and
perhaps what is more important, "to the body of the Society," phrases not present in the 1691 vow formula. This theme is so critical, it
is repeated in another paragraph in the 1694 version, and has served
as a basis for subsidiarity and community-based decision-making.[6]

In both his letters and meditations as well as elsewhere, De La
Salle further explained his understanding of this vow. In an early
May 1702 missive, he reminded Brother Hubert of the importance
of being "a child of obedience," whose purpose is "to obey" so we
can "carry out God's will." We must avoid "I want," "I won't," and
"I must," and our "principal virtue" must be obedience. He reiterated this last idea in a number of letters to Brothers. To Brother
Robert, probably in May 1708, he wrote that obedience "is a virtue
you should have very much at heart" for "it is the principal one you
should practice in community." De La Salle understood how difficult the vow could be. In a later note to the same Brother, he had
"no difficulty in believing that you have a dislike for obedience."
The Founder did not limit pleas for exact obedience to his Brothers.
In a letter to a woman religious, he reiterated the need for "total submission" and our responsibility "to carry out commands indiscrim-
inately, no matter how opposed they are to our feelings and
inclinations." In these directives, De La Salle mirrored the spiritual
advice of his time.[7]

Obedience must be absolute and without answer. "Do this," he
wrote, "no matter how foolish what you are told to do or what is
said to you may seem." If you obey because it makes sense, "you

are no longer acting through obedience." He further connected obedience with a reflective state (recollection), and the ability to be flexible in terms of accepting different assignments within the Institute.[8]

Our relations with superiors obviously form a backbone for the vow in practice. De La Salle emphasized the value of a frank, open dialogue between the Brothers and their superiors, perhaps a precursor to our concept of discernment. The Brothers must not view the Directors or other superiors as supermen; rather, they must differentiate between the imperfect individual and the will of God, whom he represents.[9]

While the role of superiors posed one issue that needed to be confronted, life in community also presented itself as a difficulty. Without a true spirit of brotherhood, any type of discussion/confrontation over faults would be useless. The Director played an important role in reminding community members of their specific need for self-improvement. De La Salle emphasized the personal approach and need for "good example," "winning cordiality," and "an engaging manner." He saw the community's effort to help individual Brothers recognize their failings (advertisement of defects) as a vital key to developing interpersonal, healthy relationships.[10]

As we know, De La Salle's predilection toward strict obedience to the Church caused him much pain, especially in the age of Jansenism. His own last words—"I adore the will of God in all things in my regard"—underscored the impact of this vow in his own life.[11]

The post–Vatican II years witnessed a careening yawl away from these views but a yawl in no discernible direction. Martin Helldorfer's observation in the mid-seventies that "you have to hunt for someone to tell you what to do" still makes more than a little sense. Our efforts to see the vows in a behavioristic way leaves us to some extent with "the phenomenon of emptiness" because "the world of behavior has changed and we feel empty." Brother John Johnston, Superior General, viewed the pre–Vatican II period as a "model of dependence" in which "authority was heavily centralized." In following years, he observed, "we successfully dethroned" this concept "with amazing rapidity," moving to a "model of independence."[12]

Given the tumult of the Vietnam era, it is easy to see this reemphasis on the individual and community as opposed to the strict chain of command. The use of words such as "collegiality and coresponsibility," "dialogue," and "subsidiarity" swept the church. As Jeffrey Calligan noted, the stress was on the move toward "a new sense of authority which is communal in base and horizontal in structure."[13]

Interpersonal relations and communication became more important, for, as David Detje told us in 1984, "how successfully we prepare for our role in the future of the church" rested on "our ability to become interdependent." Our accountability to the Brothers we live with provided a basis for discussions that could be confrontative as well as affirming and healing. Meetings and prayer accompany this journey. The emphasis on the individual vis-a-vis the group rather than the superior was not an easy one, for "no longer exist 'they' who 'should do something about that.'" Perhaps Detje summed up our state best with his view, "We are satisfied with independence and not yet ready for interdependence."[14]

This quest for communal accountability was only one ingredient in an effort to fill a void left by the dismantling of the traditional view of obedience. The 40th General Chapter (1976) stressed the role of the Spirit and the "principle of subsidiarity." The Director's position required him to be able "to issue a command when it becomes necessary"; however, "his influence comes more from his attitude of service than from domination and power." While the wording is modern, the sense of obedience echoes De La Salle. The Brothers should "respect decisions" as well as "give honest, intelligent cooperation, even when they personally consider another course of action to be better." Certainly, specific application of the vow "will sometimes be difficult and can often go contrary to legitimate personal conviction." If consensus can't be agreed on, then the Brothers "accept the final decision in the spirit of sacrifice and prayer, trusting that what God expects of them will become more clear." Community meetings and personal interviews become important means of communication. The Visitor's role emphasizes the interpersonal nature of his responsibilities. He is "one who serves," whose position is to "know them [Brothers] personally" and to continue "trustful relations with them." Within the framework of District Chapter directives, "with due respect for the persons concerned," he "arranges the composition" of the different houses of the Province. The section on obedience observes that, as a member of the Institute, a Brother "accepts the authority structure therein established." The same emphasis on service pervades the *Book of Government*'s view of the Director.[15]

Obedience in the Present Age

Thus far I have examined, albeit superficially, differing views of obedience, all rooted in their historical context. In each case, words have reiterated a need for following directives. Yet in practice, we have continually moved toward individuality, a process accelerated no doubt by the last decade. In the election campaign of 1980, Ronald Reagan may have won victory with basic questions aired in a TV debate concerning the state of our own welfare and America's place in the world. Given the soaring misery index and sense of social frustration triggered by affirmative action, Iran, and a less than sluggish economy, the answers propelled the "Great Communicator" into the White House. Yet those questions may well define the eighties as a self-centered decade, a period in which decision-making became committee-oriented and thus in reality individualized. "That we have been so influenced by our fast-evolving culture is disappointing," the Superior General observed in his 1989 Pastoral to the Brothers, "but not surprising or difficult to understand." The eighties accelerated the move toward the Director's role as coordinator and the Brother's ultimate role in deciding a plethora of issues. Imperceptibly we have shifted to an individual approach.[16]

There is a geometric dimension to this emphasis. Visitors, Directors, even the center of the Institute now basically exhort. Within broad (and broadening parameters), the individual's input has widened to direction in some critical areas: attendance at exercises, money, friends, role in community (I can do my job but not be there), retreat, attendance at District gatherings, summer work, careers, and so on. This is not an attempt to set up a straw man argument. There are many good reasons why, for example, a Brother might not teach, might not do research, or might not attend school, but perhaps we need more accountability or at least information-exchange. Thus, we may need a clearer focus on the who, what, when, where, and why of our lives.

Our involvement with the democratic model leads to community acceptance of annual programs and individual responsibilities. Phrases like "Leave me alone," and by extension, "Where I'm at and what I'm doing," can be watchwords heard more often, not automatically with negative overtones.

Certainly, our recent rhetoric offers rich diversity. We continually underscore the value of reflective prayer and constructive dialogue as vital aspects of the discernment process. In its opening article on this vow, The *Rule* of 1986 reemphasized the role of the Spirit. We are reminded of the need for "availability within a community." The final decision-maker in each community remains the Director (in theory). The *Rule* does recognize that to obey on occasion "seems difficult and it can go contrary to one's personal convictions." Ultimately, however, the Brothers should obey "through an attitude of faith."[17]

The roles of the Director and Visitor both stress the importance of service. The former's decision-making involvement is carefully couched in the almost journalistic vein: when ("at the appropriate moment") and what ("intervene, endorse, settle"). Most of the section deals with specific responsibilities including personal interviews, the Director's appointment, and finances.

Besides a variety of nondirective responsibilities, the Provincial assigns Brothers, ensures adherence in legal matters, and has a determining voice in certain financial issues. Once again, practical matters are key factors.[18]

The current *Guide for Formation* provides an interesting glimpse into our direction of younger members. There is a clear reminder of the specific commitments including the willingness "to be prepared to go to any place to which they are sent and to do there whatever the ministry requires of them." "Fraternal correction" is valuable as a "Christian duty." Further, as in other Institute documents, we see obedience discussed in the context of one of several possible "crises of faith," as we personally deal with "the way in which authority is exercised in the Institute and the Church." The document also notes potential problems inherent in community living ranging from the theoretical to the practical.

Brothers Today

Thus far, I have observed the basic black and white statement of obedience which, as it turns out, has many gray shades. While the Institute has recently underscored the concept of collegiality, service, and community responsibility, our documents still discuss the final authority in both placement (Visitor) and interpersonal community relations (Director) as well as the difficulty of subordinating our own will to that of another. [19]

Understandably, we see a clear gap between theory and practice. Some Brothers have, consciously or not, adopted a philosophy that puts responsibility on the Visitor to make a case for transfer or policy as opposed to the individual Brother, starting from the premise that a move or change of lifestyle might be better for the common good. Our discussions about accountability and responsibility have rightly focused on community and the place of discernment in the Brothers' lives. But obedience to a group, perhaps like rule by committee, remains a difficult process at times.

Our lives as American religious must be rooted in personal accountability. The tension inherent even in the words "religious community" requires, however, a rediscovery, a reanalysis, and a new understanding of the meaning of obedience in our lives. While we, like De La Salle, are products of our time in history, we also need to step back a bit and reflect on this vow and its personal application. The Superior's Pastoral Letter on "Solidarity" emphasized our co-responsibility to interdependence, a process by which we understand our relationship with the community, district, region, and Institute at large. As Brother John Johnston explained, this "interdependence is an invitation to live, not as children or as individualists, but as mature men who are willing to love, trust, take risks, share, make demanding commitments and be faithful to them."

Practically, this may result in a changed mind-set. In many areas, we have divided the posts of Director and Principal. It seems we are willing to understand and follow (not always accept) decisions in the workplace. Yet in our community lives, the emphasis is on continued discussion, general goals, and few aids to resolving conflict. Certainly the traditional view of the vow and authority seem tyrannical, yet we should reestablish a middle ground in the area of obedience. While canonically appointed, the Provincials are usually Brothers who have received significant District support. We sometimes propose leaders with a "don't rock the boat" philosophy, and often are most comfortable with someone like ourselves in a position of responsibility. Perhaps our most pressing personal question remains: do we support Brothers in leadership posts because they will use their judgment to do what is best for the order, popular or not, or because they will keep the *status quo?* Perhaps we need to let our superiors lead. Frustration sets in for them when Brothers indicate a general interest in another apostolate, but within months, equivocate when presented with a specific alternative. Certainly, Heraclitus was right in seeing life as a continuous stream in which one never steps into the same water twice. Thus, a Brother is a different person even a day after his agreement to go elsewhere. But collectively and individually in areas as diverse as summer activities and second careers, we may need to let those in positions of responsibility have stronger involvement in our lives. Personally and communally we should review the question of whom we listen to, whom we follow, and why.

This change of heart must be a collective effort. Our answer to criticism often is, "But what about the other guy who's getting away with —— [fill in the blank]?" District annual gatherings, prayer services, or vow renewals could focus on this theme of group commitment to rediscovery. The call is for a return to balance. The most important issues involving summers, for example, revolve around retreats, apostolates, vacations, communities, and renewals. Clearly, the Province should not dictate every move or day but at least the local superior should know individual plans for these months and the Province should carefully review each Brother's program, so that there is some accountability. Our presence "in the world but not of it" mandates structure in our lives—not total structure but *some* structure and focus. Obedience, like our other vows, must have personal meaning to us. Human nature demands it, but more important, our religious commitment calls for it. The common bond of brotherhood needs strengthening. To grow spiritually, assist others, and develop continually as vibrant communities, we must, in words borrowed from July 4, 1776, "all hang together," or figuratively, we will "all hang separately."[20]

Notes

1. Richard Lacayo, "The Silent Guns of August," *Time,* 2 September, 1991, 31.

2. Clausewitz, *On War* (1812); Alfred Tennyson, *The Charge of the Light Brigade* (1854); Alfred Thayer Mahan, *Retrospect and Prospect* (1902).

3. For a view of military obedience from a half century ago, see *The Bluejackets' Manual,* 10th ed. (Annapolis: U.S. Naval Institute, 1940).

4. Geffrey Kelly, FSC, "Toward a New Expression of One's Religious Commitment," in *The Brothers and Their Vows: A Fresh Look at Religious Vows* (hereinafter referred to as *The Brothers and Their Vows*), Martin Helldorfer, FSC, ed. (Christian Brothers Seminar, 1974), 13.

5. Thomas à Kempis, *Imitation of Christ,* 1441; John Milton, *An Apology Against a Pamphlet,* 1642; Girolamo Savonarola, *Sermon,* 1496, quoted in *Cambridge Modern History,* vol. 1. See Note 4, Kelly, *The Brothers and Their Vows,* 15–16.

6. Vow Formula, June 6, 1694. See Vow Formula, November 2, 1691, *Cahiers Lasalliens* 2: 40, 42.

7. Letter 7 to Brother Hubert, May 5, 1702, *The Letters of John Baptist de La Salle* (hereinafter *Letters*). Translation, Introduction, and Commentary by Colman Molloy, FSC. Edited with additional commentary by Augustine

Loes, FSC. (Romeoville, IL: Lasallian Publications, 1988) 35. Letter 40 to Brother Robert, May 21 [1708], *Letters*, 139. Letter 46 [1709], *Letters*, 150. Letter 107, to the same member of a religious community of women, undated, *Letters*, 223. See also *Letters*, 204–205, 218.

8. Letter 107, 224. See Letters 55 and 64 to Brother Matthias, December 3 [1706], *Letters*, 165–166; 179–180.

9. See *Meditations*, nos. 72–73, Nineteenth and Twentieth Sundays after Pentecost, De La Salle *Meditations* (hereinafter *Meditations*), W.J. Battersby, ed. (London: Waldegrave 1964) 304–310.

10. Letter 66 to a Brother [Director], September 14, 1709; *Letters*, 185. See also 202–204.

11. See no. 106, *Meditations*, 414–417, "On the Submission We Owe to the Church."

12. Martin Helldorfer, FSC, "The Vows as Hidden Realities," in *The Brothers and Their Vows*, 23; John Johnston, FSC, "Solidarity," *Pastoral Letter*, January 1989, 23.

13. Jeffrey Calligan, FSC, "No More Kings . . . (A Bicentennial Minute!)," *A Seminar on Power and Authority* (hereinafter *Power and Authority*). (Lockport, IL: Christian Brothers Conference, 1976) 47.

14. David Detje, FSC, "Community: Loving Confrontation" in *Brothers in the Church*, Martin Helldorfer, FSC, ed. (Romeoville, IL: Christian Brothers Conference, 1984) 64–67.

15. Brothers of the Christian Schools, *The Rule and Constitutions, The Book of Government*, 40th General Chapter, 1976, The *Rule*, "Obedience," 51–53; *Book of Government*, "Brother Visitor," 119; "Obedience," 154. See Gabriel Moran, FSC, "Is Religious Authority Possible in a Post–Critical Age?" *Power and Authority*, 38–40. *Book of Government*, "Brother Director," 135–137.

16. Johnston, "Solidarity," 23. See entire document.

17. The *Rule* of the Brothers of the Christian Schools. Rome: 1987, 48–50.

18. Ibid., 65–67, 135–139.

19. Brothers of the Christian Schools, *Guide for Formation* (Rome: General Council, 1991) 39, 95, 126, 211. See 126, 214.

20. Johnston, "Solidarity," 22, 25.

Questions for Reflection and Discussion

1. Do I compartmentalize my life regarding obedience in the following areas: ministry, community, district, personal life? If so, how?
2. What qualities do I look for in a religious superior?
3. Is obedience the vow of the 90s and beyond? Why or why not?
4. How do I view the role of the region and the Institute with regard to obedience?
5. Has my personal view of obedience changed over the years? If so, how?

Touching Hearts

Searching Sacred Texts

The Touch of God

Robert C. Berger, FSC

Life is filled with experiences of God. Our students are no exception to this reality. Their lives rise and fall as their experiences fluctuate between anxiety and restlessness on the one hand and positive thinking and awareness of social concerns on the other. Periodically their lives may be marred by complaints, discouragement, hostility, or resentment, and yet God quietly holds out to them hopefulness, faith, patience, and love. Young people need encouragement to seek God not only in these extremes but also in the intermediate moments of ordinary life.

This article will reflect on one of our tasks as Lasallian educators: to encourage our students to notice the touch of God in daily life. This challenge is as sacred as it was in the days of the Hebrew Scriptures. Thus, I intend to use the example of men and women remembered in our biblical tradition, especially Jeremiah, to show that the touch of God can be a vivid and powerful current in the lives of our students. Obviously these stories will not grasp the imagination of every student in our Lasallian schools but, at the same time, probably more students are open to these narratives than we realize. The student audience intended in this article is either of upper high

---

BROTHER ROBERT C. BERGER, FSC, DMIN, is Assistant Professor of Religious Studies at Manhattan College, Bronx, New York. He earned a Master of Divinity Degree from Princeton Theological Seminary and a Doctorate from Drew University in New Jersey. He holds a Certificate in Spiritual Direction and has conducted Eight-Day Directed Retreats. At Manhattan College he is also a Residence Hall Director, and has held the position of Director of Campus Ministry.

school or college age, young people who can freely choose how to deal with their emerging adult spirituality.[1]

Our students are caught in a precarious bind. They find themselves beyond the years of childhood and, at times, fear they will never achieve what they imagine to be adulthood. During this transition period many young people understand life as a journey in which they discover new horizons of identity. They often search for meaning with the intensity of pilgrims and proclaim their newfound message with the enthusiasm of prophets. For them this period of life is understood in terms of endless possibilities. It is a time stimulated by growth, encouraged by hope, and headed toward happiness.[2]

But how many of our students view these years as an opportunity for spiritual growth that will accompany them on the journey to adulthood? From this question a challenge emerges for young men and women to accept responsibility for their own spiritual growth. This challenge is their ability to become aware of God's action in their lives as they reach crossroads in personal development. Crossroads are times of decision and direction that lead people toward or away from wholeness. These are demanding periods of struggle and pain, usually accompanied by rewarding opportunities for self-discovery and learning.

At these crossroads many young people are conscious of God at work in moments perceived as positive and growthful, but they find it difficult to articulate the presence of God in times of ambiguity and defeat. Their lives are often based on the mistaken notion that all of life should be on the upswing. Their theology is a theology of resurrection more than of the cross. Since both elements are integral to Christian participation in the Paschal mystery, there may be danger to this one-sided approach among the young. Without the cross, growth in spirituality is able to retain its thrust only by repressing the negative side of life. In the long run, repression could lead to an eruption of resentment and frustration. Such a reaction poses a challenge for today's Lasallian educators: to help in the formation of young people as they respond to the touch of God in times of restlessness and times of peace.

Biblical and Theological Aspects of the Touch of God

Scripture gives us many stories of men and women who respond obediently to the touch of God and live out their lives as faithful followers of God. Abram and Sarai listen to Yahweh, leave the land of their kinsfolk, and many years later become parents of a people that expands into a host of nations (Gen 12:1–3). Abram was said to be "seventy-five years old when he departed from Haran" (Gen 12:4). But one does not need the experience of many years to become a serious pilgrim who listens to the word of God. One needs only the desire, like Abram and Sarai, to enter more deeply into the presence of a personal God who seeks a relationship and exacts a response.

The theology of a personal God, who desires relationship, both invitation and response, is illustrated in the lives of a number of young men and women in the Hebrew Scriptures. These young people emerge from their early adult years with an experience of being helped to see God more clearly through their association with an adult who is close to them. Isaac follows the guidance given to him by his father Abraham and learns to know the Lord as the One who will always provide (Gen 22:14). As a young widow Ruth refuses to leave her mother-in-law, and in her loyalty to Naomi embraces the God of the Hebrews (Ruth 2:16). Ruth's decision to follow Yahweh and Yahweh's people leads her to join a noble cast of characters who have as their descendant David the king and Jesus the Christ. The story of Samuel and Eli (1 Sam 3) also shows the powerful dynamic that is present when one adult who is experienced in listening to the Lord instructs a neophyte how to hear God's personal revelation. The faithful and charitable Tobit is mindful that life is a journey with God. A prayerful man, he advises his son and sends him on a mission. Tobit's mutual relationships with God and his son result in a supernatural deliverance from affliction for himself, his son Tobias, and Tobias's wife, Sarah. Tobit shows a young adult the faithfulness of God to those who are faithful to God.

In the New Testament, one example of a person trying to keep focused on the Lord is that of the rich young man (Mt 19:16–22) who approaches Jesus and requests eternal life. He is a good illustration of a young man who seeks some direction on his spiritual journey: he asks a question in an effort to gain an answer about a new direction in life. He desires growth in life, and Jesus challenges him with yet another question in order to guide him to that growth. Such a form of guidance is exactly what a Lasallian educator seeks to accomplish.

Jeremiah and the Prayer Experience

As all the aforementioned biblical people came to a particular crossroad in their journey, they were helped to focus their orientation on the meaning of God in their lives and to grow in their own faith response. Another outstanding personality who reveals the same dynamic is the prophet Jeremiah, a person of prayer and action. His life reveals a series of incidents that build around his experience of "call," a profound theological and spiritual reality.

Being called by God seems to be something very common to many people throughout history, especially people who try to live by faith. This call is particularly keen in the minds of some students who seek to discern God's will in their lives. To understand the way in which God calls the prophet Jeremiah is to get some sense of the uniqueness with which each young person experiences a call.[3]

The Call of Jeremiah

4. Now the word of the Lord came to me saying, 5. "Before I formed you in the womb I knew you, and before you were born I consecrated you; I appointed you a prophet to the nations." 6. Then I said, "Ah, Lord God! Truly I do not know how to speak, for I am only a boy." 7. But the Lord said to me, "Do not say, 'I am only a boy'; for you shall go to all to whom I send you, and you shall speak whatever I command you, 8. do not be afraid of them, for I am with you to deliver you, says the Lord." 9. Then the Lord put out his hand and touched my mouth; and the Lord said to me, "Now I have put my words in your mouth. 10. See, today I appoint you over nations and over kingdoms, to pluck up and to pull down, to destroy and to overthrow, to build and to plant" (Jer 1 NRSV).

Chapter one of the book of Jeremiah contains a classic example of the call narrative. Initially, the divine confrontation (1:4) takes the form of a word, a creative power that does not come back to God until it has fulfilled its purpose. There is no preparation for this word's coming; it is up to Yahweh, and only Yahweh can initiate the call. Second, Jeremiah is aware of a personal relationship with Yahweh in that he now senses a God who forms, chooses, and sets him apart.[4] The introductory word (1:5a) is all-encompassing, inasmuch as Yahweh chooses Jeremiah before his life even begins to stir in his mother's womb. Third, a commission is given (1:5b), a direct imperative to be a prophet to the nations. Thus, the choice is clear: Jeremiah perceives his vocation. Yet, the clarity of the message does not rule out some wavering on Jeremiah's part. This fourth aspect of the call narrative reveals Jeremiah's concern. His objection (1:6) shows the real human side of the prophet, his fear and frustration. So he boldly opposes God. In short, he doubts his call. But Yahweh speaks to the needs of his servant and gives reassurance (1:7–8). Finally, the narrative ends with God touching Jeremiah (1:9–10) and making him an overseer of God's sovereignty in history, to uproot and to plant, to tear down and to build.[5]

Journey of Students in the Lasallian Tradition

What student today could describe a personal call in such a clear and meaningful progression? A rare young adult indeed. If that person were to describe such a call, who would listen? How would the listener help the student gain confidence in such an experience of personal call from the Lord? How can the student be helped to notice the personal touch of God in such a call?

As we examine these questions it is safe to say that most, if not all, of our students wonder, at one point or another, whether there really is a God. On the other hand, many young people seem to have at least one experience that assures them that God exists. Cannot the personal call of Jeremiah (1:4–10) serve as a biblical and theological model for these people who have such ambiguous experiences? God calls and the young Jeremiah hears the invitation. But quickly doubt enters. In terms of the spiritual journey, Jeremiah is an excellent illustration of one who experiences doubt, and yet remains faithful to God. Jeremiah's faithfulness is rooted in a prayer life that is completely intertwined with his experiences.[6] Prayer enables him to view all experiences as religious insofar as he notices God in everyday life circumstances. He savors this knowledge. Thus, his words and actions reflect a response to God's touch, which is an essential part of our Lasallian tradition.

Nature of a Religious Experience

> 11. The word of the Lord came to me, saying, "Jeremiah, what do you see?" And I said, "I see a branch of an almond tree [Heb. *shaged*]." 12. The Lord said to me, "You have seen well, for I am watching [Heb. *shaged*] over my word to perform it." 13. The word of the Lord came to me a second time, saying, "What do you see?" And I said, "I see a boiling pot, tilted away from the north" (Jer 1).

The vision of Jeremiah 1:11–12 is brief compared to the call narrative of 1:4–10 but, prayerful women and men can find a rich theology in it. Meditating on these two verses could help our students discover what happens when someone like Jeremiah prays. They could gain confidence in their prayer if they took the time and opportunity to listen to the experience of Jeremiah. To watch Jeremiah in these two brief verses is to see a man open himself to God's touch.

For Jeremiah, from the experience of first seeing a "branch of an almond" (1:11) to the contemplative attitude of knowing a God who is "watching" (1:12) suggests a religious experience. Although there is word play here (both terms are very similar in the Hebrew), nevertheless there seems to be a genuine experience of divine communication.[7] Although the chronological order of Jeremiah's visions is unknown, it is possible that this vision and others are experiences that lead the young prophet to know himself as being called by the Lord. One way of helping our students to know themselves as also called by the Lord might be to examine some basic qualities of religious experience as found in both spiritual direction and Jeremiah's vision (1:11–12). This I shall try to show.

Religious Experience in Spiritual Direction

From my ministry in teaching and spiritual direction, I believe that common characteristics of religious experience can be observed as a person speaks about his or her encounter with God's touch. They are not necessarily all observable at the same moment, but they are present in a variety of combinations at various times and in different degrees. First, there is a sense of simplicity as the person becomes involved in the ordinariness of the experience. Second, a clear beginning and end to the experience helps the person to be drawn into the image that reveals the presence of God. These parameters allow the person to focus more directly on the experience. Third, this image becomes a vivid memory that gives sustenance and confidence to the person. The student gradually grows in the conviction that God is active in his or her life.

Religious Experience in Jeremiah 1:11–12

First, there is indeed a simplicity in the brief exchange between the Lord and Jeremiah. The ordinariness of the "branch of an almond" becomes an instrument by which the prophet becomes involved in the experience. Next, for Jeremiah the experience has a beginning and an end. He is apparently drawn into the almond image and becomes overwhelmed by the discovery that God is actually watching over the divine word. Third, for this image to be recorded in the Hebrew Scriptures indicates that it is a vivid memory for Jeremiah, a memory which gives sustenance. Jeremiah believes in this and other prayer experiences; for example, the vision found in 1:13. These prayer experiences give him the confidence to realize that he is receiving a "call" from the Lord, a call that reassures him that God is with him at all times, in the good and the bad.

Religious Experience and Our Students

Jeremiah's experience of call can offer an invitation to our students to become familiar with their own religious experiences. As young men and women study the dynamics that occur between God and Jeremiah, they might be encouraged to bring the ordinariness of their own lives to prayer. The simplicity of their life situations will take on greater significance as they realize that God communicates at every moment. Like the young Jeremiah, prayerful students can come to know their own sense of call as they recognize that it is a personal God who invites and who desires to communicate the divine presence to all. Students could benefit by our encouragement to look at their own experiences, no matter how brief or sustained, in order to gain confidence that God is present in their own lives, much as God was in the life of Jeremiah.

Jeremiah's attentiveness, a movement from seeing a "branch of almond" (1:11) to understanding that God is "watching" (1:12), is an illustration for young people that God invites and communicates in human history. God's touch is perceived when our students take the time to be mindful of God. This is the very richness of our Lasallian tradition and reminiscent of the Founder's concern that Brothers and students alike continually recall the presence of God. Students need encouragement to pay attention to God's touch, to notice what happens inside themselves, to savor their experiences, and, finally, to share their responses with others. Thus, the main structure of Jeremiah's call could give our students the key elements of prayer—noticing, savoring, and responding—as well as a direction in life.

Jeremiah and Spiritual Direction

As an aid to helping our students to pray, our educational ministries have a unique opportunity for fostering a renewal of an ancient ministry, the art of spiritual direction. The dynamic of spiritual direction basically involves two Christians who come together to notice, savor, and respond to God's presence in everyday life. One person may share an experience, what is happening (or not happening) in prayer or in life, or speak about how one's relationship is with others and God. The director listens and invites the student to become more aware, and possibly see the presence of God in his or her life. In short, both the director and student keep their minds and hearts focused on a mutual, mysterious friend, God.[8]

A biblical understanding of spiritual direction is demonstrated by the analogy of the potter's touch to the clay in Jeremiah 18:1–12.

1. The word that came to Jeremiah from the Lord: 2. "Come, go down to the potter's house, and there I will let you hear my words."

3. So I went down to the potter's house, and there he was working at his wheel. 4. The vessel he was making of clay was spoiled in the potter's hand, and he reworked it into another vessel, as seemed good to him. 5. The word of the Lord came to me: 6. "Can I not do with you, O house of Israel, just as this potter has done?" says the Lord. "Just like the clay in the potter's hand, so are you in my hand, O house of Israel. 7. At one moment I may declare concerning a nation or kingdom, that I will pluck up and break down and destroy it, 8. but if that nation, concerning which I have spoken about, turns from its evil, I will change my mind about the disaster that I intended to bring on it. 9. And at another moment I may declare concerning a nation or a kingdom that I will build and plant it, 10. but if it does evil in my sight, not listening to my voice, then I will change my mind about the good that I had intended to do to it. 11. Now, therefore, say to the people of Judah and the inhabitants of Jerusalem: 'Thus says the Lord: Look, I am a potter shaping evil against you and devising a plan against you. Turn now, all of you from your evil way, and amend your ways and your doings.' 12. But they say, "It is no use! We will follow our own plans, and each of us will act according to the stubbornness of our evil will."

This analogy can easily be applied to our own tradition as Lasallian educators. Jeremiah's receptivity to the message of God at the potter's house is the same essential element in our Lasallian ministry that allows educators to keep their focus on both God and the prayerful student.[9] Jeremiah's attitude of simple attention to the ordinariness of the scene allows him to watch both the potter and the object of clay, symbols of God and the student. To contemplate with Jeremiah the relationship of the potter to the clay object is to share in the ministry of a Lasallian educator who watches the intimacy between God and a student.

Dynamics of Spiritual Direction for Lasallian Educators

To see Jeremiah as a model for Lasallian educators to be spiritual directors, one must understand the answers to four questions that help illustrate the dynamics of spiritual direction. What is the attitude of Jeremiah? What hope encourages Jeremiah to look toward

God? What does the touch of God and the freedom of God mean to Jeremiah? What is Jeremiah's responsibility as he watches God?

Attitude of Jeremiah and the Lasallian Educator

Within this brief pericope (Jer 18:1–12) is a deeply meaningful simplicity. The relationship between God and the people is symbolized as a routine and unobtrusive occupation, that is, molding clay. Jeremiah's attitude is a prayerful attentiveness to the action of molding the clay. He looks at both the potter and the pot that is being molded. He watches the potter who has the ability and freedom to mold the clay into whatever form he wishes. Jeremiah also notices the nature of the clay that the potter can mold into any desired form. The clay is neither hard nor brittle. As Jeremiah watches the potter give such careful attention to the painstaking craft, he understands that the relationship of the potter to the clay object is similar to that of God to God's people.

As Jeremiah watches the potter shape and re-shape the object, so too a Lasallian educator carefully watches God gradually form and re-form a student. Thus, the educator's attitude is also one of prayerful attentiveness to both God's action in the student and the student's response to the initiatives of God's touch.

Hope Necessary for Jeremiah and the Lasallian Educator

In the act of shaping and re-shaping, Jeremiah sees the strain between the divine intention of doing good and the human inclination to evil. Jeremiah lives in the days of King Josiah's reforms to bring the people back to God; he is also aware of the idolatrous practices of Judah. There is a tension between God's will to guide the people and their freedom to refuse such guidance. Yet in the midst of this tension Jeremiah notices one profound hope in the action of the potter: God is for us—whether building up or tearing down!

God's being for us is the hope that Jeremiah or Lasallian educators need to carry out their ministries. Jeremiah knows that God is faithful in the midst of Jerusalem's destruction. The follower of De La Salle is convinced that God is faithful to the students no matter what activities are happening around them. God is attentive to each student as the potter is attentive to the clay.

"The Touch of God" for Jeremiah and Lasallian Educators

One can understand why Jeremiah so carefully watches the potter: he is fascinated by the potter's touch on the clay. For him, it is like the touch of God. He himself knows the touch of God; it is like no other touch. For Jeremiah, no marriage, no family, no security can ever equal that loving and caring touch of God on a person. Jeremiah contemplates the potter and the clay and suggests that it resembles the reality of God's touch for women and men in all places and at all times.

As Jeremiah watches the potter with the clay, so too the Lasallian educator watches the way God molds a student. The educator is humbled as he or she witnesses this touch of God on a student. Only God knows when to touch and how deeply to touch. This touch is a mystery that reminds both the educator and the student that the Holy Spirit is the only true educator.

Freedom of God for Jeremiah and the Lasallian Educator

In this pericope, Jeremiah is apparently attracted to the touch of the potter and becomes fascinated by the discovery that God actively cares for God's creation, the clay. Both touch and discovery give Jeremiah the confidence of knowing a God who desires to mold clay into a particular form. So too, Lasallian educators can rest in a similar hope and confidence that God continues to work freely with the "clay" of our contemporary students.

By reflecting on the potter's action, educators can come to know the freedom that was involved in God's action on the lives of the people of ancient Jerusalem. It was a free sovereignty that operated in the midst of a people who also exercised their freedom to choose God or false idols. This freedom is expressed in 18:7,9, where God promises to either "pluck up and pull down" or to "build and plant." The first half of each movement represents ascending action, the second half descending action. Yet, "pluck up" is the opposite force of "plant," while "pull down" contradicts the movement of "build." Here Jeremiah has two different descriptions of what can be the will of God, a will that is balanced by the choice of a people. Their lives will experience growth or destruction depending upon what they choose. Lasallian educators see a similar freedom operative in God and in their students' choices. God is free to act, yet God respects the freedom of all.

Responsibility of Jeremiah and Lasallian Educators

Jeremiah senses his own personal responsibility in the two-way relationship between God and God's people. It is a responsibility that the people have obviously forgotten, but that God painfully remembers. Jeremiah sees his relationship to God as a trust to pray for both the people and himself. In this prayer Jeremiah is invited to be as attentive to God as he is to the potter. Thus, Jeremiah looks to God with a reflective awareness similar to the way in which he stands before the potter. As Jeremiah prays, he is willing to wait and listen for God's self-revelation. When it comes, it reveals God as possessing the freedom to reshape the people into the image intended by God—as the potter reshapes the clay.

Lasallian educators also know themselves to be in a two-way relationship with God when they accompany students on their spiritual journey. Educators pray for their students as well as for themselves in order that God will be the central focus of whatever happens in a particular classroom session or individual meeting. As Lasallian educators travel with others they are willing to wait and watch for God's presence. This attentiveness acknowledges the freedom of God working in the lives of all students.

Jeremiah and Students

For young men and women who wish to understand their Lasallian education as the opportunity to grow in their relationship with God, it is important for them to note how Jeremiah stands silently, yet observantly, before the potter. Jeremiah's stance reveals a certain awe that comes when one is experiencing God's touch. This awe begets a reverence as we notice how God is so much a part of us, and we of God, that all of life makes sense only in the context of such an intimate relationship. Belief in this relationship supports our theology of God's dwelling among us and in us. To know and love a God who suffers when we suffer and rejoices when we rejoice, allows us to see a God who wants to share everything with us.[10]

Jeremiah's silent attentiveness to the actions of the potter on the clay is far from passive. A powerfully relational dynamic is at work connecting the potter, the clay, and Jeremiah. This triangular relationship of God, the directee, and the director can serve as a challenge for both Lasallian educators and students to involve themselves in spiritual direction as privileged witnesses to a God who is deeply involved in all aspects of life.

Much of what Jeremiah does before the potter and the clay is very active. Similarly, Lasallian educators, who accompany students on their spiritual journeys, also play very active roles. It takes a lot of energy to do such tasks as loving, praying for, and pondering about students. Even something as simple as not jumping in to give advice can be an active stance.

This attentive prayer of Jeremiah is an invitation for our students to walk with and delight in a God who loves each person so much that God cannot leave an individual alone, much as God could not abandon the people of Jerusalem.[11] Likewise, as in God's relationship with Jeremiah, God continuously invites all people into a more intimate and all-encompassing partnership that overflows into a specific ministry, that of becoming God's messenger at a special time and in a unique place.

In sum, Lasallian education participates in that invitational process by helping students to highlight their personal experiences of God in faith. One of our key roles, then, is to facilitate the dialogue between the student and God, slowly enabling students to discover God's intimate touch in their life. In order to help students to become more aware of God's self-communication in their life, the educator who has experienced the touch of God needs to help God touch others. We need to enjoy God's touch. It is more significant than the touch of any human being. It is the touch of life itself.

Notes

1. Scott Seethaler, "The Struggle with Prayer," *Review for Religious* 50 (July/August 1991) 602–606.

2. William F. Kraft, "Spiritual Growth in Adolescence and Adulthood," *Human Development* 4 (Winter 1983) 14.

3. R.E. Clements, *Jeremiah, Interpretation: A Bible Commentary for Teaching and Preaching* (Atlanta: John Knox Press, 1988) 16.

4. John Bright, "Jeremiah," *The Anchor Bible,* no. 21 (Garden City: Doubleday, 1985) 6–7.

5. Walter Brueggemann, "Jeremiah's Guide for Christians Who Know How To Blush," *The Other Side* 22 (October 1986) 23.

6. E. Myrna Bernadel, "Fire in Their Bones: The Active Compassion of God's History Makers," *The Other Side* 22 (October 1986) 27–28.

7. William Holladay, *Jeremiah: Spokesman Out of Time* (New York: Pilgrim Press, 1974) 29.

8. William A. Barry and William J. Connolly, *The Practice of Spiritual Direction* (New York: Seabury Press, 1982) 67–69.

9. Walter Brueggemann, *Hopeful Imagination: Prophetic Voices In Exile* (Philadelphia: Fortress Press, 1986) 18–19.

10. Dorothee Soelle, *Suffering,* Everett R. Kalin, trans. (Philadelphia: Fortress Press, 1975) 74–75.

11. Brueggemann, *Hopeful Imagination,* 31.

Questions for Reflection and Discussion

1. How do you notice God's touch in your ordinary experiences? How do you stay with God's touch? How do you respond to God's touch?

2. How do you encourage your students to notice the touch of God in their daily lives? As Lasallian educators how do we encourage each other to do the same?

3. What scripture passages speak to you of God's touch? What is that touch like?
4. To what do you believe you are personally called by God? When and how did you sense God's initiative in this call?
5. What is your attitude these days? What hope encourages you to look toward God? What do God's touch and God's freedom mean in your present experience?

An Explication of the
Meditations for the Time of Retreat

Michael F. Meister, FSC

> *They are a letter which Christ dictates to you*
> *which you write each day in their hearts,*
> *not with ink, but by the Spirit of the living God.*

In this article, I hope to explicate, primarily for our colleagues in the Lasallian family, the Founder's *Meditations for the Time of Retreat* as one of the most significant resources we have on his understanding of the nature of our ministry as Brothers and teachers. I hope that my confreres who read this "meditation on the *Meditations*" will find it a source of encouragement; I hope that my colleagues who read it will find the *Meditations* themselves a source of information and inspiration as they, like us, strive to find ever greater meaning and significance in our calling to be brothers and sisters to the youth of our time, particularly those among the poor and the disadvantaged. In the context of the theme of this year's Spirituality Seminar, "Touching Hearts," I have pursued this topic specifically that it might be another aid to those in the Lasallian family who need resources to guide them in their reading and comprehension of this aspect of De La Salle's life and writing.

BROTHER MICHAEL F. MEISTER, FSC, PHD, is an Assistant Professor in the Department of Religious Studies at Saint Mary's College in Moraga, California. He holds a master's degree in theology from Saint Mary's College of California and the PhD in theology and literature from the Graduate Theological Union in Berkeley.

The Charism of the Founder

Within the Institute of the Brothers, we encounter the concept of the Founder's *charism* a great deal; the fact that we are urged to emulate it and fashion our lives after it doesn't make it any less elusive and indefinite. A charism is something that belongs to individuals as an intrinsic part of their being. Though we're often quite good at copying what we see in others, to emulate their charism appears almost impertinent. Impertinence aside, the emulation of a charism is a positive feature to reproduce in our lives. The difficulty comes when we're forced to define exactly what it is that we're replicating and how we go about it.

The word *charism* is often synonymous with *charisma;* it suggests a rare quality or power attributed to persons who inspire us with their ability to convey an ideal through their leadership over us and our devotion to them. Theologically, this power is seen as a heavenly gift, a grace, and is most often associated with the Holy Spirit. What is significant about charismatic persons, whether worldly or spiritual, is that they have the ability to inspire or empower others with their gifts so that those who share them and use them show remarkable correspondences with the original possessors of those gifts. This is what makes charisms valuable to others and this is why we are urged, or urge others, to emulate them.

In the New Testament, Paul coined the Greek word *kharisma* (free gift of God), and he uses it often in his exhortations. In the Letter to the Romans, we find the pre-eminent list of Christian charisms:

> We have differing gifts [read *charisms*], according to the grace given us. If a person's gift is prophesying, let them use it in proportion to their faith. If it is serving, let them serve; if it is teaching, let them teach; if it is encouraging, let them encourage; if it is contributing to the needs of others, let them give generously; if it is leadership, let them govern diligently; if it is showing mercy, let them do it cheerfully.[1]

In First Corinthians, we read: "I wish that everyone was as I am. But all have their own gift from God; one has this gift, another has that."[2] When Paul wrote to the community in Ephesus he told them, "I became a servant of this gospel by the gift of God's grace given me through the working of his power."[3] James takes up this same theme: "Every good and perfect gift is from above, coming down from the Father of the heavenly lights, who does not change like shifting shadows."[4] Peter writes, "Each one should use whatever gift they have received to serve others, faithfully administering God's grace in its various forms."[5]

On the emulation side of charisma, we also find New Testament validation. In the Letter to the Hebrews, we read, "Remember your leaders, who spoke the word of God to you. Consider the outcome of their way of life and imitate their faith."[6] To the Ephesians, Paul writes, "Be imitators of God, therefore, as dearly beloved children . . . ,"[6] and to the Thessalonian Christians he writes: "You became imitators of us and of the Lord; in spite of severe suffering, you welcomed the message with the joy given by the Holy Spirit, so that you became a model for all the believers in Macedonia and Achaia."[8] Charisma, then, in the New Testament sense is a gift one possesses, the value of which is discovered only in using it. Furthermore, it is also a force for good in its attractiveness to others, and thus something to emulate.

In the Lasallian context, not only are we urged to admire the Founder's charisma, but we are urged to imitate it and pattern our lives after it as we carry forward his work, which he called the work of God. This "Lasallian charism" can become a source of great power for those of us who follow De La Salle in this ministry of educating youth. But how do we recognize this power? How do we tap into it? What are the signs that we have acquired it? What do we do with it? I hope answers to these questions will surface as I explore here *Meditations for the Time of Retreat* where, as I have suggested, we can have an extraordinary experience of De La Salle's charism (and charisma).

In reading the *Meditations* as a whole, not only do we encounter De La Salle as charismatic, but we also discover that each meditation proposes a charism to us that the Founder himself deems worthy of our emulation. Thus the *Meditations* are a place where we can have a dynamic experience of the Founder's charism and discover for ourselves those gifts he felt to be fundamental in his disciples. "The charism of the Founder," then, implies two things for me. First, a recognition of the singular gifts with which he was endowed by God; and second, a recognition of how he used those gifts as a teaching tool for his disciples. To "imitate" or "emulate" the charism of the Founder is to "intimate" the Founder; it is, ultimately, to *be* like him just as he encouraged us to *be* like Christ, or Paul, for example. It is to allow our hearts to be touched by his, to allow our spirits to be moved by his, to allow our wills to be shaped by his.

The *Meditations:* Retreat Versus Life?

The Gospels present us with several occasions when, after exhausting himself in ministry, Jesus went off by himself to pray. At times he brought his disciples apart as well.[9] Throughout its history, the church has honored the tradition of the faithful spending time apart for prayer, giving rise to the institution of the "retreat." In one form or another, the idea of going away from "the world" for a time of renewal is a common feature of all world religions. In the Christian tradition, not only has the retreat been a privileged time of renewal for the ordinary believer, it has also become an integral part of the lives of those who have entered formal religious communities and ministry.

The annual retreat of the Brothers came into being with the Institute itself. Away from the busy work of their ministry, the quiet and solitude of the retreat not only afforded the Brothers the opportunity for ongoing spiritual growth, but it also provided them with time to refocus on the significance of their ministry by strengthening the spiritual and experiential foundations on which it was built. To this end, John Baptist de La Salle wrote the classic *Meditations for the Time of Retreat* toward the end of his life.

While these meditations are not autobiographical of the Founder, we can see in them a distillation of his years of experience and growth in wisdom. Furthermore, they do tell us a great deal about the originality of his understanding of the relationship between the Brothers' ministry and their spiritual lives: HE MAKES NO DISTINCTION! I repeat: he makes no distinction between our ministry and our spiritual life. To this end, Canon Blain, the probable author of the Foreword to the original (ca. 1730) edition of the *Meditations* writes:

> Out of respect for the author it was thought proper to leave the meditations just as they were, though they have been written more in the style of instructions, exhortations, and regulations, than meditations. They are without expressions of fervent desire, feelings of tenderness, or resolutions customary in similar meditations, but this is not surprising; the author has done this intentionally, as in the meditations he wrote for all the Sundays and feasts of the year. His purpose was to instruct and exhort the Brothers rather than teach them how to express their desires, emotions, and intimate conversation with God. He had provided for this training by giving the Brothers a method of making mental prayer, in which he taught them very clearly how to express their desires, feelings, and resolutions with facility and effectiveness.[10]

What is most revealing here is Blain's suggestion that the *Meditations* were intended more as "instructions, exhortations, and regulations," than what we have come to expect as "traditional" material for meditation. There is a distinct difference between the Founder's *Method of Mental Prayer,* on the one hand, and his *Meditations for Sundays and Feasts* and *Meditations for the Time of Retreat,* on the other. The absence of "expressions of fervent desire, feelings of tenderness, or resolutions customary in similar meditations" amplifies the Founder's understanding of the inherent unity of the Brothers' ministry with their spiritual life. This inherent unity as the cornerstone of a Lasallian spirituality is, I believe, the source out of which Lasallian charism is nourished.

This unity of mission and spirit is an amazing thing, and I don't have to tell you what a problem this concept is (or can be) for many Brothers. For some, the interior life can be a place of escape (or "retreat") from their ministry. For others it is a place of communion with God on a level apart from the realities of everyday life. Some view the idea of equating ministry and spirituality as tantamount to sacrilege in that it denigrates the "pride of place" the spirit has been accorded over the vicissitudes of the world in our culture. For still others, the idea that "our work might be our prayer" is a sure sign of a weak spiritual life in the individual who endorses and lives it.

Not wanting to be disrespectful, but realizing it may be unavoidable, my response to those who hold these views is that they have not taken the Founder seriously because they refuse to accept the implication that to be a Christian Brother is to embrace a legitimate spirituality particular to our Institute and articulated by our Founder, who sought to give his Institute an entirely different character from its many cousins in the church. For me, the *Meditations for the Time of Retreat* are among the clearest articulations of De La Salle's innovative understanding of the nature of what it means to be a Brother in **this** Institute.

In light of the resurgence of Lasallian studies in the last half of this century, these meditations have become a valuable resource for those seeking to enrich themselves in the charism of John Baptist de La Salle and an understanding of his spirituality. More important, however, the recent broader concept of the Lasallian family embraces our numerous colleagues, who hunger to know and understand the significance of this charism. This explication is a way to present and briefly explore some of the key themes in these meditations, thereby inspiring and educating our colleagues in this ministry to the potential richness of a Lasallian spirituality they can and must call their own. Nowadays, though desirable, it is not always possible to go away from one's occupational commitments or one's family for extended periods of time, and so it is all the more important to bring the significant principles of the retreat to a non-stop workplace. Though the *Meditations* themselves are not the kind of work one simply reads from cover to cover, I hope that this explication will provide the contemplative reader with ample food for thought and action between readings.

The *Meditations:* An Overview

A glance through the titles of the 16 meditations will disclose the Founder's intent to present a view of the work of the Christian schools he founded as a noble and magnificent upward spiral which the Brother's ministry is intended to parallel. As a kind of *Genesis,* De La Salle begins his volume of meditations with God establishing the work of the schools in his foresight and Brothers collaborating with him[11] as agents announcing his message of salvation to young people in the conduct of those schools. Subsequent meditations frame the vocation of Lasallians in the context of their agency as co operators with Christ and examples to those they instruct. Midway through the *Meditations,* the Founder shows how the role of the teacher-brother is complementary to the mission of the church. This leads to meditations on practical matters, like reproving and correcting students, and moves to a consideration of the account of their ministry Lasallian educators will need to render to God. The *Meditations* culminate with the earthly and heavenly rewards educators can expect to receive for their fidelity.

The outward structure of these *Meditations* is apparent, as I have just outlined them. When they are viewed from within one begins to see that they rely a great deal on the New Testament, particularly Paul, to maintain their outer structure. New Testament themes such as calling and sending, stewardship and accounting, reproof and encouragement, evangelism and zeal, play themselves out again and again as De La Salle articulates our pivotal place in God's plan for the salvation of young people. I think it is no accident that the Founder relies heavily on Paul in these meditations. Of the 209 New Testament references in the *Meditations,* 145 are from Paul or works attributed to him, and he is mentioned by name 34 times. De La Salle, the Doctor of Theology, is at work here as he reinforces the foundations of his Institute's spirituality with the strength and conviction of Paul, the New Testament's evangelical and "charismatic" teacher *par excellence.* Furthermore, it is no coincidence that the New Testament should play such a significant role in the *Meditations.* As far back as the *Rule* of 1718 we read:

The Brothers of this Society shall have a most profound respect for the Holy Scriptures; and, in proof thereof, they shall always carry the New Testament about with them, and pass no day without reading some of it, through a sentiment of faith, respect and veneration for the divine words contained therein, looking upon it as their first and principal rule.[12]

As I implied above, the *Meditations for the Time of Retreat* are designed to mirror the life of the Brother back to him during a time (the annual retreat) when he can reflect on it as well. To this extent, the *Meditations* are an autobiographical account of the Lasallian educator's ministry, and as such they become, in the words of Blain, "instructions, exhortations, and regulations" against which the teacher-brother measures his life. The implied exhortation in all these meditations is that we will strive to align ourselves and our ministry with the standards or charisms laid out in this set of 16 patterns which overlay the story of De La Salle's life.

Each of the 16 *Meditations for the Time of Retreat* contains three sections or movements through which the title theme of the meditation is explored in ever greater depth. Throughout each movement, but particularly at the end of each, the Founder's exhortations can be seen in the form of advice and counsel. Collected together in other volumes, these exhortations form a major part of De La Salle's spiritual legacy to us. The new reader will also note that the meditations go in pairs: the first one in the set usually opens the title theme on a general level, the second goes into greater detail. At an annual retreat lasting eight days, the reading of one meditation in the morning and another in the evening maintained a kind of "symmetry" of thought and consideration for each day.

A View Inside

There is no substitute for a prayerful reading of the *Meditations,* but insofar as it might assist the reader, particularly the newer reader, what follows is an explication of the 16 *Meditations* which is intended to offer some insight into the major ideas, themes, and charisms that can be found there. The new reader should bear in mind that these *Meditations,* like any classical texts, have not lost their ability to address us out of the past. However, a literal reading in order to "soak up more" of their substance would do them and us an injustice, as the circumstances and situations which they address are, in many ways, different from our own. Obviously, the structure of our ministry is quite different from that of our predecessors in the Institute. Furthermore, the developments in theology over the span of three centuries bring into focus a different set of caveats. It is not far from the truth to suggest, for example, that the Founder was convinced that if the Brothers' students did not know their catechism and the basic truths of their faith, their eternal souls were in grave danger.

However, because these *Meditations* have not lost their ability to speak to us, the principles there that characterize the Founder's thinking about how we are to understand our ministry and our relationship to our students are still very much alive today. To this extent, these *Meditations* are part of the canon of sacred texts which form the "Lasallian scripture."[13] It is my belief that, in many ways, the vitality of the future Institute will depend on how deeply we allow our hearts to be addressed and our wills to be moved by what we hear in this scripture, and how charismatically we follow its exhortations.

An Explication of the
Meditations for the Time of Retreat

Meditation 1: God in his Providence has established the Christian schools[14]

You have been called by God to this ministry and you have been given the grace of teaching and the gift of exhortation for the sake of those entrusted to your responsibility. Use these gifts you have received with care and vigilance in order to fulfill the main duty of fathers and mothers toward their children.

This meditation is the "*Book of Genesis*" of the collection. In Part 1, De La Salle's imagery suggests that the ministry of the Lasallian educator is an outgrowth of God's work of creation. He weaves the fabric of faith with threads of knowledge and light in these considerations, showing how our ministry is a direct outgrowth of God's desire that all creation should come to know him. De La Salle likens knowledge to a fragrance diffused throughout the world by human ministers. Almost as he created light out of the darkness, God kindles the light of his calling in his ministers and sends them to diffuse the fragrance of his knowledge to those they teach. We are thus "the ministers of God and the administrators of his mysteries."

In Part 2, De La Salle addresses the reality of "fallen" creation: parents have a duty to instruct their children in the elements of faith, but they often have little time or ability to do so. Enter God's Providence. In his loving foresight, God cares for these parents and has a plan to assist them in their important office. He has called us to act as wise master-builders who, with our gifts of teaching and exhortation, can build a solid foundation upon which the faith of these children can be built.

In Part 3, the Founder as theologian is clearly at work. He expands on the above themes, showing us that God wants everyone to be saved and that he provides teachers who assist him in this plan. De La Salle uses a wonderful image from Paul to underscore our ministry to youth: they are "God's field,"[15] and we are sent to cultivate it by our announcement of his Gospel. He also suggests that our ministry is one of reconciliation (another Pauline theme) as we personify God's appeal to those we teach.

The charisms suggested by this meditation are teaching and exhortation. Using them, we cooperate in God's ongoing act of creation by bringing light into the hearts and minds of our students, banishing the darkness of their ignorance, and reuniting them with their creator in faith. We are exhorted to be watchful that we fulfill our obligations not only to God, for whom we work, but to parents for whom we also work, ministering to their children.

Meditation 2: What teachers must do
to procure the sanctification of their students

If you want the instructions you give those whom you teach to be effective in drawing them to the practice of good, you must practice these truths yourselves. You must also be full of zeal. It is zeal which makes your students capable of receiving a share in the grace which is in you for doing good. For your zeal draws upon you the Spirit of God. It is this Spirit Who gives your students the power to practice good.

In Part 1, De La Salle is somewhat of a sociologist as he expands a theme he began in Meditation 1 —the problems experienced by the working class relative to the education of their children. Here, though, the context is poverty which is at the root of so many social ills. Children's lives, and their souls, are wasted, he suggests, by being neglected and abandoned to forces they may never be able to overcome. Echoing the opening line of his first meditation, however, De La Salle sees God's goodness at work even here in the foundation of our Institute, and he urges us to thank God, who has called us to this ministry.

Having established the Christian school in God's plan, De La Salle is not satisfied that students should merely be kept busy and off the streets. In Part 2, he tells us that our real mission is to devote ourselves to bringing them up in a Christian spirit. Echoing Jesus' appreciation of children, the Founder boldly suggests that the spirit in which we bring up our students gives them the wisdom of God— something the "princes of this world" do not possess. So conscious is he of the value of our ministry that he exhorts us to do everything in our vigilant power to prevent any evil influence from corrupting our students.

In Part 3, the seasoned De La Salle is pragmatic. While we may be good teachers of doctrine, we must never forget to teach "the practical truths of faith in Jesus Christ and the maxims of the Gospel." What this comes down to is the notable principle in the Letter of James: "Faith without good works is dead."[16] To this, the Founder adds Paul's teaching on love, and closes with a powerful question: "Do you look upon the good that you are trying to achieve in [your students] as the foundation of all the good that they will practice for the rest of their lives?"

The charisms suggested by this meditation are piety and wholeheartedness. Piety or reverence should characterize the motivations of our ministry, and our wholehearted dedication to it should speak more than our words. The Founder exhorts us to be unpretentious in our teaching, but let our example be famous.

Meditation 3: Those who teach the young are cooperators with Jesus Christ in the saving of souls

Since you are ambassadors and ministers of Jesus Christ in the work that you do, you must act as representing Jesus Christ himself. He wants your disciples to see him in you and receive your teaching as if he were teaching them. They must be convinced that the truth of Jesus Christ comes from your mouth, that it is only in his name that you teach, that he has given you authority over them. They are a letter which Christ dictates to you, which you write each day in their hearts, not with ink, but by the Spirit of the living God. For the Spirit acts in you and by you through the power of Jesus Christ.

In Part 1 of this meditation, De La Salle echoes the theology of Paul as he returns to the theme of reconciliation and reparation he explored in Meditation 1. What concerns the Founder here is that we strive to unite ourselves with Christ by joining our wills to his. In this way, our lives become an example and a powerful lesson to our students.

Part 2 forms one of the most noble and poetic sections in the entire group of meditations as we hear De La Salle echoing the sentiments of Paul in his Second Letter to the Corinthians. In our ministry, we must consider ourselves as ambassadors of Jesus Christ—actually as other Christs to our students. The Founder urges us to live so convinced of the importance of this role that our students will come to believe that Christ's words issue from our mouths because we teach in his name. We are further urged to look upon ourselves as writing instruments in the hand of the Holy Spirit, seeing our students as letters which Christ dictates, letters we write each time we teach them. As his ambassadors, then, it is all the more important that our will be one with Christ's, to whom we must give ourselves every day.

The message in Part 3 is quite straightforward. Recalling the image of the vine and the branches from John's Gospel, the Founder reminds us that what we do as teachers is worthless if we fail to realize that our gifts come from Christ. Thus, the more nourishment we draw from the vine (Christ), the more fruit will our branches produce.

Since the chief image in this meditation is ambassadorial, I think it follows that the charism here is diplomacy. As "ministers and administrators of the mysteries of God" (Meditation 1), we have a double responsibility. We must represent his will clearly and accurately to our students, but we must also represent back to him the many needs of our students that we come to know so clearly in our relationships with them. Note that this relationship is not a mere formality. De La Salle's implication here is that we know our students so well that daily we "read" in them the letter Christ dictates to us. The Founder exhorts us to read that letter carefully and lovingly every day of our lives.

Meditation 4: How to be true cooperators with Jesus Christ for the salvation of children

> *You must constantly represent the needs of your disciples to Jesus Christ, explaining to him the difficulties you experience in guiding them. Jesus Christ, seeing that you regard him as the one who can do everything and yourself as an instrument to be moved only by him, will not fail to grant you what you ask.*

In Meditation 3, De La Salle introduced our role as cooperators with Christ, and in this meditation he explains how it works in practice. Part 1 begins with familiar Lasallian phraseology: "Be convinced . . ." Writing to us like this in various places in the *Meditations,* the Founder reveals something of the story of his own life and his complete and enthusiastic trust in God. His conviction here deals with an application of Paul's image of the garden in First

Corinthians. We do the planting and the watering, but God makes it grow. The purpose of this image (in both Paul and the Founder) is not so much to "show us our place" as it is to urge us to beseech the divine Gardener on behalf of our "plants," especially when we perceive the troubles that hinder their full growth. Thus, we come to see in this meditation that Lasallian prayer consists of bringing to Christ all the concerns that stem from our ministry, convinced that he listens to them and inspires us on how to address them when we return to that ministry.

Part 2 shows us clearly how important De La Salle considers the Gospels as a rule of life for his Institute. Advancing his practical exposition of what it means to cooperate with Christ, the Founder simply refers us to our "first and principal rule"—the Gospel—as a timeless resource when we have questions about how to proceed. His knowledge of the Gospels and his pedagogical experience blend here as the experienced teacher points out to his disciples the many ways to approach the solution of a problem they might encounter.

In Part 3, the Founder broadens his lesson by giving us a strategy. He tells us that we cannot fulfill our ministry adequately if we merely imitate Christ's actions. What is needed is that we "must enter into his way of thinking and adopt his goals." Here, again, he echoes Paul's view in First Corinthians: "We have the mind of Christ."[17] This is also a way of driving home his earlier exhortations that we consider ourselves as ambassadors, or administrators, or ministers—always representing to those to whom we are sent the mind of the one who sends us. In this way, speaking the words of Christ to our students and knowing his mind, we fill them with his spirit and life.[18] But all this power? The Founder is clear: "Name something you have in this regard that you have not received?"

As a development or unfolding of the previous meditation, this one stresses the charism of advocacy as another facet of our ambassadorial role among our students. Though we play a powerful role in our ministry, the real power comes from the one who commissions us, not from ourselves. Even more power is to be found in our prayer, during which time we review with Christ the needs of our students and how he can best meet them through our agency.

Meditation 5: Those chosen by Providence
for the work of education must fulfill the function
of Guardian Angels toward children

> *Ask God today for the grace of watching so well over the children confided to you, that you will take every possible care to shield them from serious faults. Ask Him to be such good guides through the light your prayers will obtain for you from God and the fidelity you bring to your work, that you will see clearly every obstacle to the good of children and keep away every harm that could injure their souls on the path of salvation. This is the main concern you must have for the children entrusted to you. It is the main reason why God has entrusted you with so holy a ministry, and He will call upon you to give an exact account on the day of judgment.*

As its title suggests, this meditation brings before us another notable Lasallian theme. De La Salle is not merely making a point here as our spiritual father. He is also our master teacher instructing us out of the wisdom of his experience, highlighting here and in the next meditation the guardian dimension of the educational enterprise wherein we find our ministry. As moderns we may be bothered occasionally by the idea of angels, but in an era obsessed by "forces" there may be little reason for us to wince. For the Founder, there was no question of the angels' existence and role, and they were another way to amplify his central point, which is vigilance. In Part 1 of this meditation, he spends time elucidating the nature of the angels' role: "as guardians, [they] share their understanding of the true good and they help the human race come to a more living knowledge of God, of his perfections, of all that is related to God, and the means of going to Him." He also returns to an earlier context by reminding us that young people are in great need of clear guidance when it comes to their education, especially on the spiritual plane. Enter again God's goodness. Enter again his call to us to represent his desire that all come to know him through our ministry.

Part 2 also echoes earlier exhortations. It is not enough that we instruct our students. We must live in such a way that our example speaks to them more convincingly than our words. It is in this context that we need to act like angels to our students, winning them over to the knowledge of the truth so that gradually they will live that truth without our prodding.

In Part 3 of this meditation, De La Salle apprises us of the forces or obstacles that hinder us in life, suggesting that even those of us who act as guardian angels need guardian angels to assist us. He makes his point, as he often does, by contrasting our strength with our students' weakness, thereby urging us to assist them in every way we can, realizing that what we have received by way of strength is meant for them, not for ourselves.

The charism suggested here is vigilance, a theme De La Salle raises in his pedagogical works and a virtue that must be possessed by every teacher. Throughout the *Meditations* so far (and he will continue to make this point), De La Salle instructs us in the care we must exercise to guard our students from bad influences that will hinder their growth, especially their spiritual growth. In later meditations, after he has instructed us thoroughly, he will make a radical assertion: The salvation of our students is so important that God will require us to give an account of their souls *before* giving an account of our own! We will be judged by how well we fulfilled our ministry in their regard.

Meditation 6: How the function of Guardian Angel is fulfilled in the education of youth

> *God uses the angels not only to deliver those entrusted to them from the powers of darkness and make them grow in the knowledge of Himself but also to help them lead a life worthy of Him, so that they will be pleasing to Him in every way and multiply good works of every sort. The angels are zealous for the good of those in their care because of the commission they have received from God, the Father of light and of all good. They contribute, as far as they are able, to make those in their care worthy of sharing the lot of the saints. As those chosen by God to announce the truths of the gospel, you share in the ministry of the guardian angels by making known these truths to children.*

Looking back to his explanation of the role of the guardian angels in the previous meditation, Part 1 here has the Founder broadening our understanding of their function and ours by cleverly directing our attention to the image of Jacob's Ladder in the *Book of Genesis*. Suggesting that the angels were ascending and descending with messages between God and ourselves, De La Salle urges us to see ourselves in the same capacity: the bearers of messages between God and our students. To this end, he heightens our understanding of what it means to pray as Lasallians: daily we must go up to God to learn what we must teach our students. Then we must come down to them "by accommodating [ourselves] to their level in order to teach them what God has communicated" to us for them. Without suggesting a course of action one way or the other, I think there is ample professional food for thought in this directive to accommodate which may leave many of us questioning and reevaluating our teaching style.

In Part 2, De La Salle explores another aspect of the guardian angels' function: they can inspire us and provide us with the means to do good. Accustomed to his pattern by now, we hear the Founder exhorting us to see ourselves in this role as well: inspiring our students in what is the right thing to do and providing them with the means to do it through practical instruction and good example.

In Part 3, the Founder is completely exhortative, summing up his advice by casting it in the light of Paul's Letter to the Ephesians. As Christian educators, our role is to build up the body of Christ, whose ambassadors we are. In doing this, we must see that our students do not "sadden the Holy Spirit of God," that they lay aside their former lives, and that they be kind, compassionate, and forgiving—all virtues of Christ himself.

Evangelization is the charism appropriate to this meditation. Though the vehicle for his message here is the guardian angels, the Founder would not have us be distracted from his real purpose in using them: like these angels, we are commissioned by God to spread the message of his truth and goodness. Like them, we must be zealous to inspire our students with the love of God. We must be visible guardian angels to our students.

Meditation 7: The task of teaching youth is one of the most necessary in the church

> *The reason that St. Paul gives why this ministry was so esteemed is that God's secret plan was unveiled to him, and he had received the grace of unveiling to the Gentiles the unfathomable riches of Christ, so that those, who in former times had no part in Jesus Christ and were excluded from the covenant of God without His hope and promises, now belong to Jesus Christ and are strangers no longer but fellow citizens of the saints and members of God's household; they form a building which Jesus Christ has built and raised on the foundation of the apostles; they become the temple where God dwells through His Holy Spirit. This is also why you must have an altogether special esteem for the Christian education and teaching of children, since it is the means of helping them become true children of God and citizens of heaven.*

The *Meditations for the Time of Retreat* can be imaged together as a kind of ascending spiral, because from time to time it is obvious that De La Salle looks back on earlier expositions, thus bringing us to ever greater heights of understanding. To a certain extent, this is the case in this meditation. The title is almost an understatement, given all that we have read and explored already. Here the Founder banks on Paul for his primary focus and returns to his theme of laying the foundation of faith in our students as good master-builders (a theme he used in Meditation 1). In Part 1, while he holds the Apostle up as our model, he also reminds us of the proportionate difference between our ministry and his. Nevertheless, he urges, we must see our work as corresponding to this great Apostle's, and thus come to view it as one of the most important and necessary in the church.

In Part 2, the Founder points us toward the example of the early Church Fathers who took the ministry of teaching as their main duty. More significant is that he makes a point that radiates outward to illuminate all the other meditations: "Teaching was the first ministry Jesus Christ gave his holy apostles." Furthermore, the mission to teach formed the centerpiece of Christ's great commission at the end of the Gospel. Recalling that the Founder has consistently made an issue of the power of the teacher's example, he ends this section by pointing out that Christ not only commissioned his disciples to teach, but he himself was a teacher and saw this as the prime focus of his own mission.

Part 3 repeats much of the earlier material in this meditation, but in the context of another pedagogical principle the Founder extracts from Paul. De La Salle reminds us that this Apostle told the Corinthians, "Christ did not send me to baptize but to preach the gospel, and not with the wisdom of human eloquence, so that the cross of Christ might not be emptied of its meaning."[19] I believe this is near the heart of the matter when we grapple with what it means to be Lasallian in the way we teach and the way we are with our students. Paul's (and the Founder's) point is that clever words, while they may impress our audience, leave the message of the Cross void of its meaning. Paul recognizes that the greatest charism he has received from Christ is "the grace of unveiling to the Gentiles the unfathomable richness of Christ," so that those who were once without hope of any relationship with God are now "fellow citizens with the saints and members of God's household."[20] Talk about touching hearts! The Founder couldn't be clearer: if we are going to follow the example of this charismatic Apostle and teacher *par excellence,* we must read his above words to the Ephesians into our own ministry as well. Thus, our calling to teach is great and necessary because it builds the household of God. But it must be done without clever words—and this is what makes our ministry (like Paul's) appear absurd in the eyes of the world.

While the gift of teaching is the unmistakable charism held up for our consideration in this meditation, the Founder's emphasis is on the implications of this gift we have received, the power of our ministry, and the faith and reliance we must put on Christ to empower us to speak his words so that our students will always be able to understand them.

Meditation 8:
How to make your ministry useful to the church

It will not, then, be enough to have taught your disciples the mysteries and the truths of our religion, if you have not helped them learn the chief Christian virtues, and if you have not taken a very special care to help them put these virtues into practice, as well as all the good of which they are capable at their age. For no matter how much faith they may have, nor how lively it may be, if they are not practicing any good works at all, their faith will be of no use to them.

In the previous meditation, the Founder urged us to see our ministry as one of the most necessary in the church, and now he pursues this theme by exploring the ways in which it is useful. Recalling a Pauline theme he raised in the previous meditation—building up God's household—De La Salle focuses his considerations here on the practical ways in which the household of the church is built up by our ministry. In Part 1 we are presented with the model of the Apostles' early preaching of the Gospel as presented in the *Acts of the Apostles*. Their zeal had a direct bearing on the increase in the number of believers, and the Founder suggests that our zeal will have similar effects among our students. Reminding us again that Christ was a teacher, he urges us to be filled with our Lord's zeal for the salvation of those we instruct, and to see ourselves as successors to the Apostles in this task.

In Part 2, the Founder again places heavy emphasis on the example of teachers as their most significant teaching tool. Pointing to the Apostles, he urges us to see that they were not satisfied with mere teaching, but that their real power came from the way they lived their own message, Christ's message. The Founder then narrows his focus here and makes a special appeal to us. Just as the Apostles considered it a vital part of their ministry to introduce their converts to the sacramental life of the church, so we must also provide frequent sacramental opportunities for our students, convinced that this is as much a part of our ministry as our teaching.

In Part 3, the Founder modifies his teaching on example by changing the focus from us to our students. He suggests that our teaching about the faith will be worthless if we do not also teach our students how to practice it. Thus, it is important that we instruct our students in virtue and good works, since these are what nourish their life of faith.

I would characterize the charism embedded in this meditation as spiritual parenthood or mentoring. On several occasions, the

Founder has encouraged us to see the importance of our role as surrogate parents. Here, he is suggesting that we must also see ourselves as spiritual parents. As such, our concern must be not only to instruct our students in secular subjects, but also to teach and care for them spiritually. De La Salle's exhortation echoes that of James: Faith without good deeds is useless. A Lasallian education without instruction in virtue is similarly worthless.

Meditation 9: The obligation of those who teach youth to have great zeal to fulfill well so holy a ministry

What ought to encourage you to have much zeal in your vocation is the fact that you are not only the ministers of God, but also of Jesus Christ and of the church. This is what St. Paul says when he expresses the wish that people should regard those who announce the gospel as ministers of Jesus Christ, whose role is to write the letter dictated by Christ, not with ink but with the Spirit of the living God, not on tablets of stone but on tablets of flesh which are the hearts of children. For this reason, and in this spirit, you must have the love and the glory of God as your single aim in teaching these children, since the love of God impels you, because Jesus Christ died for all so that those who live might live no longer for themselves but for him who died for them. This is what your zeal must inspire in your disciples, God as it were appealing through you, since you are ambassadors for Christ.

In Part 1, De La Salle introduces his subject by showing us that our ministry is one of the three major charismatic forces in the Christian church: the apostolic, the prophetic, and the educational. His enthusiasm is evident as he urges us to consider the greatness of God's gift to us who have been called by him to do this noble work. We are God's ministers, "acting with love, with a sincere and true zeal."

In Part 2, the Founder recapitulates a theme he offered for our consideration in Meditation 3. Not only are we ministers of God, we are also ministers of Jesus Christ, and of the church. As such, our role as announcers of the gospel message is to write that letter dictated by Christ in the hearts of our students. Through us, his zealous ambassadors, Christ addresses them, urges them, appeals to them.

Our zeal must empower those we teach to enter into the building we are constructing for them—the house of God, to use Paul's image. The education we provide our students is really a gift God gives them through our agency. Through it they become "heirs of the kingdom of God and of Jesus Christ our Lord."

Not only is our good example to our students a cardinal pedagogical principle for De La Salle, he also teaches us about good example by holding up even greater examples for us to imitate. So he tells us in Part 3 that we must imitate God whose zeal to restore his creatures to grace led him to send his only son to redeem them. The Founder's own zeal is so explicit, he tells us here:

> The zeal you are obliged to have in your ministry must be so active and so alive that you are able to tell the parents of the children entrusted to your care what is said in scripture: "Give us their souls, keep everything else for yourselves."

The Founder's fervor and intensity are apparent in this meditation, where zeal for souls plays so charismatically central a role. His enthusiastic conviction is itself our exhortation and instruction here. We are called by God to imitate God by speaking the word of God in order to bring our students back to God. This is the cyclical message of the *Meditations* as a unit, almost a refrain at the end of each one.

Meditation 10: How a Brother of the Christian Schools must show zeal in his ministry

> *Your zeal toward the children you teach would not go very far and would not have much result or success if it limited itself only to words. To be effective, your teaching must be supported by your example. This must be one of the chief characteristics of your zeal.*

Following his pattern, in the previous meditation De La Salle focused on our obligation to show zeal in our ministry. Moving from theory to practice, as it were, he now explores the application of this zeal. He begins Part 1 with a bold assertion: Christ came into this world to destroy sin, and the main purpose of our schools and the focus of our zeal must be the same—to destroy anything that might separate our students from the love of God.

In Part 2, we can almost predict that the Founder will tell us what he does: it is not enough that we keep our students from evil, we must lead them to actively avoid it themselves. Notice the methodology here. First there is an instruction; next there is the application; and finally there is the practice. I suspect the Founder is suggesting that unless the students can put into practice what they have learned from us, they have not learned the lesson.

Again, in Part 3, the Founder insists that our instruction is meaningless if it is only words. Rather, the chief characteristic of our zeal must be that our teaching is supported by our example. Note, of course, the important implication here: the teacher whose example is his or her greatest lesson is also growing in holiness. If our lessons in virtue must be backed by a virtuous life, we must be striving toward goodness long before we open our mouths to teach. There is necessarily much food for thought here.

Once again, the charism presented for our emulation and adoption is zeal, but zeal tempered by practice; instruction tempered by example.

Meditation 11: The obligation of the Brothers of the Christian Schools to reprove and correct the faults committed by those whom they teach

> *Since you are substitutes for their fathers and mothers and their pastors, you are obliged to keep watch over these children as men who must render an account for their souls. He has entrusted you especially with the care of their souls, which is what God had most at heart when He made you the guides and guardians of these young children.*

Like several other pairs in this collection, Meditations 11 and 12 form a unit whose focus is on reproof and correction, necessary elements in any educational venture. The phrase "reprove and correct" in the titles of these meditations is obviously from Paul's advice to Timothy,[21] and in Part 1, the Founder is quick to link it to the charism of zeal he has so prominently illustrated thus far. As an educator, the Founder knows both the need and the value of reproof and correction and he urges us in our watchful instruction to use these tools so that our students might be saved from even greater faults.

In Part 2, the Founder writes not only as an educator but also as a developmental psychologist. He instructs his disciples about the nature of habitual behavior in impressionable young people and uses the image of captivity to express his conviction that bad habits result in a loss of freedom. He urges us to see correction and reproof as God's tool against the wiles of Satan as we wrest our students from his clutches and deliver them to the freedom of the children of God.

The issue of responsibility is the keynote of Part 3, where De La Salle reminds us that if we fail to correct the bad habits of our students we are failing in our responsibility to their parents and ultimately to the one who has called us. In blunt terms, the Founder warns us: "If you do not watch over their conduct, you had better realize that, since these children are not able to guide themselves, you will render an account to God for the faults they commit just as if you had committed them." For the Founder, failing to correct and reprove our students is an abuse and negligence of the ministry with which God has honored us.

Thus, the charism here is vigilance—a virtue extolled throughout the New Testament (our first and principal rule). If we think of our students as our own children, we must act responsibly toward them in light of their development and do all we can to guide, encourage, and correct them toward the virtue and goodness which make them children of God.

Meditation 12: The proper manner for reproving and correcting the faults of those for whom we are responsible

The result of wise correction is that those receiving it are disposed to correct their faults, whereas when correction is administered through uncontrolled emotion and without having God in view, it serves only to turn the disciple against his teacher and to arouse in him feelings of revenge and ill will, which sometimes last a long time. Results are generally related and similar to the cause that produces them: If you want your corrections to have the results they ought, administer them

in a way that can please God and those who receive them. Take care,
above all, that it is love and zeal for the salvation of your pupils that
lead you to correct them.

The Founder now addresses the practical ways in which reproof and correction are to be administered by his disciples in their
ministry. If we recall that when the Founder gives advice about
teaching he generally looks back to his counsel on good example,
we see here that he is careful to note that our corrections must be
tempered by the Spirit of God and given only under the Spirit's
guidance. The Founder's wisdom in suggesting this approach to correction can be seen in its effect: one avoids acting from tainted motives, and the correction is tailored to the individual receiving it.
Thus, not only is Lasallian education a way of being with our students as individuals, it is also a way of correcting them as individuals.

In Part 2, though he espouses the hard line on correction, the
Founder is quick to follow his own advice by looking at the example of Paul who also urged his disciples to reprove with kindness
and patience. Holding up the example of the prophet Nathan in his
confrontation with King David, the Founder urges us to reprove in
such a way that the recipients enter into themselves and become
aware of the error of their ways. Finally, he urges us to "cool off"
before giving any correction so that it will be given and received in
wisdom and gentleness.

Part 3 is a recapitulation of the Founder's advice: moderate
your discipline with affection, and remember it is God who reproves
through you. Once again De La Salle links correction with zeal and
places it in the context of love: love for those corrected, and love for
God who calls us to do it.

Though reproof and correction could be considered charismatic, particularly since they have a basis in Paul's teaching, I think the
real charism evident in this meditation is healing. This is the case
because of the moderation and tempering the Founder urges upon us
before we correct, and because of the concern we should have that
what we do be tailored to the person receiving it.

Meditation 13: Teachers must give an account to God on the way they have fulfilled their ministry

Consider that the account you will have to give to God will not be inconsequential, because it concerns the salvation of the souls of children whom God has entrusted to your care. On the day of judgment you will answer for them as much as you answer for yourself. You must be convinced of this: that God will begin by making you give an account of their souls before asking you to give an account of your own. For when He entrusted them to you, He made you responsible to procure their salvation with as much attention as your own, and you have committed yourselves to be entirely dedicated to the salvation of their souls.

With the end in sight, as it were, this meditation shows us De La Salle beginning to move from considerations dealing with the recipients of our ministry to considerations that deal with us ministers ourselves. Thus, we begin to approach the end of the *Meditations* by examining the account we will have to give at the Judgment of how well we fulfilled the duties laid out in the previous meditations. In Part 1, the Founder reiterates Pauline themes on which he has grounded other meditations: we are co-workers with God, and our students are his field that he cultivates through our efforts. Using gospel imagery, the Founder paints a scenario of the judgment we will face before Christ, who will examine every detail of our ministry. What the Founder has been implying here he now tells us directly: we must carry out a kind of daily judgment, examining *ourselves* unsparingly to make sure we are fulfilling our responsibilities thoroughly.

In Part 2, the Founder reminds us that the account we will be required to give Christ will not be inconsequential, because it concerns the salvation of those who have been entrusted to our ministry. Here, De La Salle makes one of the most significant theological statements in the *Meditations:* "God will begin by making you give an account of their souls before asking you to give an account of your own." The reason for this is elementary in his mind: God has entrusted our students to us. By reason of our commitment to them, their salvation has become as much a responsibility for us as our own. Here is where we begin to find the heart of our spirituality, I believe. No Lasallian's prayer to God is complete without relating it to the zealous concern we must have for our students' salvation. In praying this way, De La Salle tells us, our students will be given the graces they need for their salvation, and we can then be assured that God will take responsibility for ours. Once again, this section offers considerable food for thought and needs much reflection on our part.

Part 3 addresses a further set of responsibilities. The Founder reminds us that we are accountable for building up the body of Christ by our concern for the souls of our students. Realizing that young people are quite impressionable, he reasons that they stand to benefit most from the workings of grace—which comes to them through our agency, and for which we will be held accountable. Telling us that our students will be our character witnesses before Christ, the Founder urges us to teach them well and fulfill our ministry with the greatest care.

Stewardship is one of the more outstanding themes in the New Testament, and it is the charism underlying this meditation. Perhaps our most important realization as Christians is the gifted nature of our faith. The second most important realization may well be the responsibility that gift of faith brings with it. The faith of a Lasallian minister is not his or her own private possession. Rather, it is a tool of empowerment that gives us ears to hear our calling, eyes to see what must be done, a heart to love our students, and power to bring them to the knowledge of Christ. Using this tool of faith properly, we come to see that the salvation of our students is more important than your own.

Meditation 14: Matters of his ministry on which a Brother of the Christian Schools must give an account to God

To give account for their [your students'] souls means to give account for everything that concerns their salvation. To watch carefully means to watch over everything with attention, omitting nothing,

neglecting nothing. If you have not applied yourself to all these du-
ties, consider yourself guilty before God and realize how fearful it
will be to appear before Him at the moment of your death after you
have lived in such negligence of all that concerns His service.

As an accompaniment to the previous meditation which focused more on the recipients of our ministry, this one follows De La
Salle's pattern of laying out the specifics for the ministers themselves. In Part 1, he notes that we will be asked to give Christ an accounting of how well we have taught our students (in this case, he is
speaking of the teaching of religion, specifically). His concern is not
simply whether we have taught the material well, but whether we
have been conscious of the persons of our students, whether we
have neglected the slowest or poorest students, whether we have
shown favoritism to the rich or more pleasant or more gifted among
our students, whether we have wasted time, and whether we have
stayed abreast of our subject matter.

In Part 2, we are held accountable for our students' conduct,
not merely their lessons. This brings to full circle the Founder's previous exhortations about good example. Perhaps the most frighten-
ing sentence in all the *Meditations* is found in this section:
"Consider well what it means to give an account to God for the salvation of a soul that is damned, because you did not take care to
lead it to what is right and assist it in living accordingly."

In Part 3, De La Salle approaches accountability from the angle of intention, suggesting that our intentions are even more important than our words and deeds. The prime question of intention
for the Founder is whether we have done all things in our ministry
in the name of Jesus Christ. Along with intention, the Founder also
addresses the manner of carrying out our ministry as a matter for
judgment—whether we have worked with wisdom and seriousness,
with patience and control of our feelings—something he asks us to
consider very seriously.

Again, the charism of stewardship is evident in the fabric of
this meditation but with a slightly different emphasis from the previous one. Here we are asked to consider the utter seriousness of our
commitment to our students and examine within ourselves whether

we have used the gifts we have been given in the proper way: namely, for our students. The foundation of these two meditations is the
gospel story of the rich man who calls his steward to him and tells
him, "Give me an account of your stewardship."[22]

Meditation 15: The reward that those can expect even in this life who have taught children and fulfilled this duty well

*You can expect yet another reward which God will give you in
advance in this life if you devote yourselves generously to your
duty and, if through zeal and the grace of your state, you know
how to strengthen your disciples in the Christian spirit. This is
the very special satisfaction you will experience when they
grow up and you see them living honorably and reverently, far
from any unjust association, and performing good deeds. For
the teaching you give them is not a mere matter of words, but
accompanied by a great abundance of grace for those who respond well, which will maintain them in the practice of good.*

In these next two meditations, De La Salle begins to draw his
considerations to a close by having us contemplate the reward aspect of our ministry as a natural consequence of having accomplished it well. In this meditation, the Founder concentrates on the
rewards given to us in this life, and in the next and last meditation,
he concentrates on the rewards given to us in heaven. In Part 1, he
urges us to anticipate God's rewards as an aspect of his goodness.
First, he tells us, God will reward us with an abundance of grace.
The Founder's theological logic is clear here. If grace is the energy
of God's life within us, it follows that his ambassadors should have
a great deal of it in order to pursue their calling. Our next reward is
"typical" of God, if I may say so. Far from being a rest from our
labors, this reward is more work in a broader field. We must remember, however, that we are his ambassadors, and if he sees the
need for his message in another area, we must be ready to leave at a
moment's notice.

In Part 2, the Founder pursues a further reward for us in this
life: the knowledge that those whose lives we have touched are

closer to salvation. To amplify this point, he relies again on Paul who looked upon his converts "boastfully" as those he had begotten in the Lord. Our glory, the Founder says, is to be identified with Paul, and this idea makes good sense considering how many times he has held this Apostle up as our model.

In Part 3, a fourth reward in this life is laid out for those of us who fulfill our ministry well: that of seeing our students living honorably and performing good deeds. Note how each of these rewards is an outgrowth of a particular aspect of our ministry that he has exhorted us to attend to in an earlier meditation. In this case, we must realize that our teaching is accompanied by an abundance of grace for our students which, as the Founder indicates, maintains them "in the practice of good," and in their "perseverance in the faith." These, then, are the rewards we can expect in this life: rewards that surely grow as the fruit of our ministry.

The charismatic dimension of this meditation is subtle, but I think it is best characterized by insight and discernment. Through these gifts, we are enabled not only to see the results of our ministry but its inestimable value each day as we live it. This insight is a gift that grows through the years; I think the Founder's wisdom of experience is evident here as he exhorts his disciples to strive toward that same wisdom and experience, knowing that God will reward them handsomely.

Meditation 16: The reward that a Brother of the Christian Schools can expect in heaven if he is faithful to his ministry

Consider, then, that your reward in heaven will be as great as the good that you will achieve in the lives of the children who are entrusted to your care. It is in this spirit that St. Paul told the Corinthians: "You will be our glory in the time to come on the day of our Lord Jesus Christ." You can say the same thing of your disciples, namely, that on the day of judgment they will be your glory, if you have taught them well and if they have profited from your teaching, because the lessons you have taught them and the profit they have received will be made clear before the whole world. Not only on that day, but throughout all eternity you will receive the glory of having taught them well, because the glory that you have procured for them will reflect on you. Oh, what joy a Brother of the Christian Schools will have when he sees a great number of his students in possession of eternal happiness, for which they are indebted to him by the grace of Jesus Christ!

In Part 1 of this meditation, another aspect of De La Salle's spirituality is apparent in the way he approaches the issue of our reward in heaven. He assures us that our reward—we who have labored for the salvation of others—will be greater than those who have labored only for their own. His principle is simple: "Your reward in heaven will be as great as the good that you will achieve in the lives of the children who are entrusted to your care."

Part 2 is filled with enthusiasm as the Founder, in the context of the prophet Daniel's statement, "Those who instruct many unto justice will shine as stars for all eternity,"[23] repeats again and again his conviction that our joy will be unbounded when we see in heaven the great number of those whose lives (and hearts) we have touched in our ministry. His only advice to us is to carry out our responsibilities with fidelity.

Part 3 is quite simply De La Salle's *Paradiso!* It is a spirited vision of heaven which may well have inspired him to write these *Meditations* in the first place. Here he recapitulates all his major themes: zeal, Providence, guardian angels, fidelity, salvation, judgment, and so on. Reminiscent of Dante, the Founder tells us that those who have procured the salvation of others will be "entirely plunged within the divinity and totally imbued with God Himself." Evoking imagery from the Book of Revelation, the Founder promises us that we who have procured the salvation of others will be met by those we have saved and brought before Christ with songs of praise urging a favorable judgment, so that there will be no delay in our taking our place in their midst. To gain such glory, De La Salle tells us, simply "act with goodness and wisdom in the care of those who are entrusted to you."

The charism so evident in this meditation stems from the Founder's own joy in describing his vision of heaven to his disciples.

Writing these *Meditations* toward the end of his life, and having spent himself tirelessly on the ministry he has so carefully laid out here, one can only imagine the powerful faith that energized him through the years of darkness and uncertainty that marked the emergence of our Institute as a significant ministry within the church. Surely the Founder himself will be among that company of students, confreres, and colleagues who will come to meet us at the end—though I believe that in the meantime their inspiration and intercession go a long way to support us who still strive for the good of those to whom we minister.

Conclusion

The *Meditations for the Time of Retreat* are much like a conversation with John Baptist de La Salle, one we can continue any time we take them up. They are a resource from which we can and must continually draw fresh insight and inspiration. Though these meditations were written almost 300 years ago, the Lasallian reader will find them echoed and affirmed in this passage from the Institute's most significant twentieth century document, the *Declaration*.

> The brother ought to have no fear of losing God when he goes among the young to serve them, nor of being estranged from Christ when he spends himself for [them].[24]

Though it is not written by the Founder himself, this affirmation clearly restates for us today what he so firmly believed: we cannot fully understand or appreciate the nature of our vocation unless we realize that its focus is first and foremost our students and their salvation. Everything we are as Lasallians, everything we do makes sense only in the light we kindle in the hearts of those we touch.

Notes

1. Rom 12:6–8.
2. 1 Cor 7:7

3. Eph 3:7.

4. Jas 1:17.

5. 1 Pt 4:10.

6. Heb 13:7.

7. Eph 5:1

8. 1 Thes 1:6–7.

9. See Mk 6:31, for example.

10. This Foreword comprises Appendix A in *Meditations for the Time of Retreat,* translated by Augustine Loes, FSC, with a critical introduction by Miguel Campos, FSC, 1975, Saint Mary's Press, 107f. I think it is fair to say that this is presently the definitive English edition of the *Meditations,* and it is the edition I will use to throughout this article.

Brother Miguel Campos is, in my estimation, one of the finest Lasallian scholars of our day, and I cannot recommend his critical introduction to this edition of the *Meditations* highly enough! I am both indebted to and inspired by him in the writing of this article.

11. In deference to De La Salle's text and his culture, I will use the masculine pronouns to refer to God throughout this article.

12. The *Rule* of 1718, Chapter 2: "The Spirit of this Institute."

13. I am indebted to Peter Gilmour, DMin, a member of the Christian Brothers Spirituality Seminar, for this concept of canon, sacred text, and scripture. For a greater elaboration of his fine insights, I refer the reader to his article, "Canons and Religious Fundamentalism: Obstacles to Change," in last year's Seminar publication, *Challenged by Change,* Michael F. Meister, FSC, ed. (Romeoville, IL: Christian Brothers Publications, 1991) 115–126.

14. Each of the 16 explications which follow is preceded by what I consider to be the key idea/passage from the text of the meditation itself.

15. 1 Cor 3:9.

16. Jas 2:17.

17. 1 Cor 2:16.

18. See Jn 6:63 ("The words I have spoken to you are spirit and life.").

19. 1 Cor 1:17.

20. Eph 3:8 and 2:19.

21. See 2 Tm 4:2.

22. Lk 16:2.

23. Dn 12:3.

24. *The Brother of the Christian Schools in the World Today: A Declaration.* Thirty-Ninth General Chapter: Second Session, 1967, 42.

Questions for Reflection and Discussion

1. How does the Founder's view of the unity of our ministry and our spiritual lives play out in your life?
2. What are your special charisms? In what way have you adapted them to your particular ministry?
3. Write a seventeenth *Meditation* whose foundation would be your special charism.
4. Which of the 16 *Meditations* appeals to you the most? In what way does it exhort you or energize your ministry?
5. Describe a charism(s) necessary in today's ministry that would not have had a place in the seventeenth century ministry of the Brothers.
6. In what manner can you retreat from a busy ministry to refresh and renew your zeal?
7. How do you reconcile and balance your Lasallian duties to your students and your family duties to your own children?
8. In what ways might a nuclear family be Lasallian?
9. How do you let your students know that they play a central role in your life?

The Heart of the Matter: Faith Working Through Love

Robert J. Smith, FSC

> For in Christ Jesus neither circumcision nor uncircumcision is of any
> avail, but faith working through love. (Galatians 5:6)

For Paul the evangelist, the heart of Christian morality and
ethics is found in God's love freely extended to humanity in Jesus
Christ. No longer can the law suffice; all is grace. The only sufficient and proper response to the gracious gift of God's very self,
which has come close to us in the person of Jesus Christ, is faith.
For Paul, as for John, it is not that we chose God but that God chose
us. To accept freely the gift which God has offered is to be changed
and transformed. Life can never again be the same. One might use
the image of a "changed heart" to capture what happens to a life
committed to and rooted in Christian faith. Such a symbol or image
is doubly fitting: first, because hearts *are* changed—changed radically—by the understanding and acceptance of what God has done
for humanity in Jesus Christ and, second, because the "heart" was
for Paul and the Jews of his day the center of life, of relationality,
and of morality.

This article is an attempt to explore Paul's understanding of
morality as being rooted in the relationship between God and those

---

BROTHER ROBERT J. SMITH, FSC, PHD, is a moral theologian. He has a
master's degree in Religious Studies from the United Theological Seminary of The Twin Cities and a doctorate from Marquette University. He
presently teaches in and chairs the Department of Theology at Saint Mary's
College of Minnesota in Winona, Minnesota.

who accept in faith and live out in action the implications of what God has done in Christ Jesus. Paul's ethics are first and last rooted in faith, and such faith has immediate and necessary demands on and in our individual and communal lives. Christian faith, if genuine, changes hearts; changed hearts affect and determine the quality and tone of our relationships which are, or ought to be, the heart of the matter when it comes to morality.

Introduction

Paul's letter to the churches in Galatia is by no means the definitive statement of his understanding of Christian ethics. The letter does not contain a fully developed ethical system; it does not provide a systematic approach to morality; nor does it offer very many concrete and specific moral directives or ethical exhortations. Any attempt to claim that this letter can answer every question regarding Pauline ethics disregards the way in which Paul's experience in the Christian community and his reflection on that experience provided the necessary impetus for him to articulate more fully and expand the ethical task of Christians in his other writings. It follows, then, that in order fully to appreciate Paul's ethics, it is important to be aware, and appreciate the ethical flavor, of all of his writing. At the same time, this relatively brief letter does suggest the fundamental elements—building blocks, if you will—of Paul's approach to and application of Christian ethics. In other words, I do not believe Paul's understanding of ethics in Galatians is particularly unique or distinctive when compared with, or seen in the light of, the larger Pauline corpus. This article will begin with and concentrate on an exploration of Pauline ethics in Galatians, and will refer to other letters in the Pauline corpus in order to support and expand upon the themes Paul introduces in this significant letter.

Galatians 5–6 is certainly recognized as the ethical or exhortative section of the letter. It is there Paul takes up the expectations of conduct and requirements for Christian living that are placed upon a person who has experienced the salvation of God in Jesus Christ and who has been given a share in the Spirit's life. Although these chapters are the most obvious and direct presentation of Pauline ethics in the letter, Paul actually lays his ethical foundation, provides a summary statement of his ethics, and offers clues to what Christian behavior ought to include in earlier portions of the letter.

In this article, then, I will attempt to construct the larger theological picture within which Galatians 5–6 is situated. The first section will address the general theological underpinnings of Paul's ethics in Galatians and in other of his writings. The second and major section, followed by a brief conclusion, will suggest five particular characteristics of Paul's ethics, as well as his understanding of community relations in his letter to the Galatians.

Theological Foundation of Paul's Ethics in Galatians

If Paul's theological system can be understood as constituted by faith, his ethical theory is grounded in love. Faith in Christ leads to love of neighbor and love of God. The letter to the Galatians reveals Paul's belief that such faith is expressed in freedom *from* the requirements of the law as well as from the temptations of the flesh. At the same time, faith in Christ and the experience of the Spirit are expressed in freedom *for* loving service of neighbor and the readiness to work toward building up the community. Just as faith leads to freedom and the loving service of others, so too such loving service is an expression and reflection of one's faith and one's freedom in Christ and the Spirit.

One of the major theological tenets of this letter is the "indicative of salvation." In his study of Galatians, Hans Dieter Betz suggests the presence of this indicative of salvation at a number of junctures. It is used by Paul three times in the *Exhortation* portion of the letter (5:1—6:10).[1] Most significant for the present study is the fact that the indicative of salvation is always followed closely by an ethical or behavioral imperative. In other words, the ethical mandate flows out of, is the "result" of, and is motivated by, the indicative of salvation.

This indicative-imperative structure is a favorite of Paul and is also found in other biblical (and non-biblical) writings in both the Hebrew and Christian Scriptures. The indicative implies a statement of fact or a condition already established by God; the imperative issues a command or a directive that could be understood to end with an exclamation point. The indicative and imperative phrases are always understood to be part of the same sentence structure, joined by a conjunction such as "therefore" or "so." In the Book of Exodus, for example, the pattern looks like this: "I am the Lord your God who brought you out of the land of slavery; therefore, you must worship me on my holy mountain." The first clause is the indicative: a statement of fact about what God has done; the second clause is the imperative: the command or expectation directing specific and concrete behaviors. Such behaviors arise out of and must of necessity be preceded by God's work—the indicative of salvation.

In Galatians, the indicative-imperative structure looks like this in Paul's voice: "You were freed from the law by the Spirit of God; therefore, act accordingly and do not go back to the law." Paul urges the Galatians to remember that they are *already* free; therefore, they must act, and are empowered to act, accordingly. What is key in the whole indicative-imperative paradigm is the theological and temporal priority of the indicative over the imperative. God's action must necessarily come before, because it enables and empowers human behavior while such behavior is a direct result of and response to God's gracious activity in our lives. Paul's understanding of ethics flows out of his experience of, and his theological convictions regarding, the salvific act of God in Christ and manifest in the Spirit. Being in Christ, putting on Christ, and living in and walking by the Spirit all imply a present reality, the reality of God's fulfillment of a divine promise made to Abraham and his heirs. This present reality of being saved by God, made righteous in Christ, and living in the age of the Spirit demands, as well as enables, ethically responsible and morally upright behavior.

The Galatians' attempt to fulfill the commands of God by way of the law only leads to failure. The very real possibility of their giving in to the desires and works of the flesh was easily realized because they could not counter such temptations on their own initiative. However, in and through the suffering, death, resurrection, and exaltation of Christ, a new age of the Spirit was inaugurated and people were empowered to fulfill the law and control the flesh. God's promise made to Abraham in faith was fulfilled in Christ; as heirs to that promise, the Galatians are ushered into the new age. As a consequence, they are called upon and expected to live a new life, one guided by the Spirit—not the law or the flesh.

The behavioral specifics of Paul's ethics were not all that bold or nontraditional for his day. The vices and virtues found in Galatians 5:16–25 are not exceptional; Jewish and Gentile communities would have agreed with Paul on the need to fight against the former and cultivate the latter. What was different for Paul was the motive, source, and enabling power which made possible the realization of the virtues and the suppression of the vices; namely, the power of Christ in the gift and presence of the Spirit. *Because* people lived in the Spirit, they were called and enabled to walk in the Spirit—that is, to live a life worthy of their calling. Here we see the inextricable connection between faith (the means by which we are saved) and ethics (the way we are to live). For Paul, ethics and morality are "directly resultant from his doctrine of salvation through faith."[2] While the connection is inseparable, Paul clearly understood salvation through faith and the gift of the Spirit to be theologically and temporally prior to the human ability to live ethically.

The letter to the Galatians contrasts a life lived under the demands of the law and a life lived in the Spirit. The prior is doomed to frustration and constant failure while the latter affords freedom from the law and the desires of the flesh. Further, life under the Spirit makes real the possibility of fulfilling the law. For Paul, the fulfillment of the law

> is not the result of an obligation to observe the demands of the law, but the inevitable outcome of a life lived under the guidance of the spirit of God.[3]

While the Galatians were tempted to return to some aspects of the law as a requirement of faith, Paul was at pains to convince them that the Spirit was all that mattered. He wanted the Galatians to understand that all people are dependent upon the Spirit and that the Spirit serves as the source of their salvation in faith and as the "source of morality."[4]

God's action in Christ has brought about a new age and a new creation. No longer are the Galatians required to live according to the law; they now are free of the law and animated by the power of the Spirit. While particular behaviors have not drastically changed, the rationale and motivation for them have. No longer living in fear of the law, Christians eagerly accept the promptings of the Spirit to serve one another in love as an expression, as well as a result, of their faith. The Spirit is a fact (the "indicative of salvation"): persons need not act certain ways in order to merit God's giving it to them. The Galatians already possess the Spirit; hence, they are called, expected, and enabled to act a certain way. Neither are they (or any Christians) expected to act a certain way in order to attain or "earn" the Spirit.

Those who live in the Spirit should and will walk in the Spirit; those who do not possess the Spirit are unable to act spiritually. Although the experience of the gift of salvation in faith precedes the possibility of acting morally, individuals' actions are clues to whether or not they do in fact live in the Spirit. Peter Richardson argues that for Paul, "ethics is a basic test of the reality of Christian experience."[5] This is not unlike the Gospel criterion that we shall know the tree by the fruit it bears.

Paul's ethics in Galatians could rightly be called an "Ethics of the Spirit," as long as one keeps in mind the theological and temporal priority of the "indicative of salvation" out of which, and as a consequence of which, come the "ethical imperatives of behavior." E. P. Sanders summarizes this quite succinctly.

> The Spirit, as is well known, plays a major role in providing the grounds of Paul's *paraenesis* [ethical exhortation]. Since a man [sic] has the Spirit in him and is in the Spirit, he should *walk* by the Spirit, be *led* by the Spirit or produce the fruits of the Spirit (Rom 8:9–14; 1 Cor 6:19; Gal 5:16–25). . . . Christians received the Spirit by faith rather than by works of law. . . .[6]

Faith, then, is the absolute necessity and the constitutive element for all Paul's ethical thought. That is why Galatians 5:6*b* serves as such a fine summary of his entire ethical approach: faith working through love. Not surprisingly, Paul refers to this phrase as the "truth" (Gal 5:7*b*) of his testimony and his preaching. It is only because of faith in Christ, experienced in the Spirit, that one is able to live a life of loving service. Human beings can never accomplish such loving service on their own; it is possible only through the gift which is theirs in Christ Jesus and the fellowship of the Spirit. Such faith frees Christians from the demands of having to *do* the law and enables them actually to *fulfill* the law. Faith frees people from the law and frees them for the service of God and others. Since Christian existence is marked by being and living in the Spirit, the Christian's exigency is to walk by and under the guidance of the Spirit, building up the community through mutual service. As Gerhard Ebeling puts it: "Christian freedom is freedom to love and therefore freedom to serve. According to Paul, this is the Magna Carta of Christian ethics."[7] If this, then, is the theological foundation upon which the "Magna Carta" of Pauline ethics is built, I will now explore some of the unique characteristics of Paul's ethics as found in his letter to the Galatians.

Characteristics of Paul's Ethics in Galatians

One could say that there is both a vertical and a horizontal dimension to Paul's ethics. In the previous section of this article I suggested the vertical dimension insofar as God's action in Christ is the constitutive and necessary first element in establishing any ethics. The more horizontal dimension of Paul's ethics, which I will consider in this section, is more immediate, concrete, specific, and "verifiable." W.D. Davies suggests that the vertical dimension of Christian ethics

> is linked to the understanding of an event—the life, death, and resurrection of Jesus [and the horizontal dimension] is the living out in daily conduct what it means to have died and risen with Christ. . . . For Paul, morality is inseparable from the life, death, and resurrection of Jesus.[8]

Put another way, "Christian morality finds its source not in an ethical code but in a living relationship to Jesus Christ."[9] As a result of this "living relationship to Jesus Christ," this "vertical dimension," Christians are given the desire, motivation, and ability to live ethically upright lives. What follows, given in no particular order of importance, priority, or significance, are some of the specific characteristics of Pauline ethics.

1. An Ethic of Desiring to Please God

Although little seems to have been written on it, it strikes me that Paul's ethics is one that places a very high priority on the *desire* to please God. This would, of course, put him in continuity with his Jewish roots. The rhetorical question put to the Galatians in 1:10 suggests that Paul is not seeking the favor of humans but of God. The answer implied in his second rhetorical question is that he is trying to please God, not humans. Were he still trying to please men and women, Paul would not be a servant of Christ. The unwritten implication is that it is because he is trying to please God that he is a servant of Christ.

It was "through the law" that Paul "died to the law" so that he "might live to God" (Gal 2:19). Paul's desire to live for God reflects the primacy of God in Pauline ethics and the mystical union that has taken place: it is no longer Paul who lives but Christ lives in him (Gal 2:20). This is what ought to happen in the life of every believer. Christ should be so intimate to the believer that it is Christ himself who reaches out in loving service to the Christ in one's brother or sister. "Living to God" suggests the theocentric nature of Paul's ethical framework. Not only does ethics flow out of God's gift to us of salvation in Christ; Christian ethics returns full circle and no less rich to God when Christians walk by the Spirit.

In light of the fact that the Galatians now know God, or even more intimately and graciously are known by God (Gal 4:9), Paul cannot understand their "backsliding" into their earlier ways of adherence to the law and indulgence of the flesh. Paul here seems to be confronting the Galatians with the highest moral imperative and the greatest ethical demand: maintain the knowledge and intimacy God has established with them. How can they now return to the *stoikea* ("elemental spirits," compare Gal 4:3,9) after having experienced the gift of God's very own Spirit in Christ?

Paul's appeal to God and his suggestion that pleasing God is the highest and the ultimate of all ethical demands is in line with Jewish tradition and appears in other of Paul's letters. One Thessalonians 4:1–8 ties together the ethical imperative of pleasing God with a listing of concrete behavioral activities. In Ephesians 5:1–2, Paul encourages his readers to be "imitators of God" and to "walk in love." The command to walk in love is echoed in various parts of Galatians as well, which I will point out below. Both 1 Corinthians 10:31 and Colossians 3:17 encourage Christians, whatever they do, to "do all to the glory of God." Romans 12:1–2 suggests that because God has been merciful to them, the Romans ought to conform their hearts and minds to God, that they "may prove what is the will of God." Not only does Paul suggest that pleasing God is the highest ethical imperative and motive; he also suggests, as reflected in Ephesians 5:1–2 and various other places, that for Christians God (or Christ) is the primary model and example of the ethical life.[10]

Herman Ridderbos gives some attention to the theocentric nature of Pauline ethics when he states: *"The theocentric point of view . . . constitutes the great point of departure of the Pauline paraenesis."* [11] He offers a cogent and helpful perspective that can serve as a summary and conclusion here.

> Man's [sic] freedom is in subservience to God, and without this servitude freedom has no place in the Pauline paraenesis. This servitude to God likewise does not come into view only insofar as it is necessary to give man freedom, joy, and peace; on the contrary, "for God" and "to God" are the motive and ultimate object of this obedience. . . .[12]

In other words, the highest and most noble ethical command, motivation, and imperative is to live in a way pleasing to God. This is accomplished within the context of the community of one's brothers and sisters in Christ, expressed in loving service toward them and made possible by the empowerment of the Spirit.

2. An Ethic of Freedom

One of the ways in which Paul describes the "indicative of salvation" is through the use of the term "freedom." As stated in the first major section of this paper, this freedom which the Galatians gained in Christ and the Spirit does not exist in a vacuum. It is not simply freedom *from* something; it is also freedom *for* something. Having experienced the Spirit, the Galatians are freed from the obligatory demands of the law and the passions of the flesh; at the same time, they are freed for loving service to others. One of the constitutive elements of Paul's understanding of God's salvific activity in Christ is freedom. This gift of salvation in Christ through faith leads to "the awareness that the most important freedom, ultimately, is freedom *for others*. . . ."[13] Freedom, then, is an important aspect of both Paul's theological understanding and his ethical system.

Galatians 2:4 is Paul's first statement about the freedom the Galatians have in Christ Jesus. The ethical or exhortative section of the letter is introduced with a statement of the indicative of salvation in terms of the freedom it affords the Galatians: "For freedom Christ has set us free; stand fast therefore, and do not submit again to a yoke of slavery" (Gal 5:1). The theological statement of the indicative of salvation is closely tied to the behavioral imperatives which follow in the succeeding verses of Galatians 5–6. Paul's plea that the Galatians ought not to "submit again to a yoke of slavery" refers back to the Galatians' tendency to continue to live by the ordinances of the law. Because "yoke" has the connotation of burdensome moral rules and regulations, the freedom to which Paul calls the Galatians is all the more precious.[14]

In Galatians 5:13 Paul sums up in a single verse his understanding of ethics and the relationship of ethics to the indicative of salvation: "For you were called to freedom, brethren; only do not use your freedom as an opportunity for the flesh, but through love be servants of one another." Here, just as in Galatians 5:6*b*, the intimate link between the indicative of salvation and the ethical or behavioral imperative is revealed. The freedom the Galatians have in Christ is an enabling and empowering freedom which manifests itself in loving service within the community. Indeed, in Galatians 5:13 we can recognize "the kernel of [Paul's] social ethics with its intimate connection of love and service. . . ."[15] Freedom and love, as mentioned in the section addressing the theological underpinnings of Paul's ethics, are mutually interdependent. Both have a theological component (the vertical dimension) and an ethical component (the horizontal dimension) which, while distinguishable, are not separable. Ebeling is perceptive when he concludes that freedom is freedom only as love, and love is love only as freedom.

> To serve one another in love does not limit freedom. It is rather the unfolding and fulfillment of freedom. The very warning not to let freedom become an opportunity for self-emancipation of the flesh does not lead to a demand to rein in freedom and limit it but to encouragement to live the freedom opened through Christ to the uttermost, after the model of Christ.[16]

It might not be too far off the mark to link Ebeling's suggestion about the "unfolding and fulfillment of freedom" with Paul's contention about the fulfillment of the whole law through loving service of neighbor (Gal 5:14 quoting Lev 19:18) and the fulfillment of the law of Christ through the bearing of one another's burdens (Gal 6:2).

Paul uses freedom in similar ways in Romans and in his first letter to the Corinthians. In both instances the context has to do with a theological statement (the indicative of salvation) as well as with its ethical implications. Romans 8:2 shows how the law of the Spirit of life in Christ Jesus has freed Paul from the law of sin and death. In 1 Corinthians 9:1 Paul asks a number of rhetorical questions intended to prove the freedom he has in Christ and the grounding of his ministry in that freedom. In all Paul's writing, freedom is not only intended to serve as a statement of faith in Christ; it is also an ethical command and moral directive to act on and out of the gift which is ours in Christ and the Spirit.[17]

3. An Ethic of Sensitivity of the Strong Toward the Weak

As has been pointed out numerous times in the preceding pages, freedom is a constitutive element of Paul's theology and of his ethics. At the same time, because this freedom does not exist in a vacuum and is dependent upon the community for its exercise, it is necessary that it be tempered and relativized in practice in light of its effects on the larger community in general and the community's weaker members in particular. "Freedom is essential, but it is always to be exercised in a way that will not destroy others."[18] This is not developed in as great a length or detail in Galatians as it is in other of Paul's letters, but it is there.

Paul's sensitivity to the weaker members of the community is most striking in Galatians 6:1, where he encourages the stronger, more spiritually mature members of the community (*pneumatikoi*) to "restore" those who have been overtaken in trespass, doing so in a "spirit of gentleness." This reveals Paul's concern for those who are not yet spiritually mature, as well as his concern for the overall well-being of the community. Paul encourages the Romans in much the same fashion. "We who are strong ought to bear with the failings of the weak, and not to please ourselves" (Rom 15:1). The manner in which Paul resolves the occasional tension between freedom of the individual in Christ—a freedom from the law and the flesh, a freedom for the up-building of the community in loving service of one another—and the need for sensitivity to the weaker members of the community is clear in those letters in which Paul introduces the notion of conscience (*syneidesis*). Unfortunately, an excursion into this issue would go too far afield from the immediate concern here.[19] Suffice it to say that such a study would show clearly that "consideration for the pain of the weak becomes for Paul a principle of conduct."[20] One would look in vain for anything near perfect equality in Pauline ethics. Christian community lived under the influence and guidance of the Spirit, worked out in loving service toward one another, "requires the strong to bear the infirmity of the weak, and not the weak to bear the strong."[21] For Paul, Christian ethics requires a great deal of selflessness on occasion: a selflessness modeled on and empowered by the very selflessness that Christ exhibited in his willingness to suffer and die on a cross to set us free.

4. An Ethic of Love in Community

The primacy of love in action is a fundamental element of Paul's ethics in Galatians and in his other letters. Paul connects the indicative of salvation with the imperative of ethical behavior through faith working in love (Gal 5:6). The freedom of the Galatians in Christ necessarily works itself out in sacrificial and loving service within the community (Gal 5:13). It is through such service—motivated, empowered by, and modeled after, Christ—that the whole of the law is fulfilled (Gal 5:14; 6:2). For Paul, love is the first fruit of the Spirit (Gal 5:22) because it sums up and envelops all the other marks of life in the Spirit. The love Christians bear for one another is sustained by, and serves as a reflection of, the love of God in Christ for them. According to Victor Furnish,

> for Paul the power of the New Age is *love*—not just love in general, but *God's* love, the love through which God has created all that is, in which God wills that it be sustained, and by which God acts to redeem it. . . . This is the love, *God's* love, to which faith is a response, and by which faith itself is empowered to express itself in the believer's life.[22]

Here again, as shown above, the theocentric nature of Pauline ethics is unambiguously recognized. *God* and *God's* love are primary.

In Galatians 5:6, the passage which serves as the key to the relationship between Pauline theology and Pauline ethics, "love" assumes a double meaning: as God's love which empowers and makes possible faith in the believer, and as the believer's active love as a natural outcome and expression of his or her faith. Because love's source lies in God, given out through Christ and in the outpouring of the Spirit, it is especially significant for the Christian. The loving service Christians extend to one another and the way in which they bear one another's burdens is only possible because of the power of the Spirit. Were they to attempt such things on their own, or by way of carrying out the precepts of the law, they would inevitably meet failure. The fulfillment of the law is possible only in and through Christ and the Spirit's power.

Christian love, working through faith and in freedom, is anything but individualistic. It is concerned preeminently with the building up of the community, particularly with gently aiding the weaker members of the community (Gal 6:1) to come to a fuller appreciation of and reliance upon Christ. Far from being concerned only with oneself, the Galatians are encouraged by Paul to bear one another's burdens (6:2) and never to weary of doing good (6:9) to and for each other. "Christian love is not individualistic, proudly separate, but always above everything else concerned with the body and not the individual."[23]

The parallels in other of Paul's letters to his emphasis on love, expressed in service to and for the purpose of building up the community, are too numerous to list. A few samples will serve to reinforce this dimension of Paul's ethics. Paul desires that everything the Corinthians do should be done in love (1 Cor 16:14). The Ephesians are encouraged to act with all lowliness, meekness, and patience, "forbearing one another in love, eager to maintain the unity of the Spirit and the bond of peace" (Eph 4:2–3) because they are "members one of another" (Eph 4:25). Galatians 5:14 is echoed in Romans 13:8–10.

> Owe no one anything, except to love one another; for he who loves his neighbor has fulfilled the law. The commandments . . . are summed up in this sentence, "You shall love your neighbor as yourself." Love does no wrong to a neighbor; therefore love is the fulfilling of the law.

Of course, Paul's hymn to love in 1 Corinthians 13 is one of the strongest evidences of his "ethic of love." In its broader context, 1 Corinthians 12–14 is concerned with the ordering and regulating of spiritual gifts, all of which are given for the common good (1 Cor 12:7) and as a way of building up the church (1 Cor 14:12).[24]

This concern for building up the community is clearly present in Paul's concluding exhortation in 1 Thessalonians. He wants the community members there to encourage one another and build one another up (5:11); to be at peace among themselves (5:13); to be helpful and patient with everyone (5:14); to do good to everyone (5:15). Paul is able to write all of this in confidence because he knows that the Thessalonians have been given the Holy Spirit by God (1 Thes 4:8) and that they "have been taught by God to love one another" (1 Thes 4:9). It is the Spirit who empowers and commands this loving service toward each other within the fellowship of believers. When the fruit of the Spirit is enumerated in Galatians 5:22–23 and Colossians 3:12–14, both texts list love as the crowning virtue and both are concerned with the unity, peace, and building up of the entire community. "Thus," R.E.O. White concludes,

> *to love is enough.* Within this supreme command, the multitudinous provisions of Judaist law and Torah are summarized and unified. All Christian insights, virtues, aims, disciplines, precepts, and valuations ultimately derive from this single principle.[25]

5. An Ethic of Universalism

At the end of his ethical paraenesis in Galatians, Paul gives a final exhortation: "So then, as we have opportunity, let us do good to all men, and especially to those who are of the household of faith" (6:10). One might think, given the intensity of Paul's own conversion experience and the fervor with which he preaches and admonishes, that anyone not "of the household of faith" would receive only his wrath or pity. Not so. He encourages the Galatians to treat kindly and do good to *all* people, not only fellow Christians. There is present in Paul's writing a certain acceptance of and solidarity with the unbelieving, hence unredeemed, world on the part of Christians. Ernst Kasemann has suggested that such solidarity "rests in the fact that church and world are together waiting expectantly for the manifestation of the liberty of the children of God."[26] Kasemann also offers some insight into Paul's understanding of the relationship between Christian liberty, liturgy, and worship in the context of the world.[27]

Paul prays that the Lord may increase the love the Thessalonians have for one another and for all people (1 Thes 3:12). In 1 Thessalonians 5:15, Paul encourages believers to "seek to do good to one another and to all." Likewise, Romans 12–13 suggests Paul's relative openness to and respectful attitude toward those who are not believers. He wants the Romans to bless those who persecute them (12:14), to live peaceably with all (12:18), and to cooperate with civil authorities (13:1–7). Interaction with nonbelievers was unavoidable. Indeed, it must have been presumed that believers would be invited to take meals with them on occasion (1 Cor 10:27). Paul's primary advice in all such situations was to be kind, to act maturely, and to not bring disgrace upon the Lord or upon the believers. In 1 Thessalonians 4:10–12, Paul encourages believers to love everyone, to live and work in such a way that they are examples to believers and unbelievers alike, so that they may "command the respect of outsiders."

One of the conclusions that can be drawn from these and similar passages is that it becomes "evident in various ways that Paul extends the commandment of love as widely as possible and that every suggestion that this commandment holds only for Christians among themselves is entirely foreign to him."[28] The universality of the love command in Paul's ethics shines forth perhaps most brightly in the pastoral epistles, but again, that would take one too far away from the letter to the Galatians in particular and the Pauline corpus in general.[29]

Finally, while Paul wants to extend the love of Christ to everyone, it cannot be denied that a "setting off" or "separation" exists between those who are believers and those who are not. It is not that a different kind of love is to be shared among "insiders" and "outsiders," since it is all God's love, but its expression might take on different forms because of a differentiation in fellowship. Although a certain kind of solidarity does exist among all human beings, believers and nonbelievers alike, "the thought is never that the same solidarity exists between believers and unbelievers as between believers and other believers."[30]

Conclusion

Attempting to capture the spirit of Pauline ethics, while trying to say something accurate about those ethics, is a challenge. To do so in a brief article is a sometimes frustrating experience. I have attempted to do two things here. First, I have tried to show that Paul's understanding of ethics in Galatians and elsewhere flows out of, is grounded in, and follows upon his indicative of salvation; that is, the indicative of salvation is theologically and temporally prior to Paul's ethical imperative(s)—and necessarily so. Second, I suggested a number of elements that characterize, or themes that permeate, Pauline ethics in a general way. In doing so, I deliberately tried to avoid dealing at great length with the well-known virtue and vice lists in Galatians 5:16–25 because I wanted to suggest a broader context for and perspective from which to view Pauline ethics.

There are at least five issues that I did not explore which are important to a more accurate and complete study of Pauline ethics. Additional research and more extensive analysis would address, among other things, the following topics: (1) the eschatological dimension of Paul's ethics in light of the "new age" and "new creation" motifs;[31] (2) the relationship between an "interior" ethics and an "exterior" ethics in terms of the "law written in our hearts" and the "written law," and Paul's understanding that the written law kills but the Spirit gives life—and the relationship all this has to Paul's understanding of conscience;[32] (3) the paradigmatic role Paul assumes and the importance of his own experience in his ethical teaching;[33] (4) the varied sources Paul used or was influenced by in the formulation of his ethics: the Jewish Scriptures, Jesus traditions, Hellenistic thought, oriental mystery cults, Qumran;[34] (5) Paul's conceptualization and understanding of Christian sin.[35]

There is also a need to study the implications of Pauline ethics for the current day and to appropriate and apply Paul's ethical principles and moral insights to contemporary Christian ethics in general and questions of ethical methodology in particular. It is clear that Paul has much to contribute to ethics today given his understanding of and emphasis on an ethics that is theocentric, communitarian-based, grounded in faith in Christ and the gracious guidance of the Spirit, action- (servant-) oriented, love-centered, respectful of the freedom of individual conscience, and sensitive to non-Christians. Some commendable work has already been done along these lines, especially in terms of the theocentric nature of ethics,[36] and the communitarian dimension of and basis for Christian ethics.[37] Finally, appreciative of all the scholarly study that has been and can still be done relative to Pauline ethics, the bottom line of all Christian morality—the "heart of the matter"—remains: faith working through love.

Notes

1. Hans Dieter Betz, *Galatians: A Commentary on Paul's Letter to the Churches in Galatia* (Hermeneia; Philadelphia: Fortress Press, 1979) 253–311.
2. Morton Scott Enslin, *The Ethics of Paul* (New York and Nashville, TN: Abingdon, 1957) 64.
3. Stephen Westerholm, "Letter and Spirit: The Foundation of Pauline Ethics," NTS [New Testament Studies] 30 (1984) 244.
4. W.D. Davies, *Jewish and Pauline Studies* (Philadelphia: Fortress Press, 1984) 281.
5. Peter Richardson, *Paul's Ethic of Freedom* (Philadelphia: Westminster, 1979) 107.
6. E.P. Sanders, *Paul and Palestinian Judaism: A Comparison of Patterns of Religion* (Philadelphia: Fortress Press, 1977) 458, author's emphasis.
7. Gerhard Ebeling, *The Truth of the Gospel: An Exposition of Galatians,* David Green, trans. (Philadelphia: Fortress Press, 1985) 252.
8. Davies, *Jewish and Pauline Studies,* 281.
9. John W. Drane, *Paul: Libertine or Legalist? A Study in the Theology of the Major Pauline Epistles* (London: SPCK, 1975) 55.
10. Raymond Corriveau, *The Liturgy of Life: A Study of the Ethical Thought of St. Paul in His Letters to the Early Christian Communities,* Studia Travaux de Recherche 25 (Brussels and Paris: Desclee de Brouwer, 1970) 192–200.
11. Herman Ridderbos, *Paul: An Outline of His Theology,* John De Witt, trans. (Grand Rapids, MI: Eerdmans, 1975) 260, author's emphasis.
12. Ibid., 259; also 258–265.
13. Robin Scroggs, *Paul for a New Day* (Philadelphia: Fortress Press, 1977) 30, author's emphasis.
14. Ridderbos, *Paul,* 304–305.
15. Enslin, *The Ethics of Paul,* 242.
16. Ebeling, *The Truth of the Gospel,* 252.

17. Ridderbos, *Paul*, 301–304.

18. Richardson, *Paul's Ethic of Freedom*, 135.

19. For an excellent general overview of conscience in the New Testament see C. A. Pierce, *Conscience in the New Testament* (London: SCM Press, 1955). See also Eric D'Arcy, *Conscience and Its Right to Freedom* (New York: Sheed and Ward, 1961). In regard to Paul's understanding and use of conscience, in addition to the above, see Davies, *Jewish and Pauline Studies*, 243–254; Enslin, *The Ethics of Paul*, 75, 243–249; Richardson, *Paul's Ethic of Freedom*, 118–119, 126–136; Ridderbos, *Paul*, 295; R.E.O. White, *Biblical Ethics* (Exeter, England: Paternoster Press; Atlanta: John Knox, 1979) 180–182.

20. Davies, *Jewish and Pauline Studies*, 251.

21. White, *Biblical Ethics*, 182.

22. Victor Paul Furnish, *The Moral Teaching of Paul* (Nashville, TN: Abingdon, 1979) 26, author's emphasis.

23. Ridderbos, *Paul*, 296; also see 293–301.

24. Richardson, *Paul's Ethic of Freedom*, 120–121.

25. White, *Biblical Ethics*, 160, author's emphasis; also see 158–160.

26. Ernst Kasemann, *Perspectives on Paul*, Margaret Kohl, trans. (London: SCM Press, 1971) 127.

27. Ibid., 136–137.

28. Ridderbos, *Paul*, 209.

29. Ibid., 300.

30. Ibid., 300–301, 304–305; also see Enslin, *The Ethics of Paul*, 202–203, 237–277; Scroggs, *Paul for a New Day*, 51–55; White, *Biblical Ethics*, 185–186.

31. See Bernard H. Brinsmead, *Galatians—Dialogical Response to Opponents*, SBLDS [Society of Biblical Literature Dissertation Series] 65 (Chico, CA: Scholars Press, 1982) 165–170; also see Furnish, *The Moral Teaching of Paul*, 21–22.

32. Drane, *Paul: Libertine or Legalist?*, 53; Enslin, *The Ethics of Paul*, 130; Richardson, *Paul's Ethic of Freedom*, 80, 165–166; Ridderbos, *Paul*, 288.

33. See Beverly R. Gaventa, "Galatians 1 and 2: Autobiography as Paradigm," *NovT* [*Novum Testamentum*] 28 (1986) 309–326 and Scroggs, *Paul for a New Day*, 66–71. In addition to Gal 4:12, there are other places in which Paul offers himself as a model to be followed: Phil 4:8–9; 1 Cor 4:6–7; 1 Thes 3:7–9.

34. Brinsmead, *Dialogical Response*, 170–176; Davies, *Jewish and Pauline Studies*, 285–287; Drane, *Paul: Libertine or Legalist?*, 55–57; Sanders, *Paul and Palestinian Judaism*, 513; Scroggs, *Paul for a New Day*, 64–66.

35. Ridderbos, *Paul,* 270–271; Sanders, *Paul and Palestinian Judaism,* 500.

36. See James Gustafson, *Ethics from a Theocentric Perspective,* Vol. 1 of *Theology and Ethics* (Chicago: University of Chicago Press, 1981) and the succeeding volumes of this work.

37. See Stanley Hauerwas, *A Community of Character: Toward a Constructive Christian Social Ethic* (Notre Dame, IN: University of Notre Dame Press, 1981).

Questions for Reflection and Discussion

1. How have you experienced the "indicative of salvation" in your life? How has God been present to you? How do you come to know yourself as "saved"?
2. What implications does God's presence and saving activity in your life have for the way you act toward yourself, others, and the earth?
3. At least in one sense, Paul's highest moral imperative is for believers to try to "please God." Is "pleasing God" a sufficient guideline or motivation for your moral life and behavior?
4. Paul's ethics suggest that the strong must be especially sensitive to the weak. The strong must even be prepared to forego their own desires in order to strengthen and uplift the weak. What implications does such a stance have for you/us in your/our life in community?
5. In your own words and arising out of your own life and convictions, what does "faith working through love" really mean? What significance does it hold for you? How might it shape your life?

Touching Hearts

Confronting Cultural Patterns

Who, Me? A Racist?

James H. Ebner, FSC

Leonard

I first got to know Leonard Williams (not his real name) as a happy-go-lucky street urchin running up and down the main street, offering bargain trinkets such as cheap chains and rings which he had snatched on his way out of a tourist shop. Though he was older than he looked, Leonard came across as a tall and somewhat underfed truant from high school. He seemed more upright and less sophisticated than his peers, and I began to take him seriously, as someone salvageable and worthwhile.

At this time I was living in a senior citizen high-rise in downtown Saint Paul. I identified myself as a retired teacher, but I was careful not to mention that I lived downtown. In any event, Leonard never asked; his characteristic conversation was a few breathless sentences on arriving and departing.

I was careful not to delve or pry. From his hasty and often oblique comments I came to understand that his welfare mother was

---

BROTHER JAMES H. EBNER, FSC, PHD, is the author of several articles, two edited works, and a book, *God Present as Mystery: A Search for Personal Meaning in Contemporary Theology* (Saint Mary's Press, 1978). He earned his doctorate in religious studies from The Catholic University of America; he also holds advanced degrees in philosophy and Latin literature. Brother James has taught at Saint Mary's College of Minnesota, at the Aquinas Institute of Religious Studies in Grand Rapids, and at De La Salle University in Manila, Philippines. At the present time, he is a lecturer in Saint Paul's School of Divinity at the College of Saint Thomas (Saint Paul, Minnesota).

the one person he believed most loved him, and his grandmother was second. I never dared to unravel a complication: he never spoke of a real father and felt rejected by his stepfather. Everything about Leonard—his string of jail terms for minor charges, his never holding a responsible job, his making nothing of himself—seemed to betoken a male child who had never learned from a father what it means to be a reliable male and father.

In time, downtown Saint Paul ceased to be a quiet and safe village. So I moved to the neighborhood high-rise where I now live. Leonard had my address, which he used on a few dramatic occasions. One midmorning about two years ago I was returning home when Leonard came rushing up in desperation: Dolores had thrown him out! Where would he live now? Could I put him up?

In Leonard's world, apparently, all this is standard practice: to move in as long as you can, especially with a white woman. So it was nothing new for Leonard to come to a parting of the ways. He had made much of the fact that he was living with a white girl whose parents both were professionals. She had married a black man who eventually got lost in drugs, so she took up with Leonard. He sometimes complained that the baby-sitting duties were not equally shared—Dolores had a lively black child to care for—and the car was not available as often as expected.

When sober, evidently, Leonard can be a good-hearted person. But what happens when he begins to feel boxed in, and drinks? Leonard himself did not tell me that the fighting got so vicious that Dolores finally had to call the police. (Apparently the police charge got mislaid in the computer, to be retrieved and identified later.)

All right, so here I was standing in front of a fine 17-story building for senior citizens, realizing how unfair life can be. But of course Leonard knew that I could not take him in. It had never been put into words, but his needs were so total that I would not allow him to enter any of the public rooms on the main floor. For how do you push out a poor person once he's in? Leonard had always seen without remark that whenever he visited, we always remained standing in the entry. Well, to conclude a painful confrontation, I reached for my wallet to find a remaining ten-spot.

Early last December was the next time Leonard helped me realize how unequally suffering is assigned in life, where some enjoy so many compensations while others have so few. It was a freezing cold night. I arrived back home around 9:00 P.M. As I took out my key to the security door, over in a lateral entry space I saw someone lying on the floor. Lest this be a dangerous character, I did not investigate, but hurried to phone the manager, who called the police.

In my room about 20 minutes later, I was jolted when I was buzzed from the lobby. I pushed the talk button, to say I would be down at once. There in the lobby were two policemen, one with the empty bottle for evidence against a sobbing Leonard. Both officers seemed amazed, as if forced to believe that Leonard had been telling the truth about having a friend in the building. I did not begin very coherently. "Leonard, what are you doing here in town? I thought you liked your job down south." I felt torn by his sad reply: he had come back north for his mother's funeral.

Especially in the presence of two police, what can you say to someone who, in an already bleak world, has now lost his trustiest support? This question occurred to me sharply: who on this earth is now going to help this hapless young man to work through his grief? In a different world, any of the three of us would have embraced Leonard on the spot, encouraging him to weep his eyes dry. But no, there were two squad cars outside waiting. To end this gut-wrenching situation, the best I could manage was to say to the officers, "Please leave him off at some warm place." (I was indeed grateful that someone else, not I, had called the police.)

Soon after that Leonard also lost his grandmother. No more mother or grandmother to invite him to meals. Leonard had once mentioned that in his family he was considered the black sheep. This family estimate may have been made manifest in a recent event. Last New Year's afternoon I went to the downtown jail, to visit Leonard. About ten days earlier he had mailed me a note: he was back in detention, the police having retrieved the domestic strife charge made by Dolores two years ago. I was surprised to find Leonard looking more rested and better-fed than I had ever noticed before. When I asked whether he had a lot of Christmas visitors, he remarked matter-of-factly that I was the first.

Leonard did not seem apprehensive about the hearing soon to come. He had no reason to be. He avoided a trial by confessing he had beat up Dolores. Then he accepted an alternative program: testing for drugs, daily group therapy, and job training up ahead. In his late 30s, I wondered whether Leonard would finally make it? He had been in alternative programs before, and had never finished one. Also, I recalled a professional comment made at city hall. It was my first time there for a hearing. I knew the attorney handling Leonard's case from his years as an undergraduate at Saint Mary's College, Winona. Offhandedly, he sized up Leonard's career: "He's a loser."

But hope can spring eternal. Some street males reportedly grow out of delinquency. Near 40 now, maybe Leonard's time has come. He has asked my permission to list me among his sponsors: people willing to stand up and be counted for him, people willing to take time to talk with him. So I am registered with his appointed counselor, whom I have contacted by letter and by phone. But most encouraging of all has been Leonard's revealing story: a former street friend of his has finally quit drink and drugs, and is working at an honest job. He is after Leonard to follow suit.

Leonard is the first underclass African-American I ever got to know. From meeting him I realized the consequences of white racial prejudice. Actually, like nearly all the people I associate with, I have lived in a racially insulated world. It took a long time to open my eyes.

Seeing and Not Seeing

Back in the 1940s, I was assigned to De La Salle Institute in Chicago. At the end of each of my five years there, I turned in my reports, content that I had been a dutiful teacher.

The De La Salle I knew, it should be added, was a special high school. Founded in 1889, in my day it served a multitude of Chicago parishes, with sons of loyal alumni coming even from the suburbs.

The annual alumni dinner was a convocation of local "Irish mafia" and of Chicago Democrats generally. During my last few years at De La Salle, Martin Kennelly, a De La Salle graduate, was mayor of Chicago. So when teaching at the Institute in those days, one was aware that he was part of something larger than the venerable buildings at 35th and Michigan. All in all, I was indeed pleased with what went on at De La Salle.

But during my time there, De La Salle made another kind of impression on an outstanding student (whom I did not have in class). Donald F. Costello, class valedictorian in 1949, went on to college at De Paul, took a doctorate in English literature at the University of Chicago, and then went to teach at Notre Dame.

Some years ago Costello wrote an essay, "The Chicago Ghetto."[1] Looking back at his first sixteen years of school, all at Catholic institutions, he saw them as a kind of ghetto education, self-preoccupied. In high school, however, he had become an activist, befriending like-minded fellows, who were attaching themselves to Catholic Action priests. Ironically it was his going to De La Salle that had helped usher Costello into his activism.

> My birth began when I traveled to high school for forty-five minutes each way—on the "L." De La Salle and the Christian Brothers were located, or rather isolated, within the guts of the Negro slums. I never had a teacher who recognized what was outside the window, but several of us began to notice. We saw ugliness and hunger and prostitutes and hatred and faithlessness.[2]

Originally De La Salle may have been located in a fashionable part of town. But by the time I arrived, without planning to be so, it actually had long been segregated. As a child of the 1920s, I came ready to help promote whatever was already in place. That is, I was busy with classroom duties on behalf of youngsters, all of whom happened to be white. Furthermore, I must admit that my contact with De La Salle neighbors was limited to calculating which set of stairs to use in order to get to the "L" stop more safely. On my return trips the question was, would I have the right key for opening the front door quickly? So it was not until the era of sit-ins and marches that some of us older white Americans had our eyes opened.

In defense of De La Salle, however, it should be emphasized that the school was not more segregated than were the Catholic parishes. Besides, it was actually during Costello's time at De La Salle that the school was desegregated: without fanfare four black students were admitted in September 1947.[3] I remember I was glad when Brothers Matthew and Maurice made their front-office decision, and my recollection is that it was well-received by all the faculty. However, I myself had done nothing to bring on the change.[4] In any event, De La Salle kept on with its business without missing a beat, while the alumni association grew accustomed to its wider racial membership.[5] Currently— for the fifth time—a De La Salle graduate is mayor of Chicago: Richard M. Daley.

Racial Prejudice

What I am proposing here, then, is an examination of our personal record on social justice in general, and racial justice in particular. This is no small issue for professionally religious people, and especially for educators. Now of course if there are prejudice-free persons, we would expect to find them among such professionals. Yet there may be indications that this neat correlation is not automatic. Let me offer two anecdotes, one a twice-told tale.

First, the case of Clarence Thomas, the Supreme Court justice. In the fall of 1967, as a candidate for the priesthood, he entered the Immaculate Conception Seminary in Missouri. He left after the first year. Apparently it was a doubly dramatic event that most seared him. On April 4, 1968, the day Martin Luther King was assassinated, Thomas was watching television with a group of seminarians. He heard one of them remark, "That's what they should do to all the niggers."[6]

From my own experience I can match that comment. It was during summer school, also back in the late sixties. In the men's lounge a random crowd was reading the newspapers and watching the evening news. Everyone present was a vowed religious male. I was there as fellow graduate student. The TV camera focused on some black rioters in Detroit. I was shocked to see two or three religious stand up and shout, "Kill them! Shoot them!" But then maybe we should not expect too much. As the medieval adage says, "Scratch a Christian and find a Turk."

Now to get closer to my theme, let me compare early histories. Having gone through psychoanalysis late in life, I feel prepared to say that I may have had about as prejudice-free an upbringing as possible. I cannot recall hearing any racial slur ever made at home. On the contrary, I recollect two conversation-stoppers my parents likely had found their way to separately. For instance, whenever neighbors made remarks about Swedes and Norwegians, my mother, drawing on her experience as teacher, would somehow manage to praise Scandinavians for bringing up their children to be model students and good citizens.

Then there was my dad. In those days (the 1920s, before television, when radio still meant crystal sets), he and his friends would carry on discussions into the night. Endless hunting stories. And of course digressions into current events and politics—which were sometimes sidetracked, as when my dad would cut in with a line I can hear still: "But *Marcus* is a good man." At that time, even in the Midwest, there was plenty of anti-semitic feeling. It seems that such talk made my father uncomfortable. Instinctively he would cite as an exemplar a local Jewish person everyone respected, a civic-minded owner of what we used to call a dry goods store.

Nevertheless, despite such an advantage, I do harbor some racial prejudices. But before we compare notes, let me try to define terms. To begin with, taking James M. Jones as our mentor here, we could use this as our working definition of racism: "Stated simply, preferences for (or belief in the superiority of) one's own *racial* group might be called *racism*."[7] The attitude of racial superiority constitutes racial prejudice. Jones stresses the dynamic of prejudice.

> Prejudice is a negative attitude toward a person or group based upon a social comparison process in which the individual's own group is taken as the positive point of reference.[8]

Analyzed farther, prejudice has a cognitive component, ordinarily a stereotyped image of the outsiders. This simplified and likely twisted image we may assimilate early. Then there is an affective component in prejudice, a negative feeling habitually associated with the stereotype. Finally there may be a conative component, as when we proceed to carry out our negativity into action: thus, an act of discrimination.[9]

In itself, there is no fault in using simplifications or stereotypes. Daily living is so filled with onrushing data that, in order to arrive at a decision or a conclusion, we have to cut off the flow, to work with the best-investigated decision or conclusion we have thus far shaped. What makes prejudice or prejudgment reprehensible is when we do not feel obliged to question and test the prefabricated images we inherit from our culture.

Now I was starting to say that I am aware of having some racial stereotypes. I cannot account for them, in the sense that I do not know why, when, or how I picked them up. As a child, if I then had any stereotypes for blacks, it would have been the image of courteous men in white jackets: the stewards and waiters in dining cars, and the porters in Pullmans. However, one has to graduate from childhood. For example, today I must confess that alarm bells go off when I notice a "street dude" squiring his "white chick" around town. Similarly I feel uncomfortable when I see a white woman fondling a black child who must be her son.

Contemporary Racism

It could be health-giving and even therapeutic to look into the psychology of race prejudice, to understand better what may be going on inside of ourselves as we, the majority, look down on the minority.

Also it may be timely to do so as a nation. For on the political front racism apparently will go on as a deeply divisive issue. Gains made by the civil rights movement may perhaps have to be fought for over again, state by state, if the Supreme Court moves in the direction it now seems destined to. In the tradition of Reagan's welfare queens and Bush's Willie Horton, a David Duke lives on in the hope of exploiting such racially-coded images in his drive for power. For a long time to come this observation will likely remain a true statement: "Racism is an elusive, emotional, and historically pervasive fact of American society."[10]

Let us now take up the two major patterns of U.S. racism. We turn first to those white Americans who see themselves as above racism: possibly most college graduates, and others who consider themselves educated. One trait seems to mark this group: they are polite racially, maybe even painfully so. But to some researchers, the politeness of the educated and of liberals generally conceals ambivalence, an interior split.

John Dovidio and Samuel Gaertner are prominent among those who discern this subtle but widespread form of racism.[11] They analyze it as

a particular type of ambivalence in which the conflict is between feelings and beliefs associated with an egalitarian value system and unacknowledged negative feelings and beliefs concerning blacks.[12]

This can be called *averse* racism in the sense of reluctant and unwilling. Like it or not, beneath their polite demeanor these averse or reluctant racists are pulled interiorly in opposite directions.

That is, on the one hand, "aversive racists sincerely embrace egalitarian ideals," such as open competition, the American dream, democracy.[13] In fact, "most whites . . . have convictions concerning fairness, justice, and racial equality."[14]

But on the other hand, there is the negative side of such an altruistic stance: many of the well-wishers cannot accept the practical consequences of their openness to African-Americans. This retraction is

"not hostility or hate" for blacks, but rather a feeling of personal "discomfort, uneasiness, disgust, and sometimes fear, which tend to motivate avoidance rather than intentionally destructive behaviors."[15]

Liberal whites, for instance, may discover with a start that they personally are not ready culturally and socially to accept the African-Americans they feel should be given a square deal.

More than that, liberal whites can appreciate the fact that somehow there has to be a way to make up for slavery's past and its subsequent disadvantages. Yet the moment blacks are helped with housing, education, and jobs, even liberals may join the protests: Not on our street! Not in our school! (As long as such protests do not make the liberals look bad). What happens, it seems, is that such whites tend to fall back on their cultural and traditional stereotypes—likely learned in childhood—which continue to "characterize blacks as lazy, ignorant, and superstitious; they portray whites, in contrast, as ambitious, intelligent, and industrious."[16]

It is true that due to an increasing success of blacks in politics, in sports, in movies and television, the white stereotype for blacks may have brightened. But it seems that for many the childhood images have a long life. Clearly, then, a white person's real commitment to fairness and equal opportunity can be maintained separately from genuine respect and sympathy. Hence, contrary to some of their colleagues, Dovidio and Gaertner warn against optimism concerning the demise of racism: "We do not assume the widespread existence of genuinely pro-black . . . racial attitudes that are independent of egalitarian values."[17]

With their polite ambivalence, the educated and the liberals have no way out of their dilemma. Dovidio and Gaertner emphasize that "averse racists do not recognize their negative racial feelings."[18] For there is no overt bigotry to convict oneself of, and no obvious opening for self-criticism. Their blindness is self-inflicted. In fact, in order to preserve their noble image of themselves, they have to deny any anti-black feeling. "Aversive racists are very concerned about their non-prejudiced self-images."[19] This does not mean "however, that contemporary white Americans are hypocritical; rather, they are victims of cultural forces and cognitive processes that continue to promote prejudice and racism."[20]

It should be added that the averse racist's need to maintain a correct public image can be manipulated by clever African-Americans. For example, Shelby Steele relates his youthful experiences in lashing whites into fits of guilt.

> Those were the days of flagellatory white guilt; it was such great fun to pinion some professor or housewife or, best of all, a large group of remorseful whites, with the knowledge of both their racism and their denial of it. . . . And how could I lose? My victims—earnest

liberals for the most part—could no more crawl out from under my accusations than Joseph K. in Kafka's *Trial* could escape the amorphous charges brought against him.[21]

Steele suggests that one factor in explaining the huge success of certain African-American entertainers is this: they give off signals that they would *never* make their white audiences feel guilty. Thus, as head of the TV Huxtable family, Bill Cosby never discusses affirmative action. Huxtable home life is "a blackface version of the American dream," a black stamp of approval on the American way. "Cosby, like a priest, absolves his white viewers, forgives and forgets the sins of the past."[22]

One lesson of this section could be: any do-gooder or liberal, in which group I would have to put myself, who owns up to this racial ambivalence knows that he or she has lots of honorable company.

Conservative Racism

So much, then, for white liberals. But what about white conservatives? It appears that they too may experience a certain ambivalence. But the polarities are reversed. Thus, conservative white ambivalence is the mirror image of white liberal ambivalence. Whereas white liberals seem to emphasize racial equality, the political conservatives can focus on rights of the individual, on hard work, on antibusing—all the while as free as they dare to be in expressing their anti-black feeling. (Of course one can oppose busing for non-racist reasons.)

The ambivalence here is how to reconcile one's underlying anti-black feeling with the limitations on speech imposed by public opinion. For with the successes of the civil rights movement, old-time bigotry had to be put aside with segregation and the rest. Thus David Duke, for example, has found that old-fashioned racism is nationally counterproductive.

Publicly, then, how can conservatives oppose political programs that they consider to be reverse discrimination? Without fear of reprobation "anti-black attitudes can be expressed today in the form of opposition to busing, or to a black candidate, or to preferential treatment for blacks."[23] What is distinctive about this new form of racism is that busing and voting are respectable topics for debate. But in an implicit, unspoken racial context, the respectable words can really be heard as anti-black. Actually "such issues take on a 'symbolic' connection to deeper fears; for example deep-seated rejection of blacks can be expressed as fear of what will happen to white children bused into black neighborhoods."[24] Hence the name *symbolic racism,* our second general pattern of U.S. racism. The coded language we hear today is a sophisticated if sometimes cynical form of symbolic racism.

As studies indicate, this conservative racism has been "positively correlated with political conservatism and religious conventionalism."[25] Among some right-wingers and fundamentalists, political activity seems to be thinly veiled bigotry. The religious inspiration for symbolic racism has not been entirely dimmed.

> The original conception of symbolic racism was that it represented a blend of anti-black affect with traditional Protestant values. The latter have been enumerated variously as including values of hard work, individualism, thrift, punctuality, sexual repression, and delay of gratification, as opposed to laziness, seeking of favoritism and handouts, impulsivity, and so on.[26]

By themselves, the Protestant values have no direct connotation of race, but once they are associated with anti-black feeling, they become symbols or indicators of it. That is, while today it is bad form to promote naked discrimination, under cover of patriotism and of religion one can still do a lot to keep all those undesirables in their proper place!

The ultimate thing to say about symbolic racism is that it can be publicly tolerated as proper free speech. Yet it is a form of racial harassment, an injustice. "Symbolic racism may really be composed of resistance to racial equality; only the battlefield has changed, not the war."[27]

By using symbolic racism as his measure, David Sears professes to find "that racism continues to pervade white America."[28]

In fact he doubts that any American can be free of anti-black feelings: "If there is a single individual in the Unites States, white, red, yellow, or brown, who is not somewhat racist and prejudiced against blacks," then what we will have discovered is "a remarkable feat of resistance to a quite overwhelming saturation of centuries of cultural socialization."[29]

Black Family Values

In this process of self-examination I have surveyed something of the psychology behind racism; next I will confront the anti-black content of a few common stereotypes.

Let us adopt as our own some realistic questions posed by Robert Staples, himself a long-time student of marriage and family among blacks. His theme is this: With such strong family traditions among African-Americans, why so much broken existence? He asks three particular questions which no doubt articulate some of the charges whites level against African-Americans.

> How is it that a group that regards family life as its most important source of satisfaction finds a majority of its women unmarried? Why does a group with more traditional sexual values than its white peers have a majority of its children born out-of-wedlock? Finally, we must ask how a group that places such importance on the traditional nuclear family finds a near majority of its members living in single-parent households?[30]

Staples responds in terms of African-American family arrangements among the underprivileged. He puts his finger on the spot where male inadequacy meets female black tradition. When an African-American lives at the bottom of the socio-economic heap, he or she conforms to a hierarchy of priorities that pivot on the role of women *as childbearers and childkeepers*. Much hangs on this crucial premise: "Among the most traditional of values is that of motherhood and childbearing." Except for some college-educated women, almost all other black women bear children. "The role of mother is regarded as more important than any other role, including that of wife."[31]

The ideal, of course, would be motherhood within marriage. But in a poverty context a legal husband may be a luxury that one cannot afford. Thus an impoverished African-American woman nowadays will consider marrying only a man with at least the "minimum prerequisite . . . that he be gainfully and regularly employed."[32]

Up to the 1960s an uneducated black male could get a good-paying job in industry. But with the advance in technology, some schooling and skills are required—rendering young blacks unemployable by the thousands. The unemployable African-American male, then, is rejected by respectable employers and consequently is not wanted as a husband, not even by teenage girls. In an effort to maintain his sense of importance, the rejected male has to depend upon his street-corner friends—with unlimited possibility for mischief.

Her rejection of the jobless male reduces an impecunious woman's alternatives to one: she can still have her child, outside of marriage. Due to the lack of marriageable males, "over half of all black births today are out-of-wedlock."[33] Underclass teenage girls read their fate early and adjust to the inevitable: a baby but no husband. ("Bastard," by the way, is a white category, not a black one.)

Standing by, ready to institutionalize the situation, the U.S. welfare system rewards the unmarried women. "Black women realize that the meager welfare payments are more reliable than a class of men who may never know gainful employment in their entire lives."[34]

The total human frustration and wastage here is prodigious. Staples estimates that there may be "an excess of three million black women without the opportunity to find an available or desirable mate."[35] Some of that total will be college-educated black women who cannot locate eligible educated black males.

Now we white bystanders can question the wisdom, to say nothing of the morality, of these women. Yet, ironically, "their decision to bear the children and raise them alone reflects their traditional values and limited options in life."[36] Perhaps in the past it may have been the fashion for some social science people to dwell upon the inadequacies of black family life. But some recent researchers have not hesitated to express their admiration. What may not be respectable (or even moral?) may yet be a humane adaptation.

For instance, her close work with African-American poor families has led Carol Stack to be highly impressed by "the adaptive resiliency and strength that Black families have shown."[37] She has been struck particularly by the black family kinship network, an association of blood "kinsmen related chiefly through children." This is the ordinary extended family multiplied, a "cluster or domestic network . . . diffused over several kin-based households."[38]

To survive, then, underclass blacks work out complicated group arrangements, where the nurture of children is primary. Grandparents babysit while the younger women go out to jobs. (But, of course, as I will show in a moment, those who can afford it follow the traditional pattern of father, mother, and children, in their own apartment or house.)

If the head of a kin network (ordinarily a woman) has been married officially, her husband will be subtly but effectively reined in. All the moves of the network will be at the expense of any male-female tie, married or otherwise. Blood kinship generally takes precedence over juridical or legal relationships. Nothing can be allowed to endanger the fragile network.

The double losers in all this deprivation—in jobs and in the networks—are the more or less useless unemployed males.

> Black men have been made transitory family members, that is to say, they have been made absent fathers, boyfriends, uncles, and stepfathers who live on the margins of the female-centered household networks.[39]

"The future of the black family is inextricably tied up with the current and future status of the black male."[40] This means that for the oncoming waves of young African-American males and females, their hope of having the nuclear-type family—a household with father, mother, and children, to whom can be added one or more relatives—may be denied most of them.

What is immeasurably sad is that contrary to appearances, African-Americans want a properly wedded life. Billingsley is emphatic on this point.

There is no need to focus on inculcating values of marriage and stability among African-American youth because they already exist. The need instead is to create the conditions which make it possible to consummate and sustain the marital bond which they value.[41]

Actually, studies bear out the fact that when they can afford it, African-Americans do carry out their dream of a stable father-mother household. Billingsley, for example, finds that among upper class blacks "an overwhelming 96 percent are husband-wife families."[42] Among middle class blacks, "an overwhelming majority of 83 percent . . . were husband-wife families."[43] Among the blue-collar working class (non-poor) about 60 percent are husband-wife households, the rest being single-parent families.[44] Only one-third of the working class (poor) are husband-wife families, the rest being one-parent families.[45] Then among the underclass (non-working poor) we find "fully 75 percent single-parent and only 25 percent husband-wife families."[46]

Until the times improve, impoverished African-Americans will have to continue hanging on somehow, making the most of the extended and network models of home life. We middle class professionals may continue to drive hurriedly through a shabby black neighborhood, wondering when these people will take advantage of their opportunities, and researchers may continue to appreciate the solidarity and altruism that show up amid bleak surroundings.

Today's social science research on black female-male relations tells us what our common sense should have indicated long ago—that the essence of black family and community life has been a positive, constructive, and even heroic experience.[47]

Social Injustice

We older Catholics may find it awkward to discuss the moral dimension of social injustice and of racism particularly. We tend to think of evil in terms of personal sins—at which point we fall back on our confession-box categories: detached, individual sin-acts which we can classify and count. Since the Council of Trent, Catholic morality has been shaped largely by the textbooks used in seminaries up to recently. To meet confessional needs the books have elaborated a morality grid on which every kind of sin-act could be pegged.

Then where to locate racism? The grid works best with specific sin-acts, which are seen as isolated free-willed events. On the other hand, today we may recognize within ourselves how our white racism is a tough, enduring predisposition to look down (even if only a little bit) on people of color. We take for granted that with an occasional exception (a star athlete, entertainer, and so on) no African-American, no Hispanic, no Asian is superior to us White Americans. Until some prophetic event opens our eyes, we may remain blind to our deepest propensities.

Of course our racist attitude can express itself in sin-acts, as when deliberately and consciously we belittle a person of another race. Such an act we can feel guilty of and confess, likely under the category "injustice." For it is only lately that we have come to understand how racism is a specific type of sin deserving its own identification. But then what to say of racism as a blind tendency—beyond what we allow knowingly and willingly?

Now that we Catholics have found our way back to the Bible, we realize that one of its leading themes is the evil latent in all people, activated and embodied in all their transgressions. Genesis, chapters 1 through 11, suggests that there really is in human beings a universal resistance to God's reign on earth. Cain schemed to kill his younger brother. Their parents already had sinned. From the beginning a kind of original sin pressured the human race to resist grace.[48] "It is sin in its most basic and elemental sense, sin as a situation, sin as a reality, sin as a curse under which we all stand."[49] In Christian Scripture Paul and John speak easily of original sin in the singular—the reign of sin, the sin of the world: a malevolent force pushing upon each person within and without. In Romans 5:12, for instance, Paul ascribes to Adam the introduction of sin to the world (arriving as some resident evil power) and of death (both spiritual and physical).[50] In the light shed by Christ, Paul can lament the human condition: "Miserable one that I am!" he exclaims. "For I do not do the good I want, but I do the evil I do not want" (Rom 7:24 and 19). Similarly, Paul complains of the "sin which dwells in me" (Rom 7:17) and of his being "captive to the law of sin which dwells in my members" (Rom 7:23). Paul pictures original sin as a contagion, like someone today who learns he or she has tested HIV positive.

Now in original sin, biblically interpreted, we have a generic metaphor for racism. Both point to the overwhelming tendency of the human race to do evil instead of good. Racism is a particular, concrete way in which original sin operates through social structures. Thus racism is a common way for a society to express its predisposition toward evil. Through society's vocabulary, myths, laws, traditions, and customs racism becomes incarnated.

As "social sin," then, as sin through and in society, racist arrogance can infect all social systems: the structures which organize private and public life; the political structures ordering power in the community; economic structures by which goods are produced and distributed; legal structures by which rights and duties are adjudicated; cultural structures that make life humane: language, art, social relations. Not to be forgotten is that "social" also includes religion, which can both oppress and free.[51]

This diffusion of racism in all areas of society shows how social sin is a specialized manifestation of original sin. "Social sin is the specific concrete form that original sin takes in a particular culture and a particular generation."[52] Hence some moralists today speak of rampant "structural sin" or "social sin" of which racism is a type (among blacks as well as whites).

What marks off social evil is its coherent establishment within a group of people.

> Structural sins, then, are institutional realities, such as colonialism and imperialism, that create an unjust distribution of wealth, power, and recognition, and thus push a section of the population to the margin of society where their well-being or even their life is in danger.[53]

In order to emphasize its embodiment in persons, Baum proposes

> to define social sin with reference to its subject. What is proper to social sin is that its subject is a collectivity. Social sin resides in a group, a community, a people.[54]

The collective may be a board of directors, a parish council, a political party.

Hence there are two criteria for social sin: first, as we have seen, it must be the habit of a group which damages others through established social channels; second, the group's evil effects will not be intended consciously or explicitly.

> What is proper to social sin is that it is not produced by deliberation and free choice. It produces evil consequences but no guilt in the ordinary sense. According to the biblical description, social sin is committed out of blindness. People are involved in destructive action without becoming aware of it.[55]

Like slavery for centuries, some of the most terrible things we do to one another are done more or less blindly. (Who knows how much suppressed doubt, bad faith, and implicit personal sin flow as an undercurrent beneath such social sin?)

The social and moral components I have been exploring here are brought together by Thomas F. Schindler.

> Original sin points to the universality of the opposition to God's Reign. Social sin designates the social and historical forms that opposition takes. And personal sin . . . indicates the ways in which we as individuals actively participate in that opposition.[56]

Here, then, we have found a way to break out of our confession-box enclosure. We can still specify and count our sin-acts, but now we also see them in their worldwide context. Sin is a contagious disease so much larger than an individual sin-act. No sin-act is some sudden, isolated event out of the blue. Original sin, the sin of the world, is "a reality which precedes and affects our conscious choices."[57] No one invents sin. "Personal sin . . . is a way in which we participate in the sinfulness of society."[58] Racism is one of the distinctive areas in that mass of social sin. In a world where all is surrounded by grace, all is also steeped in sin.

"Social sin" may strike us as an innovation. Yet liberation theologies have been exploring this social model of blind evil, in line with the Hebrew prophets. In this prophetic tradition the U.S. bishops have identified racism as a virulent kind of social sin.

The structures of our society are subtly racist, for these structures reflect the values which society upholds. They are geared to the success of the majority and the failure of the minority; and members of both groups give unwitting approval by accepting things as they are. Perhaps no single individual is to blame. The sinfulness is often anonymous but nonetheless real. The sin is social in nature in that each of us, in varying degrees, is responsible. All of us in some measure are accomplices.[59]

By approaching racism from its context or background, we have a helpful way to get it into moral perspective. The notions of biblical original sin and of social sin provide working concepts we can verify in experience. But in the end we confront what baffles us: ultimately sin, like grace, is also mystery.

In Broad Perspective

By a kind of blind original sin we, the white majority, continue to trust in our inherent superiority over those whose faces are yellow, red, brown, and black. "The reality of race, then, is elitism based on a color line."[60] Accordingly, even the lowest "white trash" can feel empowered to look down on people of color.

Furthermore, we who strive to make this a better world likely find we still have work to do on our own racial prejudice, especially against African-Americans. Evidently it is "difficult for even the most well-intentioned white persons to escape the development of negative beliefs concerning blacks and to avoid feelings of superiority and relative good fortune over the fact that they are white rather than black and are culturally advantaged rather than disadvantaged."[61]

It can be a step forward, however, to empathize with those whom we deem less fortunate than ourselves. This can become one way to realize our common humanity, beneath the layers of differences. In this regard, we can profitably consider an insight expressed by Clarence Thomas during the senatorial hearings. He told how from the window of his courthouse he could look out to see buses transporting criminal defendants. His comment: "I say to myself almost every day, but for the grace of God there go I."[62]

As people in the business of educating the upcoming generation, we reflect on the awesome mystery behind each of us individuals—the selfsame mystery behind rocks and trees, birds and beasts, the sun and moon and stars. But let me make the point concrete by relating an incident. Back in the days when I was in grade school, I was out walking with my father after supper. (In those days adults talked about taking their daily "constitutional.")

As no doubt I often did, I was complaining about my brother. (We two were the only children, so that the lines of sibling rivalry were clean and clear.) I was trying to get my dad to take my side of a squabble. At some pause in the recital of evidence, my dad quietly asked a question that transcended the fray. Up to then I could not have put the question together, yet at once I recognized its rightness. I was pierced through, penetrated, speechless. "Don't you think that God loves your little brother as much as he loves you?" My memory tapes are being erased, but that moment remains with me. Yes, old and young, male and female, black and white—somehow, are we not all of us equally God's children?

Some such stance was modeled beautifully for us recently, when after six and a half years as hostage, the journalist Terry Anderson, returned to the free world. Having been treated inhumanly day after day, he could have emerged cursing and reviling those who day and night stood guard over him and tormented him. Instead, he made wondrous statements such as, "I don't hate anybody."[63] Do we not remain God's children, even when we tear at and torture each other?

Apparently few people are called to be activists for racial justice. But each of us can help make a difference. The civil rights movement showed how a country need not wait for each citizen to be personally converted before restructuring and reshaping. But the leaders had to be backed up by a critical mass, by informed and committed public opinion. Each of us can play a quiet role, giving off vibrations in our office, in the classroom, in the social project, or wherever. Despite the white flight to the suburbs, we are all still in the same boat: brothers and sisters with skins of various hues.

Notes

1. Daniel Callahan, ed., *Generation of the Third Eye* (New York: Sheed and Ward, 1965) 58–69.
2. Ibid., 60.
3. Thanks to those who checked files and archives concerning the desegregation of De La Salle: Brothers Eamon Gavin, Emery Hogan, Richard Rush, and Robert Werle.
4. What occasioned the desegregation of De La Salle? None of the files or archives support any of the hypotheses proposed. Did activist Costello have anything to do with the decision? In a recent letter, he is certain that neither he nor any of his fellow activists had any knowledge of plans for desegregating. Perhaps his conclusion (quoted with his knowledge) is the likeliest: "Blacks at De La Salle was a quiet, unpolitical, natural, and inevitable event."
5. Although "African-American" is the preferred term these days, "black" seems to remain an easy equivalent—a usage which is evident in recent pieces by respected African-Americans quoted in this essay, such as Staples and Billingsley.
6. *Star Tribune,* (Minneapolis) 4 July 1991, 4A.
7. James M. Jones, *Prejudice and Racism* (Reading, MA: Addison-Wesley, 1972) 117.
8. Ibid., 3.
9. John F. Dovidio and Samuel L. Gaertner, "Prejudice, Discrimination, and Racism: Historical Trends and Contemporary Approaches," in John F. Dovidio and Samuel L. Gaertner, eds., *Prejudice, Discrimination, and Racism* (Orlando: Academic Press, 1986) 3.
10. James M. Jones, "Racism in Black and White: A Bicultural Model of Reaction and Evolution," in Phyllis A. Katz and Dalmas A. Taylor, eds., *Eliminating Racism: Profiles in Controversy* (New York: Plenum Press, 1988) 117.
11. Dovidio and Gaertner initially studied "how liberals behaved in interracial situations." Later they studied "a relatively liberal segment of the population: college students attending northern universities." Their extensive research convinces them of "the ambivalence of political *liberals*." Dovidio and Gaertner, *Prejudice,* 22.
12. Ibid., 20.

13. Ibid., 21.

14. Samuel L. Gaertner and John F. Dovidio, "The Aversive Form of Racism," in John F. Dovidio and Samuel L. Gaertner, eds., *Prejudice, Discrimination, and Racism* (Orlando: Academic Press, 1986) 63.

15. Ibid.

16. Ibid., 64.

17. Ibid., 62.

18. Dovidio and Gaertner, *Prejudice*, 21.

19. Ibid., 20.

20. Gaertner and Dovidio, "Aversive Form," 85.

21. Shelby Steele, *The Content of Our Character: A New Vision of Race in America* (New York: St. Martin's Press, 1990) 2–3. Stephen L. Carter notes how "gushing is part of the peculiar relationship between black intellectuals and the white ones who seem loath to criticize us for fear of being branded racists—which is itself a mark of racism of a sort." *Reflections of an Affirmative Action Baby* (New York: Basic Books, 1991) 56–57.

22. Steele, *The Content*, 11.

23. Howard Schuman, Charlotte Steeh, and Lawrence Bobo, *Racial Attitudes in America: Trends and Impressions* (Cambridge, MA: Harvard University Press, 1985) 176–177.

24. Ibid., 177.

25. Dovidio and Gaertner, *Prejudice*, 22.

26. David O. Sears, "Symbolic Racism," in Phyllis A. Katz and Dalmas A. Taylor, eds., *Eliminating Racism: Profiles in Controversy* (New York: Plenum Press, 1988) 72.

27. Ibid., 78.

28. Ibid.

29. Ibid., 79.

30. Robert Staples, "Changes in Black Family Structure: The Conflict between Family Ideology and Structural Conditions," in Robert Staples, ed., *The Black Family: Essays and Studies*, 4th ed. (Belmont, CA: Wadsworth, 1991) 29.

31. Ibid.

32. Ibid., 30.

33. Robert B. Hill, "Critical Issues for Black Families by the Year 2000," in Janet Dewart, ed., *State of Black America 1989* (New York: National Urban League, 1989) 41.

34. Staples, "Changes," 32.

35. Robert Staples, "An Overview of Race and Marital Status," in Harriette Pipes McAdoo, ed., *Black Families*, 2nd ed. (Newbury Park, CA: Sage Publications, 1988) 188.

36. Staples, "Changes," 32.

37. Carol B. Stack, "Sex Roles and Survival Strategies in an Urban Black Community," in Robert Staples, ed., *The Black Family: Essays and Studies,* 4th ed. (Belmont: Wadsworth, 1991) 107.

38. Ibid.

39. Joseph W. Scott and Albert Black, "Deep Structures of African-American Family Life: Female and Male Kin Networks," in Robert Staples, ed., *The Black Family: Essays and Studies,* 4th ed. (Belmont, CA: Wadsworth, 1991,) 202.

40. Robert Staples, "The Political Economy of Black Family Life," in Robert Staples, ed., *The Black Family: Essays and Studies,* 4th ed. (Belmont, CA: Wadsworth, 1991) 254.

41. Andrew Billingsley, "Understanding African-American Family Diversity," in Janet Dewart, ed., *The State of Black America 1990* (New York: National Urban League, 1990) 87.

42. Ibid., 101.

43. Ibid., 99.

44. Ibid., 99 and 101.

45. Ibid., 98.

46. Ibid., 97.

47. Manning Marable, "The Black Male: Searching Beyond Stereotypes," in Robert Staples, ed., *The Black Family: Essays and Studies,* 4th ed. (Belmont, CA: Wadsworth, 1991) 104. Marable hastens to add that the origin and the development of black family life extensions do "not by any way justify the myth of a 'black matriarchy.'"

48. Claus Westermann does not see the sin of Adam and Eve as some *fall* from a state of primal innocence. Genesis simply stresses the human situation as shared from the beginning by all. "The crimes and transgressions mentioned in the texts of Gen 1–11 are always something belonging to a specific human being, things that can and do happen wherever a person is." *Genesis 1–11: A Commentary,* John J. Scullion, trans. (Minneapolis: Augsburg, 1984) 601.

49. Timothy E. O'Connell, "A Theology of Sin," *Chicago Studies* 21 (1982) 285.

50. It is worth adding that due to a faulty Latin translation of Romans 5:12, Augustine led the Christian world to adopt a *hereditary* view of original sin as a state of sin. See, for instance, Herbert Haag, *Is Original Sin in Scripture?* Dorothy Thompson, trans. (New York: Sheed and Ward, 1969) 95–108.

51. This paragraph summarizes Thomas F. Schindler, *Ethics: The Social Dimension: Individualism and the Catholic Tradition* (Wilmington: Glazier, 1989) 141.

52. Ibid., 142.

53. Gregory Baum, "Structures of Sin," in Gregory Baum and Robert Ellsberg, eds., *The Logic of Solidarity: Commentaries on Pope John Paul II's Encyclical on Social Concern* (Maryknoll, NY: Orbis Books, 1989) 112.

54. Gregory Baum, *Religion and Alienation: A Theological Reading of Sociology* (New York: Paulist Press, 1975) 200.

55. Ibid.

56. Schindler, *Ethics,* 140.

57. Ibid., 135.

58. Ibid., 143.

59. J. Brian Benestad and Francis J. Butler, eds., *Quest for Justice* (Washington, DC: United States Catholic Conference, 1981) 375–376.

60. Price M. Cobbs, "Critical Perspectives on the Psychology of Race," in Janet Dewart, ed., *The State of Black America 1988* (New York: National Urban League, 1988) 63.

61. Gaertner and Dovidio, "Aversive Form," 65.

62. Anna Quindlen, *Star Tribune* (Minneapolis) 17 September 1991, 13A. This classic line is variously attributed, but in the Bergen Evans *Dictionary of Quotations* (New York: De La Cort Press, 1968), it is traced back to a Bradford (1510?–1555): "There but for the grace of God goes John Bradford" (286).

63. Colman McCarthy, "Terry Anderson's Politics of Forgiveness, *National Catholic Reporter* 28, 27 December 1991, 2.

Questions for Discussion and Reflection

1. Do I find a diminution of anti-black feeling among my colleagues and friends? On the issue of racism, is U.S. society moving backward or forward? How and why?
2. What is the racial "temperature" in your (our) school(s)? Which are the more successful programs adopted in your (our) school(s)?
3. What is the secret of success of those white teachers who manage to do well in all-black or in mixed classes?
4. How do I deal with racist situations that arise in my personal, community, and professional life?

5. Do I tend to be a symbolic (conservative) racist, or an averse (liberal) racist? Are there better ways to classify the forms of racism?
6. How would I have handled "Leonard Williams"? By Christian standards should he have been treated differently?

Identity, Narrative, and Touching Hearts

Peter Gilmour, DMin

May, 1991, within the precincts of Union Theological Seminary, home to scores of Protestant theological luminaries for well over a century, including that legendary giant, Reinhold Niebuhr, whose career there spanned more than one generation of students, whose influence reconfigured twentieth century American Protestantism, whose theology burst the parochial boundaries of denomination, whose memory, now, a generation later, is memorialized by a street bearing his name adjacent to this sacred space; in a seminar room seriously overheated by unceasingly hissing radiators on an unseasonably balmy Spring afternoon on the Upper West Side of Manhattan, I heard a most unusual story.[1]

University professor Duncan Aswell, who has attempted suicide several times, decides while teaching an English class to commit another kind of suicide: he resolves to become another person, immediately, without telling anyone he now knows. After the class ends, and after he bluffs his way through an already scheduled appointment with his therapist later that day, Duncan Aswell, without ever returning to his apartment, sells his car, destroys every card in

---

DR. PETER GILMOUR, DMIN, continues his nearly 30-year association with the Christian Brothers and Lasallian educators through participation in the Christian Brothers Spirituality Seminar. Peter is assistant professor of pastoral studies at the Institute of Pastoral Studies, Loyola University, Chicago, where he also teaches many Brothers who study there.

his wallet bearing his name, and buys a bus ticket to Atlanta. Before boarding the bus, he buys a small suitcase, toilet articles, a change of clothes, pens, and notebooks. Riding toward a new life, he begins to create his new identity: he selects a name, a birth date, his parents' names, his life story.

Arriving in Atlanta, now self-named Bill Cutler registers at a YMCA under his new name, deposits the money received from the sale of his car in a bank account under his new name, and then gets a library card. "How proud I felt as I walked out of the library! I was a citizen of the town. My body cast a shadow. I had a home."[2]

"The perfect getaway,"[3] as the now Bill Cutler refers to his sudden metamorphosis, certainly was motivated by his most unhappy life. His parents, successful people in the publishing world of New York City, were, in his eyes, failures at home as parents. Their divorce during his teen age years did not help. Although he thought of becoming a writer, he did not think he could live up to his parents' impossibly high standards, so he settled for a career in teaching. At the college where he taught for several years, he initially was refused tenure, but, because of his students' activism (it was the seventies), that decision was reversed. The damage had been done, however. He left the college he loved, moved to another college he did not love, and lost his desire to teach.

His therapist told him, "Your sense of self-worth depends on your going right on with the work you've always done; otherwise your life will fall apart."[4] Twenty years later, still living as Bill Cutler and a successful free lance writer, he more than proved the therapist's advice wrong.

Looking back on his transformation,

> Bill Cutler came to realize that Duncan Aswell was psychologically a very sick man. His lack of consideration for his family and friends stemmed directly from his illness. "I was intellectually conscious of the fact that they really cared for me, but I simply couldn't feel anything. I had no contact whatsoever with my emotions or with anybody else's emotions. I certainly wasn't thinking of them or of the grief I would cause them, anymore than I had when I attempted suicide. And I didn't think of them for months."[5]

"Just the same, Bill knows that he is envied by other people for making such a complete break with his past."[6]

This story, dramatic and extreme, touched my heart. At first I thought perhaps it was the aura around the place: Reinhold Niebuhr casts a long, saintly shadow, and I, a Roman Catholic, learned from early childhood the importance of saints. But the story stayed with me long after leaving those temple precincts. Yet another thought crossed my mind: am I about to ride off into the sunset never to be heard from again? Certainly not! My friends in Chicago most assuredly tell me I am inseparably linked to this city of my birth and life.

I have learned to pay close attention to stories I can't forget, to stories that creatively haunt me, to stories I find myself telling others. I suspect these narratives somehow let me, and, I hope, others remember that, in sometimes strange and sometimes wonderful ways, we are in the holy presence of God.

Stories that touch one's heart contribute to one's identity. Whether it be narratives of the classic pagan or Christian myths, narratives of families, narratives of contemporary novels, or narratives of autobiography and memoir, these stories impact and influence one's life, one's living, ultimately, one's identity. Such narratives help a person to define, to describe, to influence, to focus, and to hone who one is, and they also help a person to mirror, to reverberate, to disclose, and to communicate that identity.

One's identity also contributes to the stories that touch one's heart. Narratives about one's own relatives are frequently far more fascinating and satisfying experiences than anonymous stories, much like cemeteries where one's relatives rest feel different from innominate cemeteries. For a woman today whose identity is strongly feminist, reading a woman's memoir such as *My Place*[7] by Sally Morgan is an experience that differs from reading a memoir of a male, and, further, an experience most always different from a male reading of that same memoir. For a person whose identity is strongly Afro-American, reading Toni Morrison's novel, *Beloved*,[8] a moving story about post-slavery life, is an experience different from either an Anglo person or one who is not a U.S. citizen reading the same book. What touches one's heart is connected to one's identity; one's identity is connected to what touches one's heart. This metaphoric palindrome reflects the ongoing, continuous, and symbiotic relationship between identity and touching hearts which manifests itself through narrative. In this article I will investigate this dynamic by centering on the personal and social dimensions of (1) physical/historical narratives, (2) intellectual narratives, and (3) spiritual narratives which contribute to identity and to touching hearts.

Part One: Physical/Historical Identity

Every person, including Bill Cutler, has a history, both personal and social. Each person comes from specific families of origin, born into a given time, a given place, and a given culture. As a person matures, one has the opportunity to become conscious and knowledgeable about one's own historical narratives. From them, a myriad of possible influences emerge.

One contemporary tool by which these influences can be traced is the genogram.

> A genogram is a format for drawing a family tree that records information about family members and their relationships over at least three generations. Genograms display family information graphically in a way that provides a quick gestalt of complex family patterns and a rich source of hypothesis about how a clinical problem may be connected to the family context and the evolution of both problem and context over time.[9]

A person constructing a genogram is encouraged to include at least three generations on both sides of one's family: two parents; four grandparents; eight great grandparents. Add to that siblings alongside oneself and alongside parents of each generation, and the field of ancestors gets crowded. Add to that the contemporary phenomenon of second marriages and blended families, and some people's genograms become extraordinarily gangly. Since one has a lot of relatives, a lot of possible influences exist for any given person.

Personal Aspects to Physical/Historical Identity

Anyone who has delved into family history, either informally by listening to family stories, or, formally, through genealogical research,[10] is aware of numerous relatives, either living or dead. If all the members of one's intergenerational families contribute equally to one's identity, the end result becomes a blandly homogenized identity. No person is an emulsoid. Something else happens.

In an interview with William Least Heat-Moon, author of best selling books, *Blue Highways*[11] and *PrairyErth*,[12] I had the opportunity to question him about his own identity.

> *Gilmour.* What led you to publish *Blue Highways* and now *Prairy-Erth* under William Least Heat-Moon?
>
> *Heat-Moon.* The first several drafts of *Blue Highways* had my other name [William Trogdon]. There was something wrong with the manuscript and some years into it, I realized what it was. What was really driving that book was that fractional part of me which is Osage (a division of the Sioux tribe). And the person writing *Blue Highways* was not simply William Trogdon. Yes, he was there too, but he was also Least Heat-Moon. That's why I used the name Least Heat-Moon and went back and rewrote the book again, trying to listen more overtly, more consciously, to this other side. And it really was a return to the person I had been twenty years earlier. Twenty years in the academic world had not erased but had covered that over. I had forgotten those things. (They were also the twenty unhappiest years of my life.) So by remembering who I really was I made my own personal peace with the troubles I'd had. It's led me to where I am now.[13]

Thus even though, on the surface, using a Native American byline looks like a clever and effective marketing strategy (and it is), something far more significant is at work here. Bill Trogdon has chosen to emphasize a particular aspect of his physical/historical identity. In doing so Heat-Moon diminishes his European identity. I was curious to find out why he selects one over another.

> *Gilmour.* Was this voluntary on your part? What I mean to say is, did you have a choice? Couldn't you have chosen another aspect of your heritage?
>
> *Heat-Moon.* It was a conscious decision. If that's what you mean by "voluntary," we can make those words interchangeable. But I also happen to believe in, for want of a better phrase, genetic memory, in

which we are inclined by the genes we have. It manifests itself in odd ways. I can only speak for my own case. I've been fascinated for years with stone work, stone masons. I almost got left behind my tour in China in 1984 by watching stone masons lay a wall. I could not take my eyes off what they were doing. It was a fascinating thing to encounter. I found out about a year later that I have a great grandfather, I talk about him in *PrairyErth,* who was a stone mason on the Erie Canal. That explains the long fascination I've had with rock masonry. He is present. He also happens to be the only man I've found in my family who ever made a buck by writing. Now I didn't know anything about that at the time of the China trip, but I did know I had a fascination with stone. So I did not choose that, that came; but now I elect, to use your term, to be aware of that and to develop it. So I think we are inclined, and I think once we learn our inclinations, then we can really begin to choose, to emphasize, certain inclinations.[14]

I liked what Heat-Moon said in response to this probe into the voluntary nature of his identity. But I was uncomfortable with this notion of genetic memory. I expressed my concern.

Gilmour. But can't that be a dangerous idea? Racists, for example, can say that a particular race is genetically inclined to negative qualities, and therefore should not be afforded rights and privileges other races have.

Heat-Moon. I think it's a question where morality comes to play, too. Surely given all the ancestors that all of us have, we each can point to numerous criminals in our background. And I've been inclined to criminal acts many times. Every time I listen to a political statement from the Republican Party I'm inclined to criminal acts. But morality comes to play too. You say: yes, I'm inclined that way perhaps by a long line of people thinking this or that about race, or religion, or politics or whatever, but I'm not going to act on those inclinations because I do have a responsibility to choose, to make ethical choices.[15]

Social Aspects to Physical/Historical Identity

Various ethnic identities and national identities, like individual identities, exist at specific historical moments. These identities can change overnight, or over a period of time. The dramatic emergence of the central Asian republics almost overnight, Kazakhstan, Uzbekistan, Turmenistan, Azerbaijan, Kyrgyzstan, and Tajikistan, for example, again much like Bill Cutler, embody current narratives of changing social identity. A slower, more subtle transformation of identity is, however, more usual for a people or a nation.

Many U.S. citizens now know that to refer to their own country as America and its citizens as Americans is both inaccurate and demeaning to other countries of the Americas and their citizens. Also, many U.S. citizens now gravitate toward narratives which stress their ethnic identities. A generation or two ago, people in this country preferred narratives which stressed their "American" identity. This is true for certain ethnic groups who are identified as underclass as well as Anglo, middle class groups, and it is not a phenomenon limited only to the United States.

What one thinks is authentic, real, and significant ethnic identity sometimes breaks down under scrutiny. Take, for example, a narrative of Scot ethnic identity, an ethnicity I select because my own surname, Gilmour, is Scottish.

> The origins of most "people" are not known, but here and there we can find accounts of people-making activities that have taken place in the modern era. One historian, Hugh Trevor-Roper, has documented various inventions of the traditions that symbolize Scotland's distinct identity, all of which took place much more recently than most of us would imagine—after, not before, the union with England. Until late in the seventeenth century, the Scottish highlanders were not a distinct people but merely an overflow population from Ireland and linked to the Irish racially, culturally, and politically. The lowlands were populated by other racial groups including Picts and Saxons. Then there began a deliberate "cultural revolt" against Ireland, which combined a good deal of creativity with a good deal of plagiarism. Trevor-Roper credits the work of two men, James Macpherson and the Reverend John Macpherson (not related) who between them invented an ancient Celtic literature for Scotland and a history to go with it.[16]

Another interesting example of the transformation of ethnic consciousness centers on identity narratives of Australia and Australians. When Australian identity centered on its colonial link to England, descendants of convicts who were shipped there as punishment were frequently hesitant to embrace narratives which reflected this heritage. Today, more than 200 years later, and just a few years after Australia's celebration of its bicentennial, being able to trace one's ancestry to convict origins is a badge of honor, not a symbol of disgrace. Australians who were able to demonstrate such linkage with the origins of their country were given special recognition by the government as part of the bicentennial celebration.

Part Two: Intellectual Identity

Families of origin narratives, represented by the genogram, are powerfully important to identity and touching hearts. Yet identity is forged by two other extraordinarily vital story lines: intellectual narratives and spiritual narratives. Alongside families of origin narratives, intellectual and spiritual narratives need to be both told and heard as part of the process of choosing identity and touching hearts. Even though there is only a small indication of Bill Cutler's intellectual narrative in the opening story, from his doctoral level studies in English one can assume that he was exposed to a wide and varied range of intellectual narratives.

Personal Aspects to Intellectual Identity

The very word, "intellectual" carries heavy negative baggage today: vague, turgid, snobbish, non-understandable, pompous, useless. I do not mean the word as such. Rather, by intellectual, I mean the appeal and influence of ideas as embodied in varied and diverse expressions of people, a process which, at this point in our understanding, seems to be uniquely human.[17] As educators we do indeed reverence ideas. Knowledges are not just necessary, but good. Why else would we work so hard at what we do: become educated ourselves and educate others? To look at how each of us became educated is, I think, to look at a long process of ideas that touched our hearts. To look at what each of us finds interesting, and, perhaps, what each of us decided to specialize in, is to look at ideas which did, in fact, touch our hearts, or, to state it from the other end of this continuing metaphoric palindrome, reflect our identity. Some subjects touched our hearts over others. Within those subjects, certain areas further touched our hearts more deeply, more dramatically.

To become conscious of our own intellectual narratives, perhaps through the process of constructing an intellectual genogram, is, in itself, a fascinating concept, and a task which leads to further understanding of the conscious election of identity, what has touched our hearts, and, ultimately, both as educators and ministers, how we touch the hearts of others.

One person who effectively demonstrates the importance of raising to consciousness one's intellectual influences is Fritjof Capra. His book, *Uncommon Wisdom,* [18] documents his intellectual identity: his own world of ideas, how they entered his life, how he pursued them, and, ultimately, how they touched his heart.

Uncommon Wisdom also well-documents how institutions can at times constrict the boundaries of ideas, particularly educational institutions. Capra's own intellectual journey involved a search for a new paradigm:

> a paradigm, for me, would mean the totality of thoughts, perceptions, and values that forms a particular vision of reality, a vision that is the basis of the way a society organizes itself. [19]

The excessive compartmentalization of ideas in higher education which excludes interdisciplinary investigations alienated Capra from the academic arena: "I had already begun my search for the new paradigm and was not willing to give it up and accept the narrow confines of a full-time academic job." [20]

Capra's search for a constellation of related ideas which make sense led him to search for a constellation of ideas which have a societal dimension, that is, to find a new paradigm. In addition to his personal, intellectual search told in *Uncommon Wisdom,* so also does the societal significance of this new paradigm get storied.

Something else emerges from Capra's intellectual narrative: ideas do not exist outside of specific people and specific personalities. He claims

> the purpose of the book you are reading is not to present any new ideas, or to elaborate or modify the ideas presented in my previous books, but rather to tell the personal story behind the evolution of these ideas. It is the story of my encounters with many remarkable men and women who inspired me, helped me, and supported my

search. . . . The stages of this intellectual journey and the meetings and conversations with the many remarkable men and women who shared with me their uncommon wisdom comprise the story of this book.[21]

Social Aspects to Intellectual Identity

At one time the societal dimension of a person's intellectual narrative was much more influential than it is today. Certainly the social dimensions of the intellectual narratives of Bill Cutler's life as Duncan Aswell were highly influential because of his highly educated parents and his own academic studies. Western Civilization, with all its traditional glories and contemporary pitfalls, has been, and, for many, still is a highly influential prescribed and proscribed social complex of intellectual narratives. *The Great Books of the Western World,* although heavily biased toward the social sciences, is a specific attempt to canonize these ideas into an orderly, disciplined, lifelong curriculum.[22] Until the great curriculum meltdown of the late sixties–early seventies, there was much more basic agreement as to what best constitutes formal education, that for better or worse, simply is not there any longer.

Any school curriculum is an attempt to present a structured, and, I would stress, favored, presentation and interpretation of ideas. By "favored" I mean something both positive and negative. The positive side of favored deals with the passion of the peoples who founded such curricula and, I hope, still deliver such curricula. The negative side of favored is, of course, what is not included in a course of study, the null curriculum.[23]

Long gone are the days when the social or institutional aspects determined one's personal intellectual narrative. Today, particularly in a pluralistic society, each person not only has the opportunity but, I would suggest, the obligation to examine many differing points of view in order to be a productive and responsible member of such a society. Each one of us over a long period of time adopts a constellation of ideas which influences our behavior, instructs our identity, and touches our hearts.

Part Three: Spiritual Identity

Identity is, ultimately, spiritual. Both William Least Heat-Moon and Fritjof Capra articulate the importance of the spiritual. Heat-Moon, a creative word artist who writes non-fiction, says in the already quoted interview,

> Any spiritual expression is an expression of some aspect of the imaginative life; that is, you can see beyond what's there in some way, you sense other existences, other forms of being. That's all dreamtime.[24]

Fritjof Capra, in his book *Uncommon Wisdom,* while in conversation with Stanislav Grof, states, "Spirituality, or the human spirit, could be defined as the mode of consciousness in which we feel connected to the cosmos as a whole."[25]

Spiritual identity, like physical/historical identity and intellectual identity, has both a personal and social dimension to it. However, the influences of organized religions, which at one time contributed mightily to spiritual identity and to touching hearts, have ebbed. More personal and personalized approaches now contribute to one's spiritual quest and, ultimately, to what touches one's heart and one's spiritual identity.

Personal Aspects to Spiritual Identity

Neither ethnic origin nor geography influence spiritual heritage in the ways these determinants once did. Marriages involving people from widely differing ethnic groups having different and sometimes differing spiritual traditions are much more commonplace than even a generation ago. Spiritual traditions at one time bound by geography have more recently found worldwide attention and attraction. Native American spirituality now influences and attracts a worldwide cadre of people. Buddhism has become attractive to Westerners.

Spirituality now stands apart from religion for some people. They describe themselves as spiritual but not religious, an unheard of dichotomy at one time. This phenomenon both limits and expands one's search for spiritual identity. Resources of religious traditions go unnoticed, unappreciated, and unused in a person's quest for spiritual identity. However, it forces men and women who accept the challenge to search for their own spirituality, and not to embrace one of the already developed, prepackaged spiritualities of a specific religious tradition.

This search for the spiritual outside any context of religious traditions leads to extremes as so well-pointed out by Robert Bellah et al. in the book, *Habits of the Heart*.[26] Such exclusively personal searches generate so many varied, different, and individual "spiritualities," that a culture could end up with as many "religions" as people. Without a common spiritual bond, essential for a communal culture, rampant individualism is inadvertently fostered. "Sheilaism," as Bellah terms it, is the logical outcome of such a stance.

> Today, religion in America is as private and diverse as New England colonial religion was public and unified. One person we interviewed has actually named her religion (she calls it her "faith") after herself. This suggests the logical possibility of over 220 million American religions, one for each of us. Sheila Larson is a young nurse who has received a good deal of therapy and who describes her faith as "Sheilaism." "I believe in God. I'm not a religious fanatic. I can't remember the last time I went to church. My faith has carried me a long way. It's Sheilaism. Just my own little voice." Sheila's faith has some tenets beyond belief in God, though not many. In defining "my own Sheilaism, " she said: "It's just try to love yourself and be gentle with yourself. You know, I guess, take care of each other. I think he would want us to take care of each other."[27]

But even if one remains within the bounds of a specific religious tradition, there are often many spiritualities from which to choose. Armand Alcazar's article, "Changing Spiritualities"[28] well-articulates two divergent spiritualities in the Catholic Christian tradition.

Social Aspects to Spiritual Identity

Yet spiritual traditions, old and new, do exist. They are embodied in narratives named sacred by those who follow the originators of spiritual traditions. They are kept alive by people dedicated to the beliefs and activities of these spiritual progenitors. John Baptist de La Salle represents one such spiritual visionary whose narratives have been named sacred, and who has attracted a group of people dedicated to his beliefs and activities, that group being both the vowed religious brotherhood and their colleagues who embrace and embody the Lasallian vision, tradition, and work.

Certainly those who consciously choose to follow in the footsteps of a specific spiritual luminary find that specific person in their spiritual genogram. In the Christian tradition, all spiritual luminaries have Jesus Christ, the Jesus of history and the Christ of faith, included in their spiritual narratives. Indeed, the Jesus of the Gospels, conscious of the spiritual luminaries who preceded him, has a host of Old Testament heroes and heroines in his spiritual genograms. It is so recorded in the genealogy of the opening chapter of the Gospel according to Matthew, and also in the genealogy of the third chapter of the Gospel according to Luke.[29] Jesus is pictured frequently in Scripture within the context of the Hebrew spiritual tradition.

As believers in Jesus, then, our own spiritual narratives are filled with these heroes and heroines of the two testaments, with the spiritual luminaries of historical Christianity, and with a vast array of twentieth century believers, from Mother Teresa to Dorothy Day, from Jose Maria Escriva de Balaguer to Daniel Berrigan, from John Paul II to George Stallings, Jr., all spiritual siblings.

Conclusion: Holistic Identity and Touching Hearts

Two focal points emerge from this discussion of the relationship between conscious election of identity and touching hearts: the first is personal, our own conscious election of identity and who touches our hearts; the second is social, our work as educators and ministers, assisting others in consciously electing their own identities, and how we best participate in touching their hearts.

These two focal points merge into one for those of us whose hearts have been touched by the narrative of John Baptist de La Salle and who are imbued with the Lasallian vision. Since our identity is educational and ministerial, it is in our nature to reach out to others, to assist them in their own search for identity, and to want to see their hearts touched with the message and spirit of Jesus Christ and his Gospel.

We live and work in an age where a multitude of physical, historical, intellectual, and spiritual narratives have the ability to contribute to identity formation and to touch our hearts. It is substantially through such narratives that we form and reform our identities, that our hearts are most deeply and profoundly touched, and that we assist in touching the hearts of others. Some of these narratives involve us as nothing else does.

As part of reaching out to touch other hearts, as part of assisting our students in the process of their own identity formation, we should, ideally, first look within, to raise this process to consciousness in our own lives. Genograms, physical/historical, intellectual, and spiritual, are helpful tools to get a handle on those narratives which shape our lives so we can better understand the mystery of who we really are and who we might become. How we become the people we are, what part each of us plays in that process, and who touches our hearts, are helpful, healthful explorations for any person, but, particularly, for people whose identities are intimately connected with both education and ministry. Only then can we most effectively turn our attention toward others.

After we have explored this ongoing phenomenon in our own lives, then, in order to touch other hearts, we must first know and respect whose heart it is we are trying to touch. What are each person's unique individual and social narratives: physical/historical, intellectual, and spiritual? As our specific populations change, including ever more races and cultures, for example, the noticeable influx of Asian and Middle Eastern peoples into our cities; as the student bodies of our schools change, for example, the increasing numbers of non-Catholic students, Islamic, Hindu, and Buddhist; as the world shrinks through communication networks, for example, school children on St. Vincent's Island in the Caribbean who, through the local news from a Chicago-based TV station, are knowledgeable about Chicago people, places, and events; it becomes both more and more difficult and more and more necessary to know and appreciate these and other identity narratives.

Once having done so, admittedly a Herculean task, in order ultimately to assist in the process of touching hearts we must then surrender appeals to authoritarian rhetoric as the only means of communication in all areas of endeavor, but, particularly in the spiritual dimension. "The Church says," even when the church speaks what we feel is impressive and overwhelmingly correct, is a stance which not only arrests the narrative process, but also erects a barrier to touching hearts.

> The magisterium's language of moral guidance often adopts a controlling voice that does not hear the voices of others who are attempting to find a moral language that is faithful both to their own experience as well as to the Gospel, a moral language that is true to their struggle.[30]

What ultimately attracts a person to one narrative over another, to emulate the character and characteristics of one person over another person, and, finally, to communicate one's own important identity narratives in the hope of assisting in the process of touching other hearts, remains one of the most profound mysteries of human existence. Why Bill Cutler did what he did, and why he chose to tell others about his transformation, has nothing to do with authoritarian rhetoric. Yet there is a mysterious authority to his life and narrative.

In order to explore this mystery, and help others to explore this mystery, we need to expand our approaches to meaning. As we encounter narratives, we should not simply ask, "What does this story mean?" Such a question asked in isolation ultimately diminishes the poetry and the power of narrative, and that answer alone becomes an exercise in *reductio ad absurdum*. It does little either to form identity or to touch hearts. Rather, the question, "What is going on inside me as I encounter this story?" is a gateway toward contributing to identity and touching hearts.[31] Since stories, whether embodied in people or texts, transcend the rational, then our encounter with these narratives needs also to transcend the exclusively rational search for meaning.

One becomes an active participant in the conscious election of identity by asking this question, "What is going on inside me as I encounter this story?" We need to ask this question of ourselves, frequently, and we need to encourage our students to ask this question of themselves. One then also becomes an active participant in what touches one's heart by asking this same question, "What is going on inside me as I encounter this story?" Only each individual can ultimately decide the answer to this question. It is the only way to know for sure that our hearts have been touched.

Like Duncan Aswell, now Bill Cutler, though perhaps not to such an extreme, we all are capable of electing a good part of our identities. What touches our hearts, what we allow to touch our hearts, is intimately linked to our chosen identities. In working with students, it is important to keep in mind that they, like us, have a significant say in their own identities, and, hence, what touches their hearts.

Notes

1. This first sentence/paragraph is dedicated to James Agee, coauthor of *Let Us Now Praise Famous Men,* a great, though little known, American classic. His prose style, emulated by William Least Heat-Moon in his most recently published book, *PrairyErth,* reveals the artistry of language and challenges contemporary readers to follow a thought expressed in more than 20 words, the average length of sentences allowed by *Grammatick,* a word-processing grammar and style proofreading software program.

2. Jo Brans, *Take Two* (New York: Doubleday, 1989) 214.

3. Ibid., 210.

4. Ibid., 212.

5. Ibid., 215.

6. Ibid.

7. Sally Morgan, *My Place* (New York: Seaver Book, 1987).

8. Toni Morrison, *Beloved* (New York: New American Library, 1987).

9. Monica McGoldrick and Randy Gerson, *Genograms in Family Assessment* (New York: W.W. Norton, 1985) 1.

10. Three hundred and fifteen of my relatives, living and dead, are listed in a book tracing my mother's side of my family: Stephen C. Gilmour, *Pioneer Settlers of Dane County Wisconsin: John and Mary (Lunny) Campbell and their Descendants* (Sparta, WI: Joy Reisinger Publication, 1986).

11. William Least Heat-Moon, *Blue Highways* (Boston: Little Brown, 1982).

12. William Least Heat-Moon, *PrairyErth* (Boston: Houghton Mifflin, 1991).

13. Peter Gilmour, "The Heartland Interview: William Least Heat-Moon," *The Heartland Journal* 37 (March–April 1992) 11.

14. Ibid.

15. Ibid.

16. Walter Truett Anderson, *Reality Isn't What It Used To Be* (San Francisco: Harper and Row, 1990) 108–109.

17. I say "at this point in our understanding" because even though I am aware of some of the thinking and research in the area of animal consciousness, I am not ready either definitively to accept or reject these opinions.

18. Fritjof Capra, *Uncommon Wisdom* (New York: Bantam Books, 1988).

19. Ibid., 22.

20. Ibid., 35.

21. Ibid., 12, 15.

22. See Peter Gilmour, "Educational Canons and Religious Fundamentalism: Obstacles to Change," in *Challenged By Change,* Michael F. Meister, FSC, ed. (Romeoville, IL: Christian Brothers Publications, 1991) 115-126.

23. Elliot W. Eisner, *The Educational Imagination* (New York: Macmillan, 1985) 87-107.

24. Gilmour, "The Heartland Interview: William Least Heat-Moon," 11.

25. Capra, *Uncommon Wisdom,* 109.

26. Robert Bellah et al., *Habits of the Heart* (Berkeley: University of California Press, 1985).

27. Ibid., 221.

28. Armand Alcazar, FSC "Changing Spiritualities" in *Challenged by Change,* Michael F. Meister, FSC, ed. (Romeoville, IL: Christian Brothers Publications, 1991) 142–155.

29. Mt 1:1–17; Lk 3:23–38.

30. William Eiler Hall, FSC, "Power, Change, and Dialogue," in *Challenged by Change,* Michael F. Meister, FSC, ed. (Romeoville, IL: Christian Brothers Publications, 1991) 130.

31. These two questions and their importance were originally brought to my attention by Rev. John Shea to whom I am grateful.

Questions for Reflection and Discussion

1. Who are the people in your life, living and dead, that comprise your physical/historical, intellectual, and spiritual genograms?
2. What attracted you toward the Christian Brothers? Toward your major fields of academic study? Toward the subjects you teach?
3. What attracted you toward your current ministry?
4. "What is going on inside me as I encounter this essay and the other essays in this book?"
5. What descriptive words and phrases come to your mind when thinking about your own identity?
6. What story or stories from your own life best capture and communicate your identity?

Reconstituting the Heart: The "Self" and Media Studies

William E. Hall, FSC

Since the time of the Enlightenment, the human being has increasingly taken center stage as an object of study and reflection.[1] Freed from the superstitions of naive religionism and confident in the growing advancements of human reason, the person became the arbiter of belief and action. Truth, goodness, and beauty could be determined by careful thought and reasoned discourse. Likewise, the advancements of science demonstrated their power by producing not just information about, but also control over, much of the material world. Life's questions and problems could be addressed to oneself, fulfilling Protagoras' assertion that "Man is the measure of all things."

Out of these developments grew an understanding of the person as holding the capacity for, if not yet actually achieving the completeness of, a unified self. The person was viewed as largely autonomous, drawing strength from the community but remaining largely singular and free. The result was a view of the person as an essentially closed or self-contained system of internal biological and psychic forces, reactive to the social sphere, but ultimately capable of some measure of wholeness and unity beyond the social. Epito-

BROTHER WILLIAM EILER HALL, FSC, PHD is an assistant professor in the Department of Communication at La Salle University, Philadelphia. He received a Master's Degree in Religious Studies from La Salle University and holds a Doctorate in Rhetoric and Communication from the University of Pittsburgh.

mized in existential philosophies, the ultimate task of human life was for the individual to take charge and make his or her own life meaningful.

These developments led to an image of the person along spatial coordinates. One could speak with common sense confidence of the "whole" person, of an "inner" self, and of a "core"of one's being. Such humanistic geometries postulated a "true" self buried beneath the "false"self of social role-taking and behavior. In religious language, this view of the person persisted in spiritualities that encourage an "inner" movement as the path to enlightenment and authentic living. To discover one's true self was to effect a transformation of will, action, and being.

As an heir to the Enlightenment project, the Founder's call to "touch hearts" appears to embrace the Enlightenment's metaphoric understanding of the person. The "heart" constitutes the center of the person, the critical place from which motive, belief, understanding, and action spring. De La Salle challenged the Brothers to touch this central place within their students so they could effect changes in knowledge, behavior, and faith—all goals of their apostolic calling.

Yet, despite its poetic and romantic appeal, the phrase "touching hearts" is not without problems. In particular, I take issue with its driving metaphor as it presents a falsely unified view of the human person. Drawing on literature from media and cultural studies, I will attempt in this article to situate the person—our students—within the web of communicative forms that render metaphors such as the "heart" troublesome guides for understanding. I contend that coming to terms with our modern technologies of communication and the cultural life that develops with them, is a prerequisite to both understanding and engaging our students. Thus, in this article I sketch a brief history of forms of communication to situate an understanding of how our electronic media transform cultural and personal constructions of the "self" and our ministry of "touching hearts."

Orality

Much provocative scholarship investigates what are termed "technologies of the word." Among such investigations are studies that identify the differences among oral, written, print, and electronically mediated cultures.[2] The general thesis is that in any given culture the reigning technology of the word—be it speech, print, or video—allows a form of consciousness to emerge that otherwise could not except through the technology or technique of its manifestation. An oral culture "thinks" through the possibilities and limits of orality; a print culture "thinks" by way of the technical possibilities of printed language. With each shift in the reigning communicative technology something is gained and lost that brings with it social upheaval and a crisis in cultural understanding. This work is important since much of what characterizes our video-dominated culture harkens back to the experience of primary orality.

Although it is difficult for us to conceive, it is necessary to begin by imagining a world where writing did not exist, a world of pristine orality. In this world where the spoken word established the dynamics and limits of human thought and consciousness and created the basis for cultural forms.

A world dominated by orality is stamped by the act of speaking. All social reality comes into being through speech and partakes of the fundamental dynamics of the speech act itself. Speaking is ephemeral: delicate, fleeting, and charged with the excitement of its radically momentary presence.[3] Words are uttered and fade into silence; reality is given voice, then expires. To speak is to create, to bring to life, making its creation an event and a reality that is coextensive with its self-contained action. This reality has a marginal past and a limited future since these are outside the dynamics of momentary orality.[4] Without the technique of writing, no trace exists to document the event which speaking produces. The moment confines the reality of its occurrence, and its reoccurrence comes again only by the creation of a new speech, a new event.

An oral culture is tied to its existential world where the concrete here and now of daily life form the web and substance of its meanings.[5] It is preeminently a world of story where human struggle, agonistic battle, and heroes and villains figure prominently.[6] Its myths and epics resist abstraction and ideation and eschew analytic differentiation, dialectical synthesis, linear progression of thought, or reflective reasoning.[7] As such, issues of validity, accuracy, logical coherence—all products of the emergence of writing—are foreign standards for judging its consciousness or social forms since they fall outside the parameters of orality's capability.[8] Instead, the "logic" of drama sets the standards of evaluation. How valiant its heroes, how noble its struggle, and how engaging its story form the criteria of use and the bases of applicability to everyday life.[9] Thus, the story as story, the form of expression itself, becomes more important than the "facts" of the story. "Truth" as a concept or value holds a very different meaning in orally dominated cultures. With no recourse to documented evidence, veracity becomes a matter of narrative fit—of dramatic coherence and relevance—between the recall of a story and the event of its telling, as, for example, legal or criminal adjudication takes place not by some written code (since none can exist), but by proverb and story which awaken the community's values and invoke its judgments.

The person or "self" in such a culture is a wholly communal person as "individual" identity achieves form within the web of the shared stories of the community's self-constitution and understanding.[10] In the dynamics of orality, speaker and hearer are fused in the event that speech produces.[11] Since one cannot speak without an audience as an integral part of the speech event, so too, one cannot form an identity apart from that of the group. The sense of reflecting on one's self as an autonomous entity is wholly outside the range of possible acts since such a level of human consciousness is disallowed in the discursive form of pristine orality.[12] Only with the advent of writing does an individuated and autonomous self begin to emerge.

Literacy

Most fundamentally, the advent of writing introduces space into human thought. Words literally take shape on a page as one graphs them in linear sequence.[13] As a consequence, writing's spatial ethos destroys the coherence of the speech event as the speaker-speech-hearer unity of oral culture gives way to a distancing of the writer from the message and the audience. One writes in solitude, isolates his or her message, and passes it along to a likewise solitary reader.[14] As a sign scrolled on parchment or etched in sand, the word subsists as a deadened object of solitary scrutiny. In this, the communal nature of the language event diminishes since no other person need be present during production or reception, thus confounding the communing function of communication.

Likewise, writing brings the gradual reconceptualization of time as a construct reflecting sequential linearity. Past, present, and future emerge as coordinates for segmenting and understanding experience.[15] The radical present of the oral world is shattered by writing, which displaces the mythic unity of time and place. Documented (that is, scripted) fact now becomes the basis for a new form of cultural and communal understanding: scientific history.

Together, the visual space needed for writing and the conceptual/historical space it inaugurates create the distance that gives rise to what we commonly call objectivity: a necessary component of all higher conceptual, analytic, and abstract thought.[16] With it, knowledge as we traditionally conceive it becomes a possibility. Under the aegis of the written word, one produces knowledge that exists outside of one's self, or one learns and takes in knowledge from outside the self. Knowledge becomes something separate from persons, and, in some fundamental way, indifferent toward persons.[17] This is most evident in the development of science, whose truths exist in large measure apart from anyone's acceptance or rejection of them. As a consequence, communal knowledge stored in the shared narratives of orality's heritage diminish in importance for the culture that embraces the developments of writing competence.

As a further development, through the invention of printing, the sense of order and control which writing carries sets the stage for routinized hierarchical and bureaucratic structures.[18] Social institutions and the various professions take shape as offshoots of the widespread dissemination of literate knowledge. Occupational and disciplinary enclosures result with their concomitant claims to ownership and power, thus setting the stage for an ethic of information and social control. The unity of mythopoetic meaning and communal life give way to the fragmentation of competing fictions and social stratification.[19] In addition, the broad distribution of information which print facilitates provides the foundation for the democratization of knowledge where personal interpretation supersedes communal meaning. Ironically, it also sets the stage for mass culture as the communally supported individual is supplanted by the collectivity.

The developments of literacy set the stage for the emergence of the self put forth in the introduction of this article. Writing's facilitation of objectivity and conceptual and semantic distance creates the space needed for critical self-reflection to take place. The "I" takes shape as a unique and autonomous entity apart from others. One could now come to know oneself as assuredly as one could know the material and physical world outside of oneself: with dispassion and a sense of separateness.[20] Essentially, literacy set loose the tether that held the individual to the community.

Furthermore, despite the dizzying advancements in scientific and social knowledge which the written word seems to bring about, and despite the allied growth in self-knowledge and personal achievement in some fundamental way, literacy also brings with it the physical and psychological alienation of persons,[21] the radical individuation and potential fragmentation of the personal self, and the collapse of a reliable and communal sense of meaning. Likewise, the formation of the state over the tribe and of power over cooperation represents the "logical" outgrowths of the formative power of literacy. It is out of these developments that electronic media must be viewed and alongside of which their effects understood.[22]

Electronic Media

Most fundamentally, mass communication technologies, especially television, transcend physical barriers and distances.[23] As such, they alter our perceptions which, in turn, alter our understanding of the social world around us and our identity with regard to that world. One leading student of mass media, Joshua Meyrowitz, concludes that, in an electronically mediated culture, individual identity is diffuse and rooted primarily in the media culture itself.[24]

As the most pervasive mass communication medium, television allows us to enter places heretofore closed to most of us. In so doing, it provides experiences that are ordinarily the privileged realm of insiders.[25] Television takes us into the back rooms and board rooms of, for example, corporate and governmental leaders and shows us the plans and practices that make up the protected realm of private behaviors. As many of these behaviors involve the construction of status and prestige, the loss of physical privacy brings the loss of social privilege which these closed regions of behavior supported.[26] Whether through real-life documentary or fictionalized drama, television allows us to witness what was previously left to speculation, rumor, or secondhand written accounts; and, once seen, the mystery of physical and social distance fades as the hidden becomes familiar.

With the breakdown of the physical structures that separated us, so too, the social structures that supported the separation of knowledge and information become more permeable through television's intervention.[27] Social roles which are played out on various stages become fluid and easily adopted through our ability to see their stagings and stylistics. The years of training and the rites of passage necessary to learn these roles—often through self-imposed institutional secrecy—are gone and with them the means for their legitimation. We can now see what it is like to be a senior partner of a law firm without the need for law school training and years of grunt work. We simply watch an episode of *L.A. Law*. Similarly, television reveals the mysteries of sexual difference that took years of firsthand, face-to-face experience to learn.[28] A recent and much ballyhooed episode of *Doogie Howser, M.D.* taught us that losing one's virginity involves setting aside the male goal of sexual conquest in favor of a young woman's need for love, sensitivity, and intimacy. A more explicit program might have taught what erotic techniques a woman prefers.

The assertion here is not that television replaces the substance of a law school education or acts as an adequate substitute for real life sexual relationships, but that it does serve to demystify status and social roles by bypassing commonplace rituals of experience that performed the social functions of gate-keeping and legitimation: once primary tasks of the social and professional institutions themselves.[29] In this, television debunks the expertise associated with special social roles, recognizing that acquired knowledge does not lead necessarily to status and prestige, but often functions in reverse: status confers knowledge and expertise through institutionalized rituals of passage and role separation.[30]

Another aspect of television's unique brand of knowledge is its concentration on image: a quality unique to the medium's capability for the closeup. Typical of face-to-face encounters, this knowledge is given off rather than self-consciously communicated and accounts for much—up to 93 percent—of what we draw upon for making judgments about a person's credibility, trustworthiness, and character.[31] While a number of critics disparage this heightening of image over substance, it is important to note that the vast majority of our important interpersonal relationships are formed on just such judgments. How we speak, manipulate space, gesture, give and receive eye contact, react facially, laugh, cry, and listen to our own musings all take overwhelming precedence over the content of words or the politics of ideas.[32] Only television provides the means for expanding what print or radio can only partly communicate. In so doing, it opens the very channels that bring us into another's most intimate space—again, through the collapse of physical and social barriers.[33]

One consequence of the blurring of physical and social space and the heightening of the importance of image is the challenge to those forms of authority that are supported by physical separation and the reliance on printed channels of communication. When the practices needed to gain power are exposed, and with them the techniques of their legitimation, then the basis for claiming social status and difference becomes suspect and open to evaluation, especially if these practices and techniques are of questionable moral or political character. On the positive side, this knowledge leads to greater egalitarianism. In this light, a case can be made for television's role in the growing trend toward greater access to information generally and to broader participation in decision-making in civic and educational organizations.[34] This counters the claims of critics who fear television's role in privatizing political matters, wherein social responsibility is relinquished by the diffusion of social events through the mass character of the electronic medium. They fear that the mere reporting of an important event subtly indicates that something is being done about it and thus removes one's own need to respond, or, that viewing others' participation suggests that civic responsibility is fulfilled by proxy.[35] On the darker side, however, television's role in the loss of authority does lead to suspicion of most rhetorics of power and to cynicism about the mechanisms for generating them.

Another consequence of television's redefinition of social roles and social status might be termed "the politicization of private life."[36] Here, the ethos of the public sphere finds its way into personal matters. At first blush, the sanctity of one's private and domestic life seems to be violated as, for example, family life evidences the loss of parental authority. Traditional family structures formed under the aegis of paternalism have been dealt a serious blow. Yet, however responsible television might be for fracturing the comfort of predictable and stable family relationships, it can also be the source of liberation from oppression and violence. It is no mere coincidence that issues such as spouse abuse have come to light through the pale glow of the television screen.[37] It is also arguable that Oprah and Phil are largely responsible for this growing awareness. As women sit and watch other women go public, telling their stories of victimization, a personal empowerment mounts, offering women the courage to find help, leave spouses, and create a new life. Again, we see that television's insinuation into private and personal places transforms the experiences of those places into public and political ones, open to contentiousness, assertive claims to authority, and, ultimately, to reevaluation and restructuring.[38]

In light of these claims about television's social effects, we can now identify some personal effects that combine to give us an image of the self formed by the technology of the electronic media. First, the self is formed with less reference to the promptings and practices of traditional communities. While not negating the influences of family, school, church, or other group associations to which individuals belong, the widespread impact of television reforms these institutions and communities as it simultaneously transforms the individual. The community of television is the community of mass culture where attitudes and behaviors are modeled without the need for direct, physical proximity. Consequently, the self is not bound by geographical markers, and identity is largely rootless in terms of place associations and the traditions that go along with them.

Second, the self is formed in an atmosphere of suspicion about authority. Television's unmasking of the practices that lead to status and privilege relocates the claims to authority directly in those practices and not in the expertise or knowledge that previously were the guarantors of authority.[39] Emblems of status are literally put on and taken off as clothing. Success, the benchmark of the impact of one's status or authority, is gauged by the places one goes, the associations one has, or the things one possesses. In the words of a popular bumper sticker, "The one with the most toys wins." While we may view this as crass materialism, it is important to remember that these emblems have a long, respected history of validity: the most powerful man in town lived in the biggest house and part of his power came from the symbolic significance of his house.

With regard to the problematic "heart" metaphor, the shift to behaviors, practices, and artifacts which we might term superficial locates the symbols of one's identity outside of some inner core of the self. Individual identity is as much constructed as it is inherited, foreordained, or *dis-covered*. Along with this, the centrality of image is obvious. Our identity or being is inextricably linked to our behaviors and the particular stylistics of those behaviors.[40]

As physical and social boundaries that previously conferred identity become porous and the status and authority associated with these boundaries suspect, the self formed by social practices becomes largely diffuse. One no longer needs to carry *a* self into all social situations and interactions. Instead, one *becomes* a self within the situations themselves. Again, the self as a constructed entity, aware of its own construction, comes to light. This need not signal a disintegration of the psyche, a self without an anchor or guiding principle. What it does signal is a multifacial self characterized by change and numerous representations.[41]

Returning to our earlier discussion, one can now compare characteristics of oral and literate culture to the experience of electronically mediated culture. Just as the primary experience of orality was one of fleeting and ephemeral presence, so too, the experience of electronically mediated culture produces a reality for the moment, unstable and driven by change. However, in orality's ethos, the fleeting quality of the speech act is balanced by the stability of the community and its mythic narratives. Although we can suggest that the whole community was created anew with its storytelling experiences, its traditions endured as the speech act was directed toward re-membering the character(s) of the community. Not so in media culture. Instead, the anchor of tradition gives way to unimpeded forces of change. The leveling of authority which comes with television's transgression of spatial boundaries so disturbs the order of social relations that no authoritative or master narrative can contain its addiction to newness. We no longer have the invigorating and creative freshness of pristine orality, but, in the language of post-modernism, the deadening reproduction of commodified image-making.

Furthermore, orality's reliance upon narrative form and its consequent confinement to thought based on narrative, non-logical processes finds a parallel in electronically mediated culture. In both cultures, a resistance to (if not incompetence in) logical and abstract thought is apparent. As television is most suited to the dramatic form, it thereby reinforces and encourages a dramatic framework of thought and action. Even television news utilizes this form in its narrative style of reporting. While this loss of higher cognitive abilities is disconcerting to some, the narrative form does contain unique and valuable characteristics. Among discursive forms, it alone appears most suited to communicating moral sensibilities.[42] Just how stable these sensibilities are remains an open question since these narratives are idiosyncratic and largely controlled by economic motives.

The differences between literate and electronically mediated cultures are even greater still. In literate culture the communicative mode stressed permanence, with continuity and objectivity as its by-products. The self was a relatively fixed and autonomous entity, moved by literacy's drive to objectify one's inner life. Electronically mediated culture appears no equivalent; its only permanence is the permanence of change itself. The self is situation specific, flexible, adaptive, and given to image and ethos. It is a self defined by its experience in the world, within the web of social relationships. The rub is that this world is a mass-mediated world with fewer boundaries to confine or define the self which develops through it. Thus, in sum, we might suggest that as the experience of pristine orality produced a communal self and literacy produced an autonomous self, electronic media produce a relativized self.

To bring this part of the discussion to a close, it is important to note that while the influences of media are forceful and dominant, vestiges of orality and literacy persist. We are clearly in a stage of transition which does not so much overthrow its previous forms of culture as it transforms them. As long as literacy persists, so will its particular consciousness-forming traits.[43] But it is important to recognize that these traits do not rule and that the young are the first to dethrone their authority.

Conclusion

The broad claim of this article has been that our students are different persons from those of the Founder's day and that a different perspective is required to understand and respond to them. This perspective should take into account the cultural situation in which our students live and through which they come to know and experience the world. In our case, the culture of electronically mediated experience provides the most relevant perspective.

More specifically, I have presented research demonstrating that a cultural period can be identified by the communicative technology that dominates it. I have tried to show that each of these technologies is instrumental in how one sees and experiences the world as well as in forming a personal and cultural consciousness. Furthermore, each of these forms of consciousness has strengths and limitations. While we may prefer a culture that supports an interiorized sense of self, for instance, and thus hold a bias toward literacy, we must also recognize that the loss of a thoroughgoing communal identity for the self was its price. The strengthening of an ascending communicative form necessarily weakens its predecessor.

Thus, when encountering an electronically mediated culture, we must be cautious about damning it out of hand. While the social, economic, and political losses appear to be great, so, too, do its benefits. Unfettered from the physical and social boundaries of past generations, young people today are offered unprecedented windows of opportunity. In the main, they are better informed about a broader range of people, places, and experiences than previous generations. In a single day they can be brought face-to-face with a famine in East Africa, the rape trial of a famous senator's nephew, and the collapse of an Eastern-block nation. Furthermore, in shattering the mysteries of social privilege and prestige, the sense of closeness and egalitarianism that comes with television holds the potential for developing a heart guided not by the metaphor of *depth* but one of *breadth*. Such a metaphor suggests that the path to self-discovery might lie in going *out* rather than *in* as television facilitates a familiarity and, potentially, an openness toward people, places, and situations.

As persons invited to ministry with young people, a deeper awareness and appreciation of the cultural forces that shape them is a prerequisite to our effectiveness. Such an awareness might call us to embrace the democratic and antiauthoritarian spirit which is television's ethos. It might also encourage us in the task of building communities based on these ideals as a way of anchoring our students, buffeted as they are by a world with few boundaries and unstable meanings. In this, we may not so much touch their hearts as give them a place from which they can develop their own.

Notes

1. Michel Foucault, *The Order of Things* (New York: Vintage Books, 1970). This volume addresses the issue of the formation of the person through discursive practices.

2. The most representative scholars in this field are Havelock, Haynes, Innis, McLuhan, and Ong. I have drawn primarily from Walter J. Ong, SJ, *Orality and Literacy: The Technologizing of the Word* (New York: Methuen, 1982); W. Lance Haynes, "Of That Which We Cannot Write: Some Notes on the Phenomenology of Media," *Quarterly Journal of Speech* 74 (1988) 71–101; and secondarily from Harold A. Innis, *Empire and Communications,* revised by Mary Q. Innis with a foreword by Marshall McLuhan (Toronto: University of Toronto Press, 1972); Eric A. Havelock, *Preface to Plato* (Cambridge, MA: Harvard University Press, 1963); and Marshall McLuhan, *Understanding Media: The Extensions of Man,* 2nd ed. (New York: Signet, 1964).

3. Ong, *Orality and Literacy,* 32.

4. Ibid., 46.

5. Ibid., 42–43.

6. Ibid., 43–45.

7. Ibid., 40.

8. Ibid., 49.

9. Ibid., 139ff.

10. Haynes, "Of That Which We Cannot Write," 75.

11. Ibid., 76.

12. Ibid., 80.

13. Ong, *Orality and Literacy,* 117.

14. Ibid., 101.

15. Ibid., 96ff.

16. Haynes, "Of That Which We Cannot Write," 79.

17. Ibid., 74; and Walter J. Ong, *Interfaces with the Word* (Ithaca, NY: Cornell University Press, 1977) 18, as quoted in Haynes, 78–79.

18. Haynes, "Of That Which We Cannot Write," 79; and Innis, *Empire and Communications,* 7 and 170.

19. Ong, *Orality and Literacy,* 130ff.

20. Ibid., 105, 178–179; and Haynes, "Of That Which We Cannot Write," 79.

21. Ong, *Orality and Literacy,* 179.

22. Ibid., 135–138.

23. In addition to the interpretive tradition of media studies discussed in the text of this article, there is also a body of literature from the empirical and administrative research tradition. Some representative examples are: Elihu Katz and Paul Lazersfeld, *Personal Influence* (New York: Free Press, 1964); Carl Hovland and Irving L. Janis, *Personality and Persuasibility* (New Haven, CT: Yale University Press, 1959); and William Schramm, *Men, Messages, and Media* (New York: Harper and Row, 1973). Two works offering good overviews and summaries of the empirical tradition of media studies are Shearon Lowery and Melvin L. De Fleur, *Milestones in Mass Communication Research* (New York: Longman, 1983); and Melvin L. De Fleur and Sandra Ball-Rokeach, *Theories of Mass Communication,* 4th ed. (New York: Longman, 1982).

24. Joshua Meyrowitz, *No Sense of Place* (New York: Oxford University Press, 1985). I draw heavily on and highly recommend Meyrowitz's work because it is the most thorough, clear, insightful, and balanced investigation of the effects of electronic media to date.

Also, in subsequent citations, I either note single pages where statements in my article are supported by Meyrowitz, or I identify chapters wherein the claims he makes are developed. In doing the latter I am condensing the discussion of a work of almost 400 pages.

For an excellent review and critique of the literature in interpretive media studies see Kevin M. Carragee, "Interpretive Media Study and Interpretive Social Science," *Critical Studies in Mass Communication* 7 (1990) 81–96.

25. Meyrowitz, *No Sense of Place,* 35–67.

26. Ibid., 169–172.

27. Ibid., 73–130.

28. Ibid., 187–225.

29. Ibid., 163.

30. Ibid., 155, 157–159.

31. As anthropologist Albert Mehrabian suggests, this knowledge is of overwhelming importance as 55 percent of interpersonal messages is communicated through facial expression, with 38 percent through vocal inflection and a mere 7 percent through verbal content. Cited in Meyrowitz, 273.

32. Meyrowitz, *No Sense of Place*, 277–279.

33. Given this ability to supply the experience of "being there," it is no mistake that the stronghold of Joseph McCarthy's anticommunist fanaticism came to end when his hearings became televised, for only then could the "true" character—and with it the questionable motives—of the man come through; or that television's intimate look led viewers to believe that John F. Kennedy had won the 1960 Nixon-Kennedy debates while radio listeners thought that Nixon had won. Thus, those who cringe at the heightening of "image over substance," particularly in the political realm, must realize how substantive an image really is, especially when it is recognized that the persona which an image projects is less malleable, less subject to opportunistic change, than a "stand" on any given issue. See Meyrowitz, *No Sense of Place*, 278ff.

For a counter-argument maligning the role of image in television, see Daniel J. Boorstin, *The Image: A Guide to Pseudo-events in America* (New York: Atheneum, 1972).

34. Meyrowitz, *No Sense of Place*, 162.

35. Ibid., 318.

36. Ibid., 315. For a discussion claiming that TV has diminished public discourse, see Neil Postman, *Amusing Ourselves to Death: Public Discourse in the Age of Show Business* (New York: Viking, 1985).

37. Meyrowitz, *No Sense of Place*, 151–152.

38. Ibid., 312–313.

39. Ibid., 324–328.

40. Ibid., 31–32.

41. Ibid., 320.

42. The claim that narrative form holds a unique capacity to express moral sensibilities is argued by a number of authors. Two good sources for this claim are found in Walter R. Fisher, "Narration as a Human Communication Paradigm: The Case for Public Moral Argument," *Communication Monographs* 51 (1984) 1–22, and Alastair MacIntyre, *After Virtue: A Study in Moral Theory* (Notre Dame: University of Notre Dame Press, 1981).

43. Meyrowitz, *No Sense of Place*, 19 and 317.

Questions for Reflection and Discussion

1. What image or metaphor comes to mind when I think of my ministry?
2. What are the positive implications that come from that image or metaphor?

3. What potential limitations does the image or metaphor produce?
4. What is my attitude toward the technological changes that have taken place in the past ten years? Awe? Fear? Regret? Gratitude? Why?
5. What attitudes do my students (or others with whom I minister) hold toward these technological changes?
6. Am I aware of how these technological changes have shaped the way my students (Brothers, colleagues) think, feel, and experience the world?

Home Is Where the Heart Is: Homelessness in the United States and a Lasallian Response

Thomas G. Lisack, FSC

And it happened that while they were conversing and debating, Jesus himself drew near and walked with them, but their eyes were prevented from recognizing him. He asked them, "What are you discussing as you walk along?" They stopped, looking downcast. One of them, named Cleopas, said to him in reply, "Are you the only visitor to Jerusalem who does not know of the things that have taken place there in these days?" And he replied to them, "What sort of things?" They said to him, "The things that happened to Jesus the Nazarene . . . we were hoping that he would be the one to redeem Israel. . . ." And he said to them, "Oh, how foolish you are! How slow of heart to believe all that the prophets spoke!" . . . Then beginning with Moses and all the prophets, he interpreted to them what referred to him in all the scriptures. As they approached the village to which they were going, he gave the impression that he was going on farther. But they urged him, "Stay with us, for it is nearly evening and the day is almost over." . . . While he was at table, he took bread, said the blessing, broke it, and gave it to them. With that their eyes were opened and they recognized him, but he vanished from their sight. Then they said to each other, "Were not our hearts burning within us while he spoke to us on the way and opened the scriptures to us? (Lk. 24:15–19, 25, 27–32)

BROTHER THOMAS G. LISACK, FSC, MA, is currently serving as campus minister and teacher of English at Pacelli High School in Stevens Point, Wisconsin. He has a master's degree in English from Notre Dame University, and has also taught at Cretin-Derham Hall in Saint Paul, Minnesota.

An Initial Failure to Recognize

Distancing and a Sense of Fear

It is of particular significance that the disciples on the road to Emmaus were not leaders of their community. They represented all followers of Jesus as they journeyed down the road in a troubled, discouraged, and preoccupied fashion.[1] It is also noteworthy that they did not immediately recognize the stranger as Christ but offered hospitality nonetheless. We, on the brink of the twenty-first century, likewise represent all followers of Jesus as we walk, meander, dance, and sometimes stumble along the road. We too fail, at times, to recognize those who are most in need—Christ among us. We fail to be willing and open to "know again" the poor. But we will not know them again, we will not recognize them if we refuse to deal honestly not only with the less fortunate, but with ourselves.

There is a variety of reasons for our failure to make this recognition. Perhaps our vision is at least partially impaired, as Matthew described, by a plank of judgment. Perhaps we fear the shadows of those less fortunate around us because they remind us of our own darker side, the shadows within. As one homeless individual stated, "I had a situation once myself. First a family problem, then no job. I got depressed and started drinking, and I just hit the street. Just gave up."[2] After two years of living in abandoned cars and vacant buildings this man began the long road back to a meaningful life. How different is this man from us? His warning could be the haunting reminder of the similarities that strike the most fear into us: "You and me are this close to being on the street [there is a slight space between his thumb and forefinger]. Half of these people here [living beneath Wacker Drive in Chicago] used to be construction workers, electricians, tradesmen. Now they're laying out here on the ground. . . . I just can't understand how we could let so much go to waste."[3] So when we really scrutinize the issue of homelessness we reach a moment of truth when we realize that ours is also a precarious state and that one day we too could find ourselves experiencing this deep sense of loss.

A sociologist described the homeless as "dancing above the abyss."[4] One way of facing the reality of homelessness is to learn about the issue. But it is most important to keep in mind the example the disciples set for us. For it is by being hospitable that *we* come to recognize Christ in the stranger and not the other way around. We can begin to confront the issue by putting ourselves in the place of the stranger.

If we place ourselves within the context of the definition of homelessness we find ourselves detached, absent, and disconnected. We ask ourselves questions such as, "Where would I be without my family? How would I manage without the support of my friends? To whom would I turn if I had no one on whom to depend or trust?" What is our response? Yet, if we look carefully at the homeless individual we find that he or she fits into this definition and is indeed completely detached from the social structure. One person in South Bend spoke from experience when he asked rhetorically, "Could anyone find themselves homeless? Less than a year ago, I was a ranking editor at one of the larger newspapers on the West Coast. After a failed marriage and a management change at the paper, I'm back in the Midwest sleeping in a spare bedroom at my mother's home. . . . "[5] But far too many are not fortunate enough to have family members or friends to fall back on.

It is very difficult to recognize the homeless, to know them again, if we do not understand who they are, where they have been, and, most important, what they have lost. We must also accept our fear and attempt to overcome it. We must begin by learning and trying to understand this profound sense of loss with which the homeless must deal. We must be willing to come face to face with their plight realistically, something that we have not done in the past.

For a variety of reasons, during the long history of homelessness in the United States our eyes have been prevented from recognizing the problem. We have deflected the issue. Often we have chosen to rationalize homelessness rather than to deal realistically with it. Rarely have we reflected upon or delved into the meaning of just what it is to have a home, to come from a home, and to frequently return home. Too often we have found a self-serving euphemism for the homeless and have used such words as detached and truncated to describe their state. We labeled them "bums" throughout the nineteenth and twentieth centuries, and as we approach the twenty-first century we find suitable contemporary labels to fit the times. Today we refer to them as "collateral damage." But we have consistently subscribed to a stance of denial. What we need to do is begin at the heart of the matter, with the concept of home and with the devastating reality of losing one's home.

A Sense of Loss

A short time before his death, former major league baseball commissioner, A. Bartlett Giamatti wrote of a spiritual, self-identifying sense of *home*. His definition links "home" with one's soul.

> *Home* is an English word virtually impossible to translate into other tongues. No translation catches the associations, the mixture of memory and longing, the sense of security and autonomy and accessibility, the aroma of inclusiveness, of freedom from wariness, that cling to the word *home* and are absent from *house* or even *my house*. *Home* is a concept, not a place; it is a state of mind where self-definition starts; it is origins—the mix of time and place and smell and weather wherein one first realizes one is an original, perhaps *like* others, especially those one loves, but discrete, distinct, not to be copied. Home is where one first learned to be separate and it remains in the mind as the place where reunion, if it ever were to occur, would happen.[6]

When one loses one's home, he or she is losing a great deal more than just shelter. That individual becomes incomplete. Home affords stability and identity as well. The person who is homeless can no longer enjoy a sense of completeness or the security of knowing that home is the place where reunion will take place. Home, in the words of Robert Frost, is no longer available as the place you can go "where they have to let you in." The homeless person loses this vital assurance and sense of security.

Giamatti provides a conceptual view of home, but, more important, he goes much farther than that. Home *is* where the heart is, and given the depth of this definition, the implications surrounding homelessness become not only much more grave but much more ambiguous. If we are to deal with the growing pervasiveness of this issue realistically, we must be willing to personalize it and embrace its gravity. We need to reflect upon times when we did a poor job of recognizing and did not serve the least of our brothers or sisters. We need to open *our* eyes and keep them open so that we too can experience hearts that are burning inside us. It is essential that we make a much more informed, meaningful response to homelessness. But before we examine life outside us, it is necessary to look within. It is necessary to ask the question, "Of what am I afraid?"

Preoccupation as Blindness

> She calls out to the man on the street, "Sir can you help me?
> It's cold and I've nowhere to sleep. Is there somewhere you can tell me?"
> He walks off, doesn't look back. He pretends he can't hear her.
> Starts to whistle as he crosses the street. Seems embarrassed to be there.[7]

In a recent publication, novelist Joyce Carol Oates illustrates the kind of blindness we have toward the homeless in a short story titled, "Shopping." In it, an affluent mother and daughter make their way through a shopping mall in a large city during the height of the Christmas season and encounter a homeless woman sitting on a bench.

> Near Baumgarten's entrance mother and daughter see a disheveled woman sitting by herself on one of the benches. Without seeming to look at her, shoppers are making a discreet berth around her, a stream following a natural course.
>
> "My God, that poor woman," Nola says. "I didn't think there were people like her here—I mean, I didn't think they would allow it."
>
> "She doesn't seem to cause any disturbance," Mrs. Dietrich says. "She just sits. Don't stare, Nola, she'll see you."
>
> "You've seen her here before? Here?"
>
> "A few times this winter."
>
> "Is she always like that?"
>
> "I'm sure she's harmless, Nola. She just *sits*."

Nola is incensed, her pale blue eyes like washed glass. "I'm sure *she's* harmless, Mother. It's the harm the poor woman has to endure that is the tragedy."

Mrs. Dietrich is surprised and a little offended by her daughter's passionate tone but she knows enough not to argue. They enter Baumgarten's, taking their habitual route. So many shoppers![8]

This homeless person is harmless. She is completely powerless in the midst of so many apparently powerful people. Yet, judging from the way Mrs. Dietrich deflects her daughter's question about the frequency of the woman's presence, this homeless woman has apparently caused at least some discomfort to this pair. Why? What do this mother and daughter see that is so disturbing? What is it about this homeless woman's state of utter loss that frightens them to the point that they feel they quickly need to anesthetize themselves amidst the Christmas trappings of a nearby department store? Is it possible that the mother and daughter fleetingly recognize something of themselves in this woman? Of what does she remind them? Might they have had a glimpse of their own souls? Here was an apparent stranger, a seemingly powerless, uninformed individual. Perhaps what they experience is similar to what the disciples experienced before they recognized Jesus as they perfunctorily walked along the road to a familiar town.

If they continue to ignore Christ among them, the mother and daughter in Oates' story will remain lost. It is that deprivation of the soul, that shared sense of loss, that they momentarily recognize personified in the homeless woman.

Annie Dillard, a novelist and essayist, reflected on the end of the Gospel of Luke in a recent essay:

> The Gospel of Luke ends immediately and abruptly after the Ascension outside Bethany, on that Easter Sunday when the disciples walked so much and kept receiving visitations from the risen Christ. . . . What a pity that so hard on the heels of Christ come the Christians. There is no breather. . . . What a dismaying pity, that here come the Christians already, flawed to the core, full of wild ideas and hurried self-importance. . . . Who could believe that salvation is for these rogues? That God is for these rogues? For they are just like us, and salvation's time is past.
>
> Unless, of course. . . .

Unless Christ's washing the disciples' feet, their dirty toes, means what it could, possibly, mean: that it is all right to be human. That God knows we are human, and full of evil, all of us, and we are his people anyway, and the sheep of his pasture.

Unless those colorful scamps and scalawags who populate Jesus' parables were just as evil as we are, and evil in the same lazy, cowardly, and scheming ways. Unless those pure disciples themselves and those watercolor women—who so disconcertingly turned into the Christians overnight—were complex and selfish humans also, who lived in the material world, and whose errors and evils were not pretty but ugly, and had real consequences. If they were just like us, then Christ's words to them are addressed to us, in full and merciful knowledge—and we are lost. There is no place to hide.[9]

Dancing Above the Abyss

Much like the disciples who perceived themselves walking above the abyss, the homeless dance above it as they make their way through the streets of our cities and towns. One of the things they have lost is a pattern to their lives. Theirs is a labyrinthine search through the downtown traffic and in the shadows of skyscrapers not only for shelter but for meaning and identity. Theirs is a profound loss of structure. Sociologist Robert Bellah, in defining institutions, describes in large part that which the homeless person is without.

> Institutions are patterns of social activity that give shape to collective and individual experience. An institution is a complex whole that guides and sustains individual identity, as a family gives sense and purpose to the lives of its members, enabling them to realize themselves as spouses, parents, and children. Institutions form individuals by making possible or impossible certain ways of behaving and relating to others. They shape character by assigning responsibility, demanding accountability, and providing standards in terms of which each person recognizes the excellence of his or her achievements. Each individual's possibilities depend on the opportunities opened up within the institutional contexts to which that person has access.[10]

The homeless person is no longer part of this whole. There is no one to give sense to his or her life. No network or collective agent exists by which to provide feedback, support, and expectations. As Christian Brothers we speak often of "the Institute," but do we take the time to recognize just what it provides and what would be lacking in our lives if we were without it?

Bellah speaks specifically about homelessness and the deinstitutionalization of the mentally ill who make up some of the homeless population. But all homeless individuals have been deinstitutionalized because they have been separated from any semblance of collective experience.

> Walking in any American city today, one participates in a ritual that perfectly expresses the difficulty of being a good person in the absence of a good society . . . we pass homeless men or, often, women with children asking for money for food and shelter. Whether we give or withhold our spare change, we know that neither personal choice is the right one. We may experience the difficulty of helping the plight of the homeless people as a painful individual moral dilemma, but the difficulty actually comes from failures of the larger institutions on which our common life depends.
>
> The problem of homelessness, like many of our problems, was created by social choices. The market-driven conversion of single-room-occupancy hotels into upscale tourist accommodations, government urban-renewal projects that revitalized downtowns while driving up rents and reducing housing for the poor, economic changes that eliminated unskilled jobs paying enough to support a family, the states' "deinstitutionalization" of the mentally ill and reduced funding of local community health programs, have together created the crisis of homelessness.[11]

Here, Bellah has described some of the recent social choices that have led to a homeless population in the United States that by some estimates exceeds three million people. It is worth briefly examining the history of homelessness in this country in order to understand it in a broader context.

History—The Old and New Homeless

The Nineteenth Century New York Bowery

In December 1991, a New York City resident, arguing against having a shelter for the homeless built in his neighborhood, stated, "That's what the Bowery is for!" This individual did not want homeless individuals to inhabit his neighborhood, but his anachronistic and insensitive comment says a lot about how Americans perceive this issue. "As a concrete measure of media attention, articles about the homeless listed in the *Reader's Guide to Periodical Literature* rose from zero in 1975 to 34 in 1984 and 48 in 1986."[12] There were 15 articles specifically about homelessness and a number of other cross-referenced articles dealing with the issue in November 1991 alone. Homelessness has become a major issue only recently, primarily because it has become a visible issue.

All of us have encountered a homeless person in the last ten years, but as early as the 1870s homeless individuals began congregating in the Bowery of New York City.[13] One hundred and twenty years after the Bowery began to be a refuge for homeless individuals, those who find the homeless threatening and unsightly want to send them back. But the Bowery is a very different place. It is no longer an alternative, a subculture, and a support system for the homeless. It is no longer a substitute family. The rapid gentrification of the urban area has extended into the Bowery vicinity as theaters, restaurants, and art galleries have enhanced real estate values. The result: the network of Bowery inhabitants has been forced to move to the streets. These are the same streets that we "inhabit" and we feel uncomfortable in their presence.

The origins of the New York city Bowery extend nearly 300 years.

> At the beginning of the eighteenth century about four hundred people lived in the vicinity of Bowery Village. By mid century, the population of the city and its environs had neared ten thousand.[14]

Bowery Lane was, at that time,

> a fair country road, bordered with comfortable homes, blossoming orchards, vegetable and flower gardens, meadows dotted with cattle and horses, and an occasional tavern or windmill.[15]

By 1790 the population of New York had reached 33,000, a figure that would double by the close of the century. Immigrants came both internally from New England and other parts of New York state as well as from abroad: Ireland, Scotland, Germany, and England. The population of the city swelled to 500,000 by 1850.[16]

As early as 1800, the Bowery began to reveal the contrasts in its altered social composition as prominent citizens lived almost shoulder to shoulder with members of the working class. While the northern portion of the Bowery retained its highly respectable reputation, the southern portion bordered on the first slum of the city. "This nascent polarization of class and urban space would characterize the Bowery throughout its antebellum period."[17] Here began the polarization and the attendant contradictions between the social classes: the poverty of the slum and the wealth of the aristocracy. The Bowery could be spatially likened to "a lady in a ball costume with diamonds in her ears and her toes out of her boots."[18]

One establishment exemplified Bowery life in microcosm. The Bowery Theater was established in 1826 and was intended as both a social and a democratic experience of the arts. "But once inside, the democratic experience became less a study of classlessness than a reflection of urban society's unraveled fabric."[19] This "unraveling" took the form of shouting matches among patrons which occasionally interfered with the theatrical performance and confused the distinction between actors and audience. One did not always know where the show ended and reality began. People sat in the theater according to social class and this distinction contributed to a variety of disruptions. Those among the laboring classes and the individuals who became known as the "Bowery Boys" gathered in the theater's pit and often carried on dialogue with the performers. The more refined and respectable families of the Bowery were seated above the pit in the dress boxes. In the next tier of boxes was a cordoned off section for the indecorous patrons such as the prostitutes. As a direct result of having such a diverse group together, "shouting matches were not uncommon between the various segments of the theater lending a bit of confusion to the distinction between players and audience."[20] During the 1850s these class distinctions were transferred to each particular theater in the Bowery. The upper class began to attend the more fashionable Park Theater, the middle class attended the Bowery theater, and this left Chatham theater to the lower class.[21]

"In the early 1900s close to 25,000 men were lodged nightly in the Bowery."[22] But while the population increased in 1914–1915 during a period of widespread unemployment, it subsequently began to dwindle. The population of the Bowery's skid row was 13,675 in 1949 and dropped to 3,000 in 1971. By the late 1970s it had dropped to about 2,000 and by 1987 it was below 1,000.[23]

> The decline of skid row has not caused the disappearance of homelessness; instead it has signaled a reconceptualization of its renewed force and decentralization. Contemporary homelessness, extensive (an estimated 36,000), scattered and incohesive, has proven to be a diffused and disoriented way of life far beyond the ordered community of skid row. In flight from its territorial base homelessness has transgressed the geographical boundaries of skid row, but in doing so it has not retained the sub-cultural identity endemic to its structure and affiliative network of supports. In its most recent development, homelessness has become uprooted, unearthing a subculture clinging to the arcane remnants of the Bowery like a vine to its fallen arbor.[24]

The homeless often walk the streets aimlessly, hoping that someone will point them in the direction of a shelter or a meal.

Chicago's Contemporary Homeless: Violence and Loneliness

Today a very similar situation exists among the homeless of Chicago who live on Lower Wacker Drive. They too experience a solidarity of survival. "They know each others' sleeping places and habits. They keep in touch and pass along bulletins of violent crime."[25] The contemporary homeless are also truncated but have far less of an opportunity to belong, to connect with other groups of people who share their plight. They live in the most deplorable conditions. They are the shadows of the city; they are invisible people scavenging like rats. Said one man who asked for anonymity, "You have to play a little bit of a head game with rats, otherwise they'll come in here and try to take what little bit of food I have."[26]

One documented incident illustrates the violence the homeless face each day. In July 1991 a 21-year-old South Side man was sentenced to 60 years in jail for killing "a Lower Wacker Drive homeless man with a razor-tipped arrow shot from a crossbow. Authorities called it a 'thrill kill.'"[27] Was this young, violent man seeking a thrill or was he attempting to kill the shadow side, the potentially destitute side of himself that he feared so much?

While families who are homeless are granted some sympathy, such as the Joad family fictionally portrayed in *The Grapes of Wrath,* there is very little sympathy for the unattached.[28] According to an October 1991 survey conducted by the Wilder Foundation, the unattached among us increasingly include an alarmingly high number of children. Researchers interviewed 81 street children in Minnesota. "Homelessness is no isolated incident for these kids. Nearly two-thirds had experienced multiple episodes of homelessness. Half had been homeless for more than 45 days, about a third had been homeless for more than 3 months and 11 percent had been homeless a year or more."[29] The report states that most of these children are attempting to escape from parents who abuse them physically, sexually, and emotionally. As described below, the increasing severity and proportion of homeless children is one way to distinguish the old and new homeless.

Five contrasts can be drawn.

1. Decentralization

The new homeless are no longer concentrated on the Bowery or on Skid Row. To make an important distinction: they have been *distributed* rather than *diminished.* Homelessness today cannot be easily ignored as in the past.[30] Because homeless people have been dispersed, their individual sense of loss is much greater. Not only do they experience a sense of loss, but often they must try to cope in isolation. This solitary existence contributes even further to their despair.

2. Families and women are more prevalent

Studies done as recently as the 1960s indicate that women constituted only a handful—64 over a period of a year—housed on the Bowery. In contrast, women constituted 25 percent of the 1985–1986 Chicago homeless population.[31] Women are facing the same potential for violent crime as men, and it is the children who are most vulnerable. Often they must survive violence at home and then face it on the streets. Some of these children have been thrown out of their homes because their parents cannot accept who they are. "This is particularly a problem for gay and lesbian youths, perhaps the most invisible of the young homeless."[32]

3. Lower age composition

Very few persons over 60 are among today's homeless. Instead, these individuals are concentrated in their 20s and 30s, the early years of adulthood. These are individuals in the prime of their lives who have lost hope. "In the 40 studies of the homeless conducted in the past few years, the average median age recorded was 36."[33] In the recent study on children, youths ranged in age from 11 to 18. The average age was 16.[34]

4. Decreased employment status

Among the new Chicago homeless, only 3 percent reported having a steady job. "Correspondingly, the new homeless have less income than the old."[35] The median annual income for the homeless was $1,058. In 1985 the median annual income was $1,198. "Correcting for inflation, the income of the current homeless is equivalent to only $383 in 1958 dollars."[36] Among children, those employed, 36 percent of those surveyed, worked an average of 17 hours per week at an average wage of $4.50. Of the rest,

> 24 percent relied on parents, 14 percent on friends or relatives, 10 percent on Aid to Families with Dependent Children (AFDC), and 9 percent on General Assistance or family's public assistance. The rest relied on prostitution or soliciting money on the street.[37]

5. Ethnic composition

Finally, the old homeless were predominately white: 70 percent on the Bowery and 82 percent on Chicago's Skid Row. But the new homeless of the 1980s are heavily made up of ethnic minorities. During that decade in Chicago, 54 percent were black and in New York's shelters more than 75 percent were black. The proportion has been increasing since the early 1980s.

In short, we can generalize that minorities are consistently over-represented among the new homeless in ratios that are some multiple of their presence in the community. The old homelessness was more blind to color and ethnicity than the new homelessness.[38]

The new and old homeless are alike in having a high rate of individuals with disabilities. Particularly evident is the significant percentage of mentally ill among the homeless. The following is the story of one mentally ill individual.

I first saw Ms. Z. in a women's shelter in Washington. She was extremely paranoid and delusional but acknowledged that she had been married to a professional man and had raised several children. She refused to take medication. She left the shelter and I next heard that she had been living on the mezzanine of National Airport for several months; it was apparently the only place she felt safe from Israeli secret agents who she believed were injecting her in her sleep and were responsible for her voices. One of her daughters, on her way back from college, accidentally discovered her mother at the airport.[39]

Much has been written about the deinstitutionalization of the mentally ill. What is most important regarding this segment of the homeless population are the current admissions policies of our mental hospitals.

Many of the chronic mentally ill homeless would have been admitted two decades ago under then-existing practices. The shelters and the streets now substitute in part for the hospitals of the past.[40]

It would be easy to subscribe to the politics of avoidance and blame the victim for his or her fate. But it is much more challenging to be proactive and face the issue by offering hospitality.

"Stay With Us!"

The Catholic Worker Movement and Hospitality

Let mutual love continue. Do not neglect hospitality, for through it some have unknowingly entertained angels. (Heb 13:1–2)

The Catholic Worker began as a monthly newspaper of the same name and was founded in 1933 in New York City by Dorothy Day and Peter Maurin.[41]

Their purpose was to present a Catholic answer to the Communist *Daily Worker* by disseminating Catholic social thought, especially embodied in the papal encyclicals and the European philosophical movement known as personalism.[42]

The central concept of Worker personalism is personal responsibility.

Throughout its history those who work with the movement continue to attempt to do what the disciples on the road to Emmaus did. Those with The Catholic Worker movement continue to view the stranger as Christ. "In the 1930s, Workers often referred to their guests as Ambassadors of Christ or Ambassadors of God."[43] This viewpoint is radically different from the one typically given to the individual in need of hospitality. It is also significant to take note of the movement's explicit and detailed definition of hospitality.

Hospitality can best be described in terms of the rights and obligations of host and guest, where those roles are assumed voluntarily and without monetary payment. The host generally has an obligation to receive the guest into his or her home and to treat the guest with respect, cordiality, and generosity. Hospitality is always done in a friendly, caring spirit—otherwise, one is not "hospitable." Although the role of the "gracious host" is often a formal requirement of the norm of hospitality, most cultures appear to distinguish between a host whose hospitality is genuine and one whose hospitality is a front.[44]

On one hand, this definition requires the person giving hospitality to take on a significant responsibility. One must treat the stranger as he or she would treat Christ and then approach hospitality with integrity and genuineness. As the Rule of St. Benedict states, "All guests who present themselves are to be welcomed as Christ for he himself will say, 'I was a stranger and you welcomed me.'"[45] As a result of the breadth of responsibility, one might assume that the worker would need to be a trained professional in order to perform this task. On the contrary, as the Catholic Worker Movement has shown, no formal training is required. In fact, the movement acts as a "cry for re-empowerment of the untrained person."[46] It argues that there are many tasks that the nonprofessional can feel competent in performing; furthermore,

> training hinders the practice of hospitality since it gives the trainee predefined categories into which to fit one's clients, and such a categorization process destroys the openness toward the stranger that is a requisite of hospitality in the traditional sense.[47]

This type of unconditional openness greatly enhances recognition and affords the volunteer the opportunity fully to attend to the needs of the person.

> . . . the movement of the various professions into the arena of homelessness prevention and cure in the wake of the "discovery" of the problem in the 1980s can be explained not only in terms of a manifest desire to help but also in terms of a latent desire to expand professional power by moving into a new area. The professions that succeed in becoming recognized as essential to the solution of homelessness will be able to expand their training programs into a new area.
>
> For over half a century, the Catholic Worker movement has advocated and practiced a different approach to the problem of homelessness—that of personalist hospitality. Helping the homeless is not a task reserved for those with professional training. Rather, it is something that anyone can do—simply by practicing the ancient tradition of hospitality—of welcoming the stranger into one's house and providing him or her with food, shelter, and companionship. For this task one needs no special training; it lies well within the competence of any member of a human community.[48]

There are more than 70 Catholic Worker Houses of Hospitality throughout the country. Dorothy Day was a visionary who exemplified the concept of hospitality found in Luke's Gospel. Like the disciples, she was present and attended to Christ in her presence. We can do much to emulate her.

Lasallian Response

As Brothers, colleagues, parents, students, and other caring members of our communities, we continue to be followers of Saint John Baptist de La Salle as we approach the twenty-first century. In the context of our contemporary setting, we can make at least two possible responses to alleviate the suffering of the homeless.

The Lasallian Youth Movement

The Lasallian Youth Movement is a general way in which to help our students put a face on homelessness. This movement acts as a forum in which students can reflect and act upon how they can make a difference in their community. They look for the spirit of God in the concrete experience of their lives and ask the question, "Where is God happening here?" In the past six years I have coordinated trips to one of the Dorothy Day Centers in Saint Paul. Whether student volunteers live in the city or come from a rural area, their enthusiastic, generous response has delighted me.

Usually the group of volunteers is diverse. There is at least one representative from each class and students who are engaged in a wide variety of cocurricular and extracurricular activities. It is not unusual, for example, for a football player or coach to pour pancake batter while a member of the debate team or a foreign exchange student flips the pancakes over. I strongly feel that the absence of required qualifications eases students' minds and helps them to concentrate on being present and attending to the needs of others rather than worrying, for example, about a personal evaluation.

During the three hours it takes to complete the process, students are profoundly affected as they encounter, many for the first time, individuals who are homeless. Several days after the experience, students hand in a personal reflection paper summing up their encounter with Christ among us. Some of the reflections are particularly poignant.

> I signed up for the Dorothy Day Center because I wanted to get involved in more service work but I didn't know what to expect. . . . What I'll always remember about working is the people I saw there, and the feelings I had afterwards. Not everyone who goes through the line shows how much they appreciate it, but you know they do. . . . One thing happened that kind of stood out and made me wonder. A woman and a young child walked through the line. He was the only child I saw. The woman asked for just one pancake and a couple of sausages. I guess it was for her child. For whatever reason she didn't take a plate for herself—her life is so different from ours that we can't really understand why.[49]

At Xavier University in Cincinnati, scholarship and service are linked. The university offers a four-year scholarship to students who demonstrate leadership and commitment to community service. Students must have demonstrated this commitment during high school and continue to serve during their four years of college. The University of Notre Dame has taken over the ownership and management of the Center for the Homeless; the Center has become an extension of the classroom. David T. Link, dean of the university's Law School, relates his experience at the shelter with his experience teaching ethics.

> I started to realize that ethics is something that has to be practiced. I discovered that I can teach more ethics in one night at the homeless center than in a whole semester in the classroom.[50]

It is also important to strengthen the community context in high schools.

> No teacher with eyes to see in school or university, has failed to notice those moments of joy that come when a student understands something important for the first time—not as a means to any end, but as an enlargement of his or her participation in reality.[51]

As a teacher, I have often experienced the most joy while engaged in a project of community service along with students, colleagues, and, on occasion, parents. But one does not have to be involved in education as a student or a teacher to help the homeless.

Lasallian Houses of Hospitality

The November 1933 issue of *The Catholic Worker* featured an article that delineated the notion of hospitality and outlined a concept of how a House of Hospitality would be organized.

> Hospitality is the keynote of civilization, its opposite is greed. . . .
> So we arrive at the idea—Catholic Houses of Hospitality! . . . The general purpose of the Houses of Hospitality is to form a center of Catholic Action in all fields, to work for, teach and preach social justice, to form a powerhouse of genuine spirituality and earnest educational and vocational work, to dignify and transform manual labor, and to work for the glory and love of God and His Church.[52]

Lasallian Houses of Hospitality need not follow these exact guidelines, but these standards could serve as a model for such a project. If Lasallian Houses of Hospitality were established, they could begin in the larger cities of the country as Dorothy Day did when she began her movement in New York City. It is in metropolitan areas that these Houses would have the greatest initial and ongoing impact. Those who are homeless usually seek out areas that are densely populated as more likely to offer shelter and food. Once the Houses began to make a positive impact and gain a good reputation, they could branch out to some rural, less populated areas where the needs might be somewhat different. Lasallian Houses of Hospitality could help to centralize the homeless in some of these rural areas and afford them at least a measure of stability.

Certainly these Houses of Hospitality would also be attractive to individuals who are interested in the life of the Brothers but are not necessarily interested in teaching. As I have stated, one does not need training in order to be a person of hospitality. Young men who are thinking about joining the Brothers could work alongside older men who have been Brothers for decades. People in various stages of formation could take part in this apostolate; while serving the poor these men could also be learning about the nature of religious life.

Conclusion

An Emmaus Psalm

> How easily, O Christ,
>> do I long for a firsthand touch
>> from you, my friend and savior,
>> risen and glorious, victorious over death,
>> radiant with luminous life. . . .
> I do not doubt the quality of my zeal
>> had I broken bread with you
>> at the sunset inn on the Emmaus road.

It's not easy to be among the living faithful
    fed by second-hand accounts
    of your resurrection visits,
    even though they have been passed on with loving care
    for millenniums mouth-to-mouth. . . .
Every time I break bread with friends or strangers
    or encounter kindness on my daily byroads,
    when I am visited by you
    even though my inner doors are locked in fear,
    let my heart be as open as the horizon
    for the feast of an Easter visit
    from you, my Risen Savior.[53]

This article has attempted to show that as Christians and followers of De La Salle, we need to experience burning hearts. We have an obligation to attend to the homeless in our midst with the same kind of zeal we approach various other ministries. As Luke reminds us, even if we don't immediately recognize Christ among us, neither did the disciples. However, it was through hospitality that they came to recognize Christ. Our willingness to offer hospitality is the precondition to being able to recognize the homeless as our brothers and sisters, and as Christ among us.

Notes

1. Raymond E. Brown, SS, et al., ed. *The Jerome Biblical Commentary* (Englewood Cliffs, NJ: Prentice Hall, 1968) 162.

2. Quoted in David Jackson, "Invisible Society Scrapes by on Lower Wacker, *Chicago Tribune,* 5 January 1992, 12-A.

3. Ibid., 12.

4. Benedict Giamo, *On the Bowery: Confronting Homelessness in American Society* (Iowa City, IA: University of Iowa Press, 1989) 191.

5. Quoted in Dana Heupel, "More Than Food and Shelter," *Notre Dame Magazine* (Autumn 1991) 9.

6. A. Bartlett Giamatti, *Take Time for Paradise* (New York: Summit Books, 1989) 91–92.

7. Phil Collins, "Another Day in Paradise," . . . *But Seriously* (New York: Atlantic Recording Corporation, 1989), audiocassette, 82050-4.

8. Joyce Carol Oates, "Shopping," in *Heat and Other Stories* (New York: Penguin Books, 1991) 58.

9. Annie Dillard, "Luke," in *Incarnation: Contemporary Writers on the New Testament,* Alfred Corn, ed. (New York: Viking, 1990) 36–37.

10. Robert Bellah et al., *The Good Society* (New York: Alfred A. Knopf, 1991) 4.

11. Ibid.

12. Peter Rossi, *Down and Out in America: The Origins of Homelessness* (Chicago: University of Chicago Press, 1989) 14.

13. Giamo, *On the Bowery,* 15.

14. Ibid., 6.

15. Alvin Harlow, *Old Bowery Days: The Chronicles of a Famous Street* (New York: D. Appleton, 1931) 50.

16. Giamo, *On the Bowery,* 6.

17. Ibid., 7.

18. Ibid.

19. Ibid.

20. Ibid.

21. Ibid., 8.

22. Ibid., 28.

23. Ibid., 29.

24. Ibid., 30.

25. Jackson, "Invisible Society," 1-A.

26. Ibid., 12.

27. Ibid.

28. Rossi, *Down and Out in America,* 25.

29. Quoted in Carol Lacey, "Survey Shows How Kids Who Can't Go Home Try to Survive," *St. Paul Pioneer Press,* 29 February 1992, 1-B.

30. Giamo, *On the Bowery,* 30.

31. Rossi, *Down and Out in America,* 39.

32. Lacey, "Survey Shows," 9-B.

33. Rossi, *Down and Out in America,* 39–40.

34. Lacey, "Survey Shows," 9-B.

35. Rossi, *Down and Out in America,* 40.

36. Ibid.

37. Lacey, "Survey Shows" 9-B.

38. Rossi, *Down and Out in America,* 40.

39. E. Fuller Torrey, MD, *Nowhere to Go: The Tragic Odyssey of the Homeless Mentally Ill* (New York: Harper and Row, 1988) 8.

40. Rossi, *Down and Out in America,* 41.

41. Peter Maurin, at the age of 14, attended Saint Privat's, a boarding school near Paris run by the Christian Brothers. He became a novice on October 1, 1893, and he professed his first vows September 18, 1895. He interrupted his life with the Brothers when he served in the 142nd Infantry

regiment of Mende in 1898–1899. Maurin left the Christian Brothers January 1, 1903. See vol. 9 of *New Catholic Encyclopedia* (New York: McGraw Hill, 1967) 507.

42. Harry Murray, *Do Not Neglect Hospitality: The Catholic Worker and the Homeless* (Philadelphia: Temple University Press, 1990) 5.

43. Ibid., 70

44. Ibid., 18.

45. For further discussion of Benedictine hospitality, see *The Rule of St. Benedict in Latin and English with Notes,* Timothy Fry, OSB, ed. (Collegeville, MN: Liturgical Press, 1981) 255.

46. Murray, *Do Not Neglect Hospitality,* 5.

47. Ibid., 4.

48. Ibid.

49. This is an excerpt taken from a reflection paper written in December 1990 by Kristen Dudas, a member of the class of 1992, Pacelli High School, Stevens Point, Wl. (Used with permission.)

50. Heupel, "More Than Food and Shelter," 10.

51. Ibid.

52. Murray, *Do Not Neglect Hospitality*, 55.

53. Edward Hays, *Prayers for a Planetary Pilgrim* (Easton, KS: Forest of Peace Books, 1988) 144.

Questions for Reflection and Discussion

1. What has been your personal response to the issue of homelessness? Has this article provided you with any new perspectives?

2. Do you experience a sense of fear regarding the homeless? If so, of what are you afraid?

3. Has there been a loss in your life that, while not so grave, helps you identify with the homeless individual's much more profound sense of loss?

4. How well do we offer hospitality to those who visit our communities?

5. How do we deal with the lonely Brothers who live in our communities?

6. How do you feel about the concept of Lasallian Houses of Hospitality? Why?

7. Are there other opportunities for Brothers, with or without students, to serve the homeless?

Summary of the 1992 Discussion

Michael F. Meister, FSC, Editor

The nineteenth annual Christian Brothers Spirituality Seminar met at the Mont La Salle Conference Center in Napa, California from April 9 to 12, 1992. We were happy to welcome two new participants this year: Brothers Robert Berger from Manhattan College in New York City, and Thomas Lisack from Pacelli High School in Stevens Point, Wisconsin. At the last minute, Brother James Ebner from Saint Paul, Minnesota was unable to attend but he was with us in spirit throughout the weekend. We were also happy to welcome two observers: Brother Robert McCann, Regional Secretary for Education, representing the Christian Brothers Conference, and Brother John Paige, CSC, President of Bishop Montgomery High School in Forestville, Maryland, and President of the National Assembly of Religious Brothers (NARB).

Discussion on the first evening of the Seminar centered on the general theme for this year, "Touching Hearts," and the experience of researching and writing articles in the context of that theme. Ed Sheehy remarked at the outset that reading the articles this year told him a great deal about the authors and that this revelatory experience included himself as well. Bob Smith agreed that this is one of several positive features of the Seminar experience, and he noted that the broad topic allowed for a breadth of perspectives in the articles.

Peter Gilmour said that he was fascinated by the idea of touching hearts, but was more fascinated by how little De La Salle actually addressed the concept directly when he researched it in the Founder's writings. In approaching the theme from a personal aspect, he discovered that there were, in fact, several experiences and stories—Peter is a narrative theologian—that touched his own heart, and he decided to approach his article from that perspective. De La Salle's words then helped Peter focus his reflections.

In agreeing with Peter, Bill Hall observed that the phrase "touching hearts" appears to exist far more than it does in the Founder's work. Armand Alcazar noted that the Founder's Meditations for Christmas and Pentecost are the major sources. I remarked that the concept has, nevertheless, been substantive in our tradition and that from what we experienced in the writing and reading of our articles, our hearts were touched as well.

As a newcomer, Bob Berger said that he didn't personally know everyone on the Seminar before arriving, but that the articles gave him certain insights into what each of us considered important. He noted that developing his own article even re-energized his work with his students at Manhattan College. Tom Lisack, our other newcomer, echoed Bob's insights, remarking that it was in the context of his own work of sensitizing his students to the needs of others that the theme really took flesh. It was out of this experience that he developed his article. Armand Alcazar also connected his article directly to his experience: especially being asked by one of his students why he became a Brother. Bill made everyone laugh when he shared a conversation he had had with Armand in which he praised Armand's article and poked fun at his own. "Yours is like one heart speaking to another. Mine is like one head speaking to another!" Kevin Griffin told us how the theme caused him to reflect on his own experiences as a Brother and those of so many of his confreres. It was out of these "growing up" experiences that he fashioned his "Quartet."

John Paige observed that having had no previous experience with the Seminar, he had a stereotypical image of dry scholars and hundreds of footnotes. He brought the house down when he told us that the first paper he received was that of Jim Ebner! He soon felt privileged, however, to read a series of articles that were so personal, intuitive, and anecdotal. Then he shared a fascinating insight. He said that the articles caused him to re-live his own Holy Cross roots. He noted that his Founder combined a community of brothers and a community of priests. The original Holy Cross Brothers were sent to the Christian Brothers' Novitiate in France. When they returned, they trained other Holy Cross Brothers. When his Founder wrote his pedagogy for the Holy Cross schools, he borrowed De La Salle's pedagogy lock, stock, and barrel. John said that the charisms I noted in my article on the *Meditations for the Time of Retreat* are all familiar to the Holy Cross community as well.

I stated, as I have before, that the breadth of the Seminar themes brings together a wealth of personal, lived experience which is condensed in the articles, and which we hope will "touch hearts" from year to year. This breadth and diversity is very much reflective of who and what we are as Brothers today. Bob McCann took up this theme, reflecting on the increased breadth of our audience, which reaches out to embrace the entire Lasallian Family. He noted that several articles in the present and recently past volumes take this family into consideration. I observed that in this volume particularly a good deal of material strives to make our experience and our primary documents accessible to a broader Lasallian readership. Bob Smith commented that our primary audience is always Brothers and that the challenges often raised by the articles are helpful and growthful for that readership. Kevin added that the Seminar publications are being welcomed and read by more and more of our colleagues, giving them further insights into the life of our shared ministry and our community. Peter spoke from his perspective as a lay colleague, saying that he sensed the Seminar's work, his own included, was aimed at an audience of professional educators who were more interested in a professional/ministerial orientation than a research orientation. The evening's discussion ended with a moment of shared appreciation and pride in the quality and professionalism of the work of the Seminar over the years.

First Day

Morning Session

The first morning session was devoted to a discussion of articles written by Kevin Griffin, Edward Sheehy, and James Ebner.

Brother Kevin Griffin. Kevin introduced his article by telling us that he had been reading men's studies and men's movements books by Robert Bly, Sam Keen, and John Friel. Some of their perspectives on what it means to be a man in the late twentieth century led him to consider a narrative exploring personal experiences surrounding growth and maturity as a male religious. He created his "Quartet" out of real and imagined experiences of his confreres and himself.

Several of us noted with appreciation the straightforwardness of the piece. I mentioned that his choice of a Brother reminiscing in the middle of his career rather than at the end of it makes the article accessible to a wide range of readers. I suggested that it also had vocation/recruitment value, not to mention its affirmation of experiences shared by so many young Brothers in the early years of their ministry. Growing in relationships is as significant as professional development. When asked about Brother Bede the Bastard, Kevin laughed and said that this man was an amalgamation of characters he had known and heard about both in the Brothers and before he joined. He said this character had value insofar as young men, himself included, often look with different feelings at the spectrum of Brothers in a local community.

John observed how so many of the experiences Kevin related are shared by others in religious life. He suggested that there was a wealth of wisdom to be seen in J.J.'s experiences with Kelly, not just for religious, but for married persons who find themselves challenged to maintain an appropriate balance in their friendships, given their commitments to others. To this end, he encouraged Kevin to elaborate on this even more in the final draft of his article.

Bob Smith expressed his appreciation for the realism and poignancy of the article and noted that it dealt with a Brother having profound relationships with persons other than Brothers. He raised a tough issue that several others echoed: many of us are good at touching hearts and being involved in the lives of people outside our communities. But how good are we at dealing with our confreres? Sometimes we know of Brothers in our communities who are "dying on the vine," but we do nothing to reach out to them. If the phone rings, however, and a student or a parent or an alumnus needs help, we're there in a flash! Bob and Bill Hall also noted that the counterbalance to J.J.'s series of joyful reminiscences is the fact that there had to be painful moments to accompany his many experiences of growth. Bill added a further note of reality, saying that, while he has many friends outside the order, there's a painfulness in the realization that they sometimes don't fully understand his life and commitments, and that he sometimes doesn't understand theirs.

Peter and Armand had similar viewpoints. Peter summed them up saying that he enjoyed the narrative quality of Kevin's article and that he was hungering for more when he had finished reading it. When Armand said that much of the "wisdom" of Kevin's article was never taught in formation, Peter noted that that's often true of life in general. Some things are often learned, though not officially taught. The question for Peter was: where does an individual or a group go to find wisdom? He suggested that the value of Kevin's paper was in its "ordinary-ness," because wisdom often comes to us through ordinary experience.

Ed Sheehy then gave the conversation an interesting twist, asking, "What about the issue of control?" He noted that often in relationships control is an issue, and that an underlying theme in Kevin's article was the possibility of losing control in a relationship. Bob Smith added that as Brothers we're often in control: in control of students, of classes, of schools, of faculties, and so forth. A hallmark of this control is that we never lose it or risk losing it. Ed suggested that this may color our relationships, especially with the confreres with whom we were trained not to develop "particular friendships."

Bob Smith added another dimension to the conversation, asking how many times we allow ourselves to be touched by those we are always controlling. He noted how easy it is for us to touch, but how hard it is for us to allow that touch to be reciprocated. Along that line, John noted that as a novice-master he has taught that one of the best things that can happen is that one falls in love, but that it's also one of the hardest challenges one will face. In light of this, he felt that Kevin's article would be particularly appreciated by younger Brothers. Bob McCann reminded us that the dark side of all this is the fact that we frequently read in the popular press of people in religious life who have "lost control" with disastrous and scandalous ramifications.

Bill gave a further twist to the conversation when he recounted how a time comes in our relationship with students where they are no longer our students but our peers. Our relationship and issues of control take a very different form. Sometimes we're touched by and learn more from a former student than we could ever have touched or taught that person ourselves. In the end, Bill suggested, vulnerability is a very real message in Kevin's article. Here Armand said that he appreciated the theme of vulnerability when Kevin had J.J. seek counsel from Brother Julius. Tom Lisack concluded the discussion by telling Kevin that what struck him the most in the article and what made the most sense in his own life were the same: what can I do to make a difference in this person's life?

Brother Edward Sheehy. Ed introduced his article by relating several discussions in councils and chapters where the issue of obedience was at the heart of the matter, though it was never discussed explicitly. One of Ed's concerns is that we spend a great deal of time talking about the other vows, especially association, but we never really grapple with obedience. So he wanted to pursue this issue in his article.

When Bob Smith opened the discussion by asking whether there was a certain tentativeness to the article, Ed agreed, saying that he wasn't sure where his article might lead him, and so he chose to reign in impulse and stay more with fundamentals. The real issue is that a discussion of obedience nowadays brings with it a great deal of uncertainty and ambiguity, though the questions that are raised as a result are often of great value. Later, Bob raised the question of the relationship between personal accountability and obedience.

Armand, on the other hand, told Ed that he found the article highly charged, and he definitely got a flavor of what was important to Ed in the context of his topic. Armand said he found himself writing lots of questions and comments to himself as he was reading the article. He told Ed that, contrary to Robert Bly's observation that we've lost the ability to lead by vulnerability, this article was direct and clear in terms of Ed's own stance on the issue. In light of the Seminar's theme, John noted that the "heart" issue was evident in the article in places where Ed suggested paths or courses of action to be taken. Bob Berger added that Ed was evidently talking about changes of heart as a collective effort of specific communities. He saw this as related to the notion of "intentional communities" in a recent circular of the Superior General.

Bill brought a different angle to the conversation about authority and obedience to an authority by recalling a definition of authority as knowledge and love coming together. He rephrased the definition by suggesting that one could say expertise and credibility come together to forge authority. He noted that superiors do not necessarily have a corner on the market in expertise. Rather, we all share a collective sense of expertise and knowledge, but we empower one individual to use these to move us in a specific direction. The tension here, of course, is the tension between the collective sense of who we are and where we're called to go, and yet empowering someone actually to get us there. Bob Smith added a further tension that we live with—that between what he called charismatic and hierarchical authority. Peter wondered whether we've actually shifted generations, finding ourselves now in a time when the almost spontaneous availability of so much information to all of us somehow changes the nature of how obedience operates.

Bill alluded to the fact that we often seem to elect our leaders, both religious and civil, more on the basis of credibility than expertise. He noted that it is not unusual for groups to elect to positions of leadership people who are most like the electorate itself. This often results in a blandness that surprises us when we see no dynamic change or development taking place. Ironically, Bill said, he believes the Brothers do want strong leadership.

Brother James Ebner. The final discussion of the morning focused on Jim Ebner's article on racism. Bob Smith had spoken

with Jim before he came to the Seminar and he introduced the article. He told us that many of the manifestations of racism in this
country had informed Jim's research and his article. Jim was also
concerned with where the Brothers are presently and where we've
come from historically on this issue.

Both Bob Berger and Ed Sheehy agreed that Jim's article, written for the vast majority of us in the Institute who are caucasian,
presents us with some provocative perspectives about whom we
reach out to in our ministry. As well, the article forces us to explore
the motivations for why we are or are not teaching people of color
in our schools. Ed gave the *tough* answer to his own question:
"What do we do about it? *I* do something about it!" Both Ed and
Bob Smith noted that racism is also found among its own victims
and that it takes many forms. One particularly destructive situation
was highlighted in a recent *Time* article about how some black students who attempt to excel academically are looked down on within their own communities.

Peter was struck by Jim's notion of racism as social sin and
how this sin actually transcends race. He said it's easy to be overwhelmed and depressed when one tries to find a way out. "How do
you touch a society's heart?" he asked. Touching an individual's
heart is so easy by comparison. Bob Smith remarked that, while it
was awkward for an all-white group like the Seminar to handle an
issue like racism, Jim seemed to have sliced through that awkward-
ness with his own lack of comfort about how he dealt with his
friend, Leonard. This observation prompted me to add how insightful I found Jim's candor in noting that Leonard's needs were so total. For me, one of the most powerful questions in the article was,
"How do you push out a poor person once he's in?" Peter responded by saying that what depressed him so much was the fact that inviting a poor person in might not necessarily change the sinful,
racist character of a society, and Bob reminded us of Ed's earlier
statement—whether or not it will change society is no excuse for
me to do nothing.

John Paige brought the discussion to a close by reminding us of
the general theme of "touching hearts," and that our own hearts

need to be touched in the extended confusion the whole complex of racist issues raises to our consciousness. He suggested that we need to grapple with the humbling realization that the issue may be beyond any individual's control right now, though each person still needs to *do* something.

Afternoon Session

The afternoon session was devoted to discussion of articles written by Dr. Peter Gilmour, Brothers Robert Smith, William Hall, and Thomas Lisack.

Dr. Peter Gilmour. Peter introduced his paper by saying that his thinking about the theme of touching hearts led him to write about what he called the "participatory nature" of the experience. Touching hearts is not simply a subject-object kind of relationship, but involves, rather, a dynamic alliance of peers. Ed Sheehy said he enjoyed the article and that he was fascinated by the idea of the genogram. Bill Hall was also intrigued by the genogram and wondered about its relationship to biological determinism. Peter responded by suggesting that there are vague hints of determinism in a genogram, but as he saw it, there are so many different influences in a genogram that no single one can stand alone. He talked about laying the historical-biological genogram alongside the intellectual-spiritual genogram as a way of looking at a host of influences, rather than just a few.

Bill observed that it appeared as if both Cutler and Heat-Moon were essentially unhappy with their identities and got satisfaction out of creating new ones, but that those identities had no continuity with the past. Peter responded by suggesting that Cutler is a rather extreme case, and that while Heat-Moon changes professions, his life shows more evidence of a unity than does Cutler's. The point was that a certain amount of dissatisfaction about who one is often initiates a quest for growth. Ed asked about consistently unhappy people, and Peter suggested that, while they may have changed the externals in their lives, they also need seriously to confront their identity.

Armand remarked that the scenarios Peter presented were quite realistic and he could imagine that others might actually envy what Cutler and Heat-Moon did to remedy their situations. What struck him the most about the article was Peter's statement: "To look at how each of us became educated is, I think, to look at a long process of ideas that touched our hearts." Thinking about that "long process of ideas" when he was first reading the article caused Armand to recall several experiences he had actually forgotten. Peter said that it was precisely this kind of consciousness-raising he hoped his article would produce.

John Paige noted that he saw Peter driving at the idea that education is a process of touching hearts in the sense that forming other persons is to enter into their story. Along the way, we might find that we are also formed by the persons we're educating. This, for John, is true education. I added that this perspective of seeing people (myself included) as embodied stories has Lasallian overtones in light of the value, respect, and dignity we accord to each of our students. Peter summed up by saying that what's important is not the story on the one hand, or the person on the other. Rather, it's the relationship that is established between the two.

Brother Robert Smith. Bob began by saying that his teaching in recent years has included much on Paul and that in his article he was interested in integrating Paul's ethics with individual and communal relationships. Peter observed the neatness of Paul's view that ethics basically follows faith, and wondered if this is really the way it is viewed today. Bob responded by suggesting that faith precedes ethics, at least theoretically. The point is that faith serves as a motive and an empowerment to act morally and ethically. Peter wondered whether the ethical foundations of modern Christians living in a pluralistic society are more eclectic as compared with the logical simplicity of Paul's view. Bob agreed that this might well be the case, but he also suggested that when you pursue Christians as to why they want to do good or behave well, they often respond, "Because God wants me to," or "Because Jesus said we should."

The discussion then turned slightly to consider the point of "arguing from an *is* to an *ought*." Bob suggested that a moralist wouldn't necessarily pursue that line of thinking. Rather, the *ought* stems from a clear understanding of what God has done for us in Jesus Christ. It is because I read in the New Testament about ways of treating people that I strive not be racist, for example, not because the government says it's wrong. Bill argued that people nowadays don't necessarily use Christ as a reason for fighting racism. Bob acknowledged this, and indicated that what was central for him in his article was Paul's view that because we are saved by Jesus we act in a new way, and that the Christian ethical view stems from this. He reminded us that salvation is a gift by which we are empowered to act responsibly, ethically. Peter put a different twist on this by pointing to the experience of Paul's conversion as a way to understand his ethical construction. He noted that the radical nature of Paul's change was not unlike Bill Cutler's. Peter also observed that violent conversion experiences are often associated with fundamentalism, and that to talk of transformation as a growth and development process in one's life makes more sense.

Brother William Hall. Bill introduced his article by saying that he was concerned that "touching hearts" not become a catch phrase, and that his inclination was to resist such phrases when they become so simplified. He suggested that the phrase is really rather complicated, and that it was in light of his interest in technologies of the word—how words form consciousness, communities, societies, etc.—that he began to construct his article. It also grew out of a realization that the students whose hearts we touch nowadays are, in fact, touched by many influences. This situation then puts us in a very different context from that of the Founder and the students of his day.

Ed expressed the feeling of the group when he said that he enjoyed the article very much. He especially appreciated Bill's examples and suggested that there be even more to amplify the significance of the communicative act. Bob Berger noted that Bill's article and Peter's had common themes, especially on the level of story. Bob Smith agreed, pursuing Bill's statement that while narrative on the oral level leaves no trace, technically speaking, it does have an effect in terms of the transformation that can take place in the hearers of the narrative. Peter pursued the theme of orality and literacy and a lively discussion ensued. His point was that words by themselves are not necessarily dead and solitary objects. Bill agreed, saying that what brings words to life is what we invest in them.

Bill remarked that a subtext of his article was a response to those who suggest that we're going to hell in a handbasket because nowadays kids do nothing but watch television. They're not reading and they're not writing. He suggested that what is really happening is a major cultural shift because of new and different technologies of the word. For Bill, the jury is still out. Armand agreed, noting that, while television can be accused of perpetrating the demise of the traditional family, it can also be credited with showing forms of oppression and awakening our society to fight against them.

Peter wondered about the validity of a statement in the article suggesting that we are better informed about a broad range of people, places, and experiences than were previous generations. Bill agreed that this point can be challenged in different circumstances, but that the dimension of depth is the real issue. At a later point, I asked where meaning comes from in this kind of culture and where one learns to mean. Does it rely on orality, on literacy, on the community? Saying that there is no easy answer to these questions, Bill suggested that meaning exists in people and between people, but not by itself. This is what makes understanding each other ultimately so problematic. We really don't know what meaning is. The more tightly we confine it, the more we lose it, and vice versa.

Brother Thomas Lisack. In telling us about his paper, Tom said that he had been involved with students working in community service projects for several years and that any student was qualified to perform acts of service for others. These service projects with students along with his reading in sociology and literature prompted him to explore a response to the pressing issue of homelessness in his article.

I began by saying that I thought the article represented an original, Lasallian approach, and that it was highly consciousness-raising. I particularly liked Tom's use of Bart Giamatti's definition of home as a way to give readers a sense of what it means to be without one. Tom responded that he wanted to get the reader to consider what's left and what it's like when an individual is separated from all the ordinary social support institutions we take for granted. What was important for him in Giamatti's definition was its link with home, self, and soul. Bill noted a recent statistic that said a majority of Americans were but two paychecks away from being on the street!

Ed pointed out other dimensions of the homelessness issue—the homeless don't vote, and the census misses a great many of them. Bob Berger noted that in many of our schools, which are located in large cities, homelessness is a difficult issue to deal with in class and in community. He appreciated the increased awareness that Tom's article brought to the reader as well as the proposal about Lasallian Houses of Hospitality. John Paige noted that oftentimes we refrain from getting involved in issues or programs because we have no training. He said that what most struck him was the simple reality that hospitality and simple human response to the needs of others requires no academic training. .

Ed took the issue of hospitality a step further by asking how hospitable we are in our own communities, to each other, to guests, to strangers. Kevin noted that the *Rule* encourages it, reminding us that our communities as homes are a source of strength and faith. Peter took us even farther in his consideration that if we are to recognize Christ in the stranger, strangers become a vital part of the eucharistic celebration. Armand recalled a spiritual writer's definition of holiness as hospitality, and said he thought of that frequently as he read the article. He said he was struck by a statement of Bellah's that Tom quoted: "Whether we give or withhold our spare change, we know that neither personal choice is the right one."

Bill moved the discussion to a different issue, which naturally grows out of the article. Is the Lasallian response Tom suggests realistic for us because it takes us down a path quite different from our present ministry? Tom thought the suggestions he was making were realistic, though ideal. For him they are a temporary ministry; in a better world there would be no need for them. On the other hand, what he was proposing does have a place as a service-oriented work in the context of our educational ministry. Its existence as a means to allow students to serve others and be sensitized by them can be a great value in our schools. Bob McCann agreed with this aspect of Tom's suggestion while holding that he didn't necessarily see Lasallian Houses of Hospitality as part of our charism. For Bob and Tom it was important that we educate students about this issue.

Bob Berger concluded by raising a tough question: how many of us would be involved in a service project if it weren't for the purpose of taking the students there? His point was that we tend to live our personal lives distinct from our ministerial lives, and he suggested that this gives us much pause for reflection.

Second Day

Articles discussed on the second morning included those written by Brothers Armand Alcazar, Robert Berger, and Michael Meister.

Brother Armand Alcazar. Armand recalled that last year someone said he hoped there would be an article this year that touched on relationships. He said that he started writing in this direction, but that his real energy came when a student he invited for dinner asked him why he had become a Brother. He noted that though he and Kevin are in the same community, they did not confer about their articles before they were written. But once he had read Kevin's, he could appreciate its relational themes, particularly since he had just celebrated his own silver jubilee.

Kevin observed that one of the clearest messages of Armand's article was that you can't give what you haven't got; if we're going to touch our confreres, or colleagues, or students we have to have been touched by someone else. Ed said that the article has a great appeal, and anyone might feel as if it were written for their age group. Bill agreed with Ed (after noting their difference in ages), and characterized the paper as having been written from one heart to another. He said he particularly appreciated Armand's citations from the *Declaration,* which amplified his overall message.

Bob Berger told Armand that he wished there was more when he had finished reading the article for the first time. He said there was a great deal Brothers can think about in the article; he and many others might resonate with Armand's anecdote about the student who said, "I've known you for five years and I don't know any more about you than when I was a senior in high school." Peter said he appreciated the article as a wisdom-piece on life experience. I observed that the tension between personal achievement on the one hand and the touching of hearts on the other was well-stated in the article. In our ministry, we tend to get pushed onto the personal achievement side with the pressure of production, production, production, and the affective side is inadequately addressed. Bob Smith agreed with this, and mentioned that the recent CARA study noted that one of the major concerns among religious today is loneliness.

Brother Robert Berger. Bob observed that while we have all had experiences of touching hearts, it is ultimately God who does the touching. He noted that from his experiences in retreat ministry, it's a very humbling experience to touch the hearts of others and realize that God is working through you. For Bob, we're most powerful in our educational ministry when we observe the touch of God working through ourselves and through others. The aspect of touch is what struck him the most, and the image that came readily to him was that of Jeremiah. These perspectives, then, came together in the writing of his article.

Many appreciative remarks about the article were expressed by the group. Peter found himself returning to Jeremiah after he had read the article, saying that he found himself wanting to read the prophet in light of Bob's perspectives. Bob McCann found the article affirming and enlightening. I noted that the article has a lot of potential for a broad readership because Bob has made his theme accessible, clear, and inviting. John said he often thought of spiritual direction only in terms of adults, and found himself looking at it with renewed enthusiasm in terms of the students we teach on a daily basis. He used some of Bob's ideas with a group of high school students quite successfully.

Bob responded that his sense was that our students are hungry for the spiritual dimension and that we have an opportunity to fill an important need by attending to this hunger. Bob Smith wondered how many students are really this "hungry," and Bob replied that, from his classroom experience, students are often very open if you present the spiritual to them. Even for those who ultimately reject it, at least it's their focus for a while. On the other hand, he said, many students say they had never thought in this way before it was presented. Peter added that he appreciated Bob's use of classic biblical narratives to convey deeper messages because they do have this power.

Bob Smith remarked that when he was reading the word "student" in the article, he would write "and ourselves" in the margin. He noted that while the focus of Bob's article was our spiritual direction and mentoring of others, we need to remember the reciprocal nature of the experience: that God may also be working with us through those we direct. I stated that Lasallian themes were very evident in the article, particularly the presence of God. Peter then said that one of the highlights of the article for him was the section on the potter and the clay. He suggested that Bob amplify it. I observed that the potter-clay image is a paradigm of education, and that Bob could amplify that as well. Bob responded that he was trying to convey the notion of Jeremiah as a role-model for Lasallian educators. In watching the potter, the clay, and the action that's taking place, Jeremiah is also actively attentive.

At this point, Bill put on his resistance hat and wondered whether Bob was suggesting that we are merely conduits between God and those we touch. He said he could understand the image metaphorically, but not humanly, suggesting that we can't disappear from the action that's occurring. Bob responded by saying that he was coming from the perspective of having lived and experienced what Bill was pointing at. He wasn't sure he completely understood it either, but he recounted situations where it was unmistakable that God was working through him even when he felt personally inadequate with regard to a spiritual directee. This was very humbling. When Bill asked Bob what he meant by seeing God touch someone, Bob gave some examples: agitation turning to a deep peace, a hidden agenda being put aside, or a person entering into the experience after initially refusing to do so. Bob added that if he had put his own agenda into any of these situations, they would have ended in disaster. Peter poked fun at himself, suggesting that he might be a bad spiritual director because he couldn't keep his mouth shut. But he wondered if one were to ask a person whether it was God or the director acting, the other would say it was the director. What he was getting at is that in this situation, the truth is often found in both testimonies rather than one or the other, and that's part of the mystery of the experience.

Bob said that in the Lasallian equation containing God, students, and ourselves as educators, God and the students are the key players. Bob Smith agreed and noted how central a role our students play in the *Meditations for the Time of Retreat*. Bill remarked that De La Salle's characterization of the Brother as a guardian angel is a very active image. Bob Berger agreed, though he suggested that our activity centers on assisting the student to develop his or her relationship with God, not ourselves.

Brother Michael Meister. I introduced my article by saying that I was also initially struck by the lack of "volume" regarding the heart in De La Salle's writings. I viewed the heart theme as an iceberg, however, and what I set out to do in my article was to turn the iceberg over (is this an excuse for its length?). What I saw was that one could look at touching hearts as the heart of the matter, and the heart of the matter, for me, has always been observable in the Founder's meditations, particularly the *Meditations for the Time of Retreat*. I stated that I believe these meditations contain a great deal of information about what it means to be Lasallian; that the Founder's charisma, which we are urged to emulate, is really an action of the heart; and that the life that results from this emulation is very much a life of the heart. With this in mind, I thought that an explication of the retreat meditations would be a splendid way to draw both my confreres and my colleagues into that life.

Armand observed that this article read differently from the rest in the sense that, like the meditations themselves, one doesn't read them all in one sitting. Noting that I had used the term autobiographical in the article, Bill asked how the *Meditations* were intended to be taken as autobiographical. I responded that they were not meant to be autobiographical of the Founder, but that they may, in fact, be autobiographical for us, the readers. Bill also asked in what sense I meant that these meditations were "classic," given the fact that until recently, their history has not been that prominent. I answered that I define a classic as something that has not lost its ability to address us out of the past, and that these meditations fit this definition. In the context of "classic," John Paige repeated what he noted on the opening night, that the charisms I wrote about in my article are used in the educational works of the Holy Cross order as well, since the first Holy Cross Brothers were trained at the Christian Brothers' novitiate in France.

Peter opened a different perspective on the article by suggesting that for the Brothers and Lasallians the *Meditations* are really a sacred text, akin to Scripture. Recalling the article he wrote for the Seminar last year, he noted that each of us—in addition to the official canon of scripture—has his or her own personal canon, and that the two lie alongside each other, one illuminating the other. In this sense, these meditations are also "classic" as important documents for Lasallian believers. Given the "scripture-ness" of the *Meditations,* Peter felt that the explication I did was very appropriate and akin to the kind of exegesis or textual study one does on a sacred text.

Armand stated that he appreciated the breadth of the description and discussion of charisma in the article and how this was then carried through each meditation. He also liked my handling of the fact that the Founder made no distinction between the Brothers' ministry and their spiritual lives. What he found here was an affirmation that suggests we don't have to tear our lives apart into segments, but that they can be a holistic unity. I noted that this issue sometimes strikes terror into Brothers when it's discussed, but that I wanted to be very clear about which side of the interpretive line I stood on. I said that I found this issue akin to Armand's discussion of the tension between the professional and affective domains in Brothers' lives.

The conversation moved to the distinction I was making in the article between the *Method of Mental Prayer* and the *Meditations for the Time of Retreat.* I said that Blain's statement about the Founder's retreat meditations seems to make it clear that they are quite distinct from the ordinary subject matter and manner that the structure of the *Method* implies. I noted that I thought the two works were unfortunately yoked together historically. The fact that the retreat meditations lack "expressions of fervent desire, feelings of tenderness, or resolutions customary in similar meditations," and that they are not connected with the *Method,* suggest that what De La Salle was doing in the retreat meditations was to articulate the various elements in a Brother's life and ministry that would, over the period of the retreat, come together as a unity, a whole.

Bob Smith asked several questions with regard to the Founder's sense of the relationship between a Brother's salvation and that of his students as it comes across in the retreat meditations. I said that in my reading of these meditations the salvation of our students is more important than our own. I admitted that this may be a bold assertion, and Bob agreed. I pointed to a statement by the Founder in Meditation 13 as my key: "You must be convinced of this: God will begin by making you give an account of their souls before asking you to give an account of your own." Bob noted that the text uses the word *before* rather than *more important.* My point, I responded, was that the Founder reminds us that we have committed ourselves to be *entirely* dedicated to the salvation of our students' souls, and we are responsible to procure it with as much attention as our own. Bill Hall observed that, in this issue of salvation, the Founder may be suggesting two things to the Brothers. First, ours is not a monastic charism, and we don't develop a one-on-one relationship with God separated from the world and those to whom we minister. Second, any separation between the spiritual and the apostolic is a false separation. Our salvation is inextricably linked to that of our students. He ended by noting that even the *Declaration* supports this by stating: "The brother ought to have no fear of losing God when he goes among the young to serve them, nor of being estranged from Christ when he spends himself for [them]."

Upcoming Seminars and Themes

After discussing all the articles, the Seminar participants spent time on the editorial details of the publication, including stylistic features of the articles and the order of articles in the publication. We also suggested new members and planned the general theme of the next Seminar.

Something New

During the last several years, suggestions have been made that there be an occasional seminar composed of members of different religious orders of men, and that the Christian Brothers Spirituality Seminar assist this group with its resources and organization. Because these suggestions haven't been accompanied by a clearly organized program, they remained simply suggestions. Within the last year, however, a constellation of suggestions, opportunities, themes, and organization has resulted in a special Seminar which will replace our usual one in the Spring of 1993. It will follow our format and result in a publication entitled: *Religious Brothers in the Church Today: Who We Are Among the People of God.* I will be the editor, and the book is slated for distribution in the Spring of 1994.

The catalyst for this Seminar is the upcoming Papal Synod on Religious Life, to be held in Rome in the Fall of 1994. The idea is to publish a series of articles on religious brotherhood in advance of that Synod and distribute them to all the Synod delegates as well as all religious brothers in North America. The organization and financial backing for this Seminar is being shared by the National Assembly of Religious Brothers (NARB), the Conference of Major Superiors of Men (CMSM), and the Regional Conference of Christian Brothers (RCCB).

By the time you read this, the project will be well under way. Brother John Paige, CSC, President of NARB, Brother Robert McCann of the Christian Brothers Conference, and I did the final planning of this Seminar during the Spirituality Seminar this past Spring. A call for papers was then circulated to all the Provincials of religious orders of men in the region, the call was announced in the NARB Newsletter, and several personal invitations were also distributed. Our intent was to gather a group of religious brothers writing about and representing a broad range of perspectives and ministries. At the beginning of July, John, Bob, and I met in Chicago to read through the many proposals for papers that were submitted, and we selected approximately 15. This group will meet in Chicago in September to become acquainted with one another and discuss together the project and the article proposals. The men will then write their articles and meet for the Seminar at Mont La Salle in Napa, California, at the beginning of April, 1993.

The Next Christian Brothers Seminar

The Christian Brothers Spirituality Seminar will resume in the Spring of 1994. Our theme for that Seminar will focus on the *Declaration*. Our choice of this theme represents a change in how we have approached the annual topics: for the first time we have selected a common text to write about. We made this choice based on the significance of this document, the fact that it's now 25 years old, and that the upcoming General Chapter will have met in the Spring of 1993.

Conclusion

All of us on the Seminar deeply appreciate the opportunity to provide you with reading that is thought-provoking, professional, and focused on aspects of our life and ministry together. We thank the various agencies of the Region who support and produce our work, we thank you for your interest, and we encourage your responses!

Spirituality Seminar Participants—1992

Armand Alcazar, FSC
Christian Brothers University
650 East Parkway South
Memphis, TN 38104

Robert Berger, FSC
4415 Post Road
Bronx, NY 10471

James H. Ebner, FSC
495 S. Hamline Avenue
Saint Paul, MN 55116

Dr. Peter Gilmour, DMin
1118 W. Loyola
Chicago, IL 60626

Kevin Griffin, FSC
Bethlehem University
B.P. 9
Bethlehem via Israel

William Hall, FSC
La Salle University
Philadelphia, PA 19141

Thomas Lisack, FSC
Pacelli High School
1301 Maria Drive
Stevens Point, WI 54481–1197

Michael F. Meister, FSC
Box 5169
Saint Mary's College
Moraga, CA 94575

Edward Sheehy, FSC
La Salle University
Philadelphia, PA 19141

Robert Smith, FSC
Saint Mary's College #46
700 Terrace Heights
Winona, MN 55987-1399

Publications of the Seminar

Order from: Christian Brothers Conference
4351 Garden City Drive
Landover, MD 20785
1-800-433-7593